W9-BFD-492

Authentic
Costumes
&
Characters
OF THE
WILD WEST

E.L. REEDSTROM

Authentic
Costumes
&
Characters
OF THE
WILD WEST

E. Lisle Reedstrom

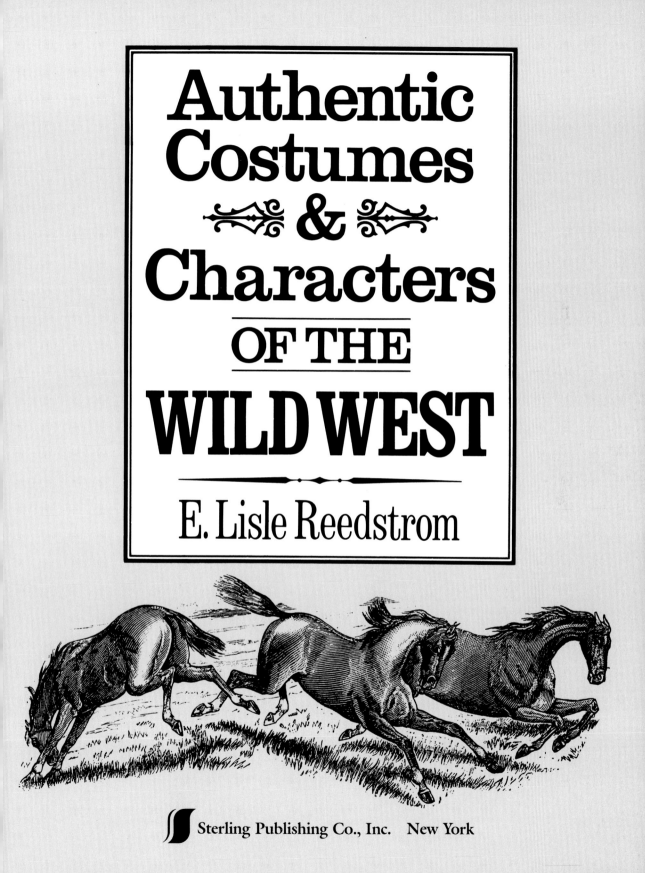

Sterling Publishing Co., Inc.   New York

Dedicated to my Mother, Helen Reedstrom,
and in memory of my Uncle, Danny Kruslak

Library of Congress Cataloging-in-Publication Data

Reedstrom, Ernest Lisle.
    [Historic dress in the old West]
    Authentic costumes & characters of the old West / E. Lisle
Reedstrom.
        p.   cm.
    Originally published: Historic dress in the old West. Poole
[England] : Blandford Press, c1986.
    Includes bibliographical references (p.   ) and index.
    ISBN 0-8069-8644-1
    1. Costume—West (U.S.)—History—19th century. 2. Frontier and
pioneer life—West (U.S.) 3. West (U.S.)—Social life and customs.
I. Title. II. Title: Authentic costumes and characters of the old
West.
GT617.W47R44 1992
391'.00978—dc20   91-43312
                                                  CIP

10 9 8 7 6 5 4 3 2 1

First published in the United States in 1992
by Sterling Publishing Company, Inc.
387 Park Avenue South, New York, N.Y. 10016
Originally published in Great Britain by Blandford Press
as *Historic Dress of the Old West*
© 1986 by Ernest Lisle Reedstrom
Distributed in Canada by Sterling Publishing
% Canadian Manda Group, P.O. Box 920, Station U
Toronto, Ontario, Canada M8Z 5P9
Distributed in Great Britain and Europe by Cassell PLC
Villiers House, 41/47 Strand, London WC2N 5JE, England
Distributed in Australia by Capricorn Link Ltd.
P.O. Box 665, Lane Cove, NSW 2066
Printed and Bound in Hong Kong
All rights reserved

Sterling ISBN 0-8069-8644-1

For description of frontispiece, see page 106.

Contents

Foreword

Lawrence A. Frost

In an effort to dispel commonly-accepted characterizations and images of Western stereotypes the well-known Western illustrator Ernest Lisle Reedstrom has turned his interest, talents and research experience toward the preparation of a volume that provides an authoritative reference and source book dealing with apparel worn by the occupants and early settlers of the West. This will be a welcome addition to the libraries of artists, authors, historians and western history buffs.

The impact made on the public by way of the printed page and television has conjured stereotyped images of the Plains Indians, soldiers, outlaws, mountain men, hide-hunters, gun-fighters, whores and the many other characters who played a role in the great move westward.

Most people have preconceived ideas as to the clothing worn by the early settlers and inhabitants of the West. In many instances those who described or sketched these peoples did so with little knowledge or background of that fascinating period of our history. The characterizations with which we are most familiar are stereotypes created by unexposed, inexperienced and highly imaginative minds.

Carlyle refered to man as a 'clothed animal', and so he is. Once the aboriginal's hunger and desire for revenge had been appeased, his next function was not that of seeking comfort but of decoration. He could find warmth in a bed of dry leaves, a cave or a hollow tree trunk. But for decorations he must have clothes.

From the beginning of time he adopted some means of adornment or covering. Though beads, tattooing, body painting and unique clothing may have had some sexual connotations, many adopted such manifestations as indications of rank, position, caste, religious belief or affiliation, profession, trade or vanity.

Clothes, though first worn as a means of adaptation to an environment, soon evolved into a means of distinction, decoration and coloring, often separating the male from the female. This could be analogous to the peacock or the brilliant coloring displayed by the male bird in most species.

The story is told of a group of literary men who, during World War I, had been stationed in a Welsh castle. In its huge hall there was an exhibit of stuffed exotic birds.

'What is that strange bird?' one officer asked.

'That is a flamingo,' he was advised.

'A flamingo! That's not my idea of a flamingo,' he responded.

'Perhaps it isn't,' was the reply, 'but it happens to be God's idea of a flamingo.'

The flamingo inherited the qualities that attract attention. Apparently early man thought he lacked these qualities. Whether it was his desire to attract attention, appear exotic, warlike, macho, handsome or wealthy, he displayed his ability to adapt to situations that temporarily or permanently confronted him. The resulting costume or apparel was evidence of his imagination, logic, cunning, inventiveness and practicality.

Lisle Reedstrom has vividly displayed these characteristics. His illustrations, classifications and descriptions make this apparent. These are real people, not Hollywood stereotypes. By their clothing you would know them out on the Great Plains or on the streets of a Western cowtown.

His sketches and illustrations are of people striving to improve upon the nudity imposed on them by an unrealistic nature.

Preface

I have always wanted to write and illustrate a book on early American costumes from the Mississippi to the California gold fields, covering just about everything in weapons and clothing styles that could be described from the 1840s to the turn of the century. I realized it would be a tedious project, but the results would certainly be gratifying. I have great hopes that it will be different from the ordinary illustrated costume books showing the many individual characters in period clothing, but to record them as they really were.

I interrogated people from all walks of life and spent many months traveling about the West and Middle West visiting numerous historians and viewing their collections. At various Gun Shows that I frequented with my editor, Gib Crontz, I purchased a great variety of material plus information on various Western subjects that I filed away until the time came to weave it into my manuscript or use for an illustration. At these Gun Shows, many knowledgeable collectors told me what they looked for in books or costume prints that coincided with their interests, and I have listened patiently and recorded anything of importance.

It is here that I wish to express my sincere appreciation to all those wonderful individuals who passed on information or historical articles so that this book might have a firmer foundation of authenticity.

For encouragement and assistance, I am indebted to my wife Shirley, who took time out of her busy schedule; to my mother, Helen Reedstrom, who believed in me, and to my good friends and editors Margaret and Gib Crontz of Cedar Lake, Indiana. Many thanks to the people who posed before me under a sultry summer sun and before the hot blinding studio lamps, wearing costumes, uniforms and leather accouterments. My appreciation to my daughter Karen Reedstrom as second editor, to Rebecca M. Crabb of Buckley Farm Homestead in Lowell, Indiana, buckskinner Don Good, Phil Rodeghiero and Jim Nemeth, military artist.

When I didn't use models, I worked from photographs supplied to me by: Arizona Historical Society; Smithsonian Institute; Newberry Library in Chicago;

Moody Texas Ranger Library in Waco, Texas; The National Archives in Washington; artist Ron Bork; Joe Gish collection, McAllen, Texas; Richard Ignarski of Albuquerque, New Mexico; Editor Phil Spangenburger, *Guns & Ammo*, Los Angeles, California; Bob Schmidt, saddle maker, Corvallis, Montana; the Union Pacific Railroad Museum Collection; Lance Cardinelli, Bounty Hunter; and the Arnold Chernoff collection. Author Carl Breihan contributed greatly.

I have reserved a special place on this page for the various frontier outfitters who have rallied to my cause with their reproductions in clothing, leather holsters, hand made saddles, books, and original military and American materials. My sincere thanks to Jim and Karen Boeke, at River Junction Trade Company, McGregor, Iowa. Their catalog has just about everything a frontier enthusiast would want. Jim and Karen work from original patterns and produce accurate period clothing and their prices are moderate. If they don't have it, they'll make it from your specs. Both of these creative geniuses have been written up in national magazines and were technical advisers for many movie and television shows.

George A. Willhauck, Military and Americana Materials in North Hampton, New Hampshire, issues an outstanding 'free' catalog twice a month, with collectable items that you seldom find at gun shows or antique shops, from original Civil War candle holders to original tobacco twists over a hundred years old; badges, beaver fur hats, documents, tintypes, sabres and boots, etc, however no firearms of any kind.

The El Paso Saddlery in El Paso, Texas, also has a free catalog offering the finest period boot made to your specs. The patterns used are from the original Ordnance Department, the leathers are close to the type used by the army contractors. They are so authentic-looking that you can't tell them from the originals. The company has five styles of boots. Three are military (1860–80), and two are early cowboy (Cuban heels with stove-pipe tops). They need at least six weeks for delivery, and boots range from $150 to $180, which is reasonable considering these boots are built for comfort and take lots of punishment.

The Red River Frontier Outfitters have been

7

making frontier clothing and military uniforms and leather goods for Hollywood's film makers for over 13 years that I know of. Associate Editor Phil Spangenburger of *Guns & Ammo*, began the company researching and cataloging cowboy gear, American dress and uniforms as a general hobby ... until it took off like wildfire. Red River will come up with almost any period costume in American History along with holsters and leather accouterments. Many colored photos have been seen in *Guns & Ammo* with their costumes accompanying a detailed article ... and Phil is always dressed as a lone cowboy, gambler or buffalo hunter. The photos look like the old-timers as it's hard to tell that they were posed. Red River's catalog is descriptive and most interesting. It can be had by writing them at Tujunga, California.

Bob Schmidt is a craftsman of repute. He operates the White Buffalo Leather Shop in Corvallis, Montana, specializing in early custom-made saddles, cowboy boots and horse furniture. Bob is very conscientious about American History and spends most of his spare time researching early saddles, horse and tack equipment. When I saw the photos of a number of saddles introduced in the 1820s, and several mountain men's saddles of the 1830s, I couldn't imagine where he even found any relics to work from ... but he did, and I received permission to show them in this book. Catalog upon request.

Burgess & Company, Military Goods, in Meriden, Ct., has one of the best catalogs on US Military accouterments. He supplies all of this county's re-enactment groups as well as the movie industry.

Rod Casteel's Old West Gun Leathers in Phoenix, Arizona, has holsters and belts of all descriptions. Here is another man who researched all his holster rigs right down to the minute blemish. His Frank James holster and belt is identical to the one in the Missouri museum. It has all the scratches, dents, nicks and scuffing that the original has. However, Rod also produces authentic holster rigs from old catalogs, making certain that they look and feel like the old-timers. His catalog has illustrations showing the types of holsters that he stocks, and anything else will take several weeks to complete; from the Forty-Niner style scabbard he also manufactures the classic Half-Flap military holster, including belt and buckle. In ordering, mention type of weapon and caliber. Barrel length is also necessary.

Joe Covais, historical tailor in Charleston, Illi-

nois, has an interesting shop, indeed. He works from original specimens which he has picked up over years of research. Both military uniforms and civilian (men's and women's) garments are his specialty. In his free catalog are illustrated fancy gamblers' vests, top hats, even underwear. Women's bustles and hoop skirts are also shown. Joe's very fussy about his historic costumes ... and he even reproduces the same stitching that was used in the early days. Cloth must be of the same weight and pattern as was used over 100 years ago. His shop and staff stop at nothing to produce an exact image of clothing from the past.

Bill Combs, Historical Cobbler, also in Charleston, Illinois, is another fanatic on authenticity. He works with original shoe-makers' tools that he either collects or manufactures himself. His work can be found in a number of local museums and in private collections. He is just beginning his business and hasn't had time to release a brochure as yet.

Finally, my dear friend of at least 15 years is William Graf, book dealer in Iowa City, Iowa. Bill and his wife Mary are old-timers in the used book business and have filled every one of my requests all these years with faithfulness and energetic performance that still amazes me. If you want an out-of-print book or a government printing, the Grafs will find it for you. His monthly catalog is lengthy, covering nearly every subject one can imagine, and he discounts some books whenever they are available. A wonderful, reliable pair of book worms to have at your side in a time of need. As for assuming total responsibility in getting manuscript and artwork to my publishers, my sincere appreciation to St John Postmaster Audrey DeArmond in Indiana.

A special thank you to Marie Dewes, who burned the midnight oil typing all my notes written in long hand, and to Debbie Higgens who finished typing the manuscript. And to my first editor, Gib Crontz, without whose knowledge on weapons, ammunition and skill with words I could not have completed this book. Since Mr Crontz took ill while working on this manuscript, Frances Katz, my new editor, took over the completion of the book. Without her assistance, talents and swiftness, this manuscript would not be in print to meet its deadline. Thank you all.

Somehow, I feel as though I have left out several individuals along the way, but, and only to them, I apologize for that error.

E. Lisle Reedstrom 1986

1 Plains Indians

The life of the American Plains Indian was almost completely dependent on the existence of the buffalo. From the buffalo came hides for clothing, shelter, containers for food and water, ornaments and boats. Bones, horns, sinews and hoofs gave weapon points, tools, implements, thread and glue. The flesh was food and the tail served as a fly swatter. And when the carcass was totally consumed, there was little that remained to show that a once great beast had ever existed. When the buffalo herd moved, so did the Indian camps. Grey wolves, coyotes and other animals of prey also followed the buffalo, ever ready to attack an old male abandoned by the herd or an unattended calf. The male bull was a magnificent animal standing six feet tall at the withers and weighing up to 3,300 pounds. In a run, at full speed he could travel 29 miles an hour, and if an Indian and horse came too close in the hunt, the animal could stop in an instant, turn and charge the hunter.

The Indian's horsemanship was unsurpassed. He trained his pony to single out one buffalo in the herd, then ride alongside of it until the beast was felled with spear or arrow (Old Warriors claim that an arrow from a good bow could pass completely through the mightiest of buffalo), continuing with others in the same manner, permitting his hands to be free when using his weapon. Riding bareback, he could hang sideways from his pony by hooking one leg over its back and with his bow arm around and over the animal's neck. Reaching underneath with an arrow, he could then shoot an enemy with a minimum of his body exposed. The same technique was used by hanging low on one side to reach out and lift up a wounded or stranded comrade and retreat on the run.

In the early days of the Plains Indian, before the horse was introduced around 1541, when DeSoto and Coronado scattered stray horses across the plains and the Southwest, the Indians hunted on foot, stampeding buffalos over cliffs, wounding and killing them. From Spring through Fall, every able hunter started out from their villages for the hunt, carrying adequate rations for several days.

While seeking a buffalo herd they lived in conical hide tents, similiar to the later tepees but much smaller, unlike their permanent villages of round earth lodges. The hunters would set up camp near a buffalo trap that they had previously constructed on the edge of a cliff. There, an area of about 150 feet in length along the cliff's edge was left open and from each end of this area two lines of piled stones, 15 feet apart, were set out in a 'V' shape formation for the distance of approximately two miles. At this point the lines were roughly two miles apart. When a herd had been sighted by the scouts, a buffalo medicine man appeared and approached the herd chanting and beating a flat shaped drum. After annoying the nearest bulls they would trail after the old man with the rest of the herd following behind into the trap area. Once the buffalos had been lured into and between the two lines of piled stones, the hunters, who had taken positions behind the stones, closed in to the rear of the animals waving their robes and shouting. This generally forced the whole herd to stampede toward the narrow end of the trap where they fell over the edge of the cliff killing themselves.

After the butchering, the meat had to be transported on a dog's back or on a travois pulled by a dog. Two poles, bound together at one end to a harness on a dog, were left to drag on the ground behind the animal. Between these poles spread out in the shape of a 'V', was fastened an oval or square frame netting woven with rawhide onto which the buffalo carcass was carried. During these early days before the acquisition of the horse, transportation was slow and difficult and the hunters stayed close to their villages.

In warfare, the greatest advantage gained through the use of the horse was mobility. The Indian pony was light in weight and grass fed, in comparison to the white man's horses, who winded easily, carried heavy saddles and were not used to much over a moderate gait.

It was not uncommon for members of a village to cover 600 miles during a hunting season and this constant migration resulted in the invention of the large tepee, which was light, compact, and comfortable in all seasons. The tepee's framework was constructed of about 15–20 slim, rigid wooden poles made of pine or cedar, approximately 25 feet in length. The thinner

9

ends of these poles were tied together about 4 or more feet from their upper ends with thongs and when raised were spread out until the bottom ends formed a circle about 15 feet in diameter. Other poles were added by laying them into the crotch of the tripod. Buffalo cow hides, as many as 30–40, depending on the size of both hide and tepee, were carefully trimmed and pieced together with sinew thread. The hide was then spread over the frame and the ends of this covering were laced together. At the bottom, the skins were pegged into the ground, and an oval doorway was covered with a cloth or a stretched skin. Very important was the upper portion of the tepee where the draft and smoke from the fireplace could be regulated at ground level. The triangular skin-flaps were held up by the upper ends of two poles by which a person standing outside could change positions of the flaps as the wind changed or weather conditions threatened.

Many tepees were renewed each year because of discoloration by exposure to the elements. Painted tepees were almost always done by the men. When a new tepee was to be painted, to tell the story of a great hunt or battle the occupants had been connected with, the owner invited 20 or more of his friends and relatives to assist him, and, as they painted and feasted, a tepee could be completed in a day. These painted tepees were owned by prominent tribal heads; chiefs, war party leaders, and medicine men. Most religious designs were handed down from one generation to another.

Tepees were always arranged in a circle or circles depending upon the size of the village and the space available. When an area was limited or when scattered divisions of a tribe got together in huge assemblies to perform their medicine ceremonies, the tepees were set up in several circles, one within the other. Family order was not haphazard. As groups assembled, each of the relatives had their own definite area. The women who set up the village on new locations knew exactly where each lodge was to be erected. This pattern of location never deviated.

In some tribes, when a village was preparing to move on, one brave was chosen to be 'keeper of the

---

PLATE 1

1 Plains Indian warrior, 1874–80
2 Central Plains Lakota Indian, 1874–80
3 Cheyenne Indian, 1874–80

1. *It was after the Civil War (1865) that most of our serious Indian battles originated with the white migration crossing Indian lands from the Mississippi to California and Oregon. Among the numerous bands of renegades were the Sioux, Cheyenne, Arapaho, Kiowa, and Comanche. Pictured here is a typical Plains Indian warrior, stripped to a loin cloth with a belt knife at the small of his back, bow and arrows slung horizontally over his chest and shoulders and an 1873 Winchester saddle carbine, .44/40 caliber, at his side. Half of his face is painted for warfare, which had hidden meanings. Mainly, however, it was a way of mental conditioning as well as a personal protective display of courage in the face of the enemy. In this case this warrior wishes to express a heartfelt meaning in his make-up: 'This is my first battle and I want to avenge my brothers of the past.' Here he has the option to use either weapon, the bow and arrow for close combat or the Winchester carbine for distance. Its magazine capacity was twelve rounds and its effective range with some accuracy was close to 200 yards. A favorite method of decorating shoulder arms was with brass tacks to ensure the warrior of good medicine when he went into battle.*

2. *Loose fitting leather shirts were worn by Central Plains Lakota Indians and highly decorated with beads, porcupine quills, human hair and cloth, and usually painted yellow and blue to symbolize the earth and sky. The wide shoulder band and quilled sleeve strips were characteristic of the Cheyenne and Lakota shirts since the mid-nineteenth century. Long locks of hair*

that hung from the shirt were contributed by each family member symbolizing the wearer's war exploits. Broad side flap leggings with decorated bands running down each side were in harmony with the shirt. The lance he is holding is light in weight and had a longer shaft than the lance used for hunting, which was shorter with a broader, heavier blade. His face is painted for battle and represents his feelings: 'I have seen my family killed, and I have come to punish you.'

3. *The Cheyenne Indian represented here is attired for warfare, stripped to a breechclout and carrying the weapons he needs. In this case a knife in a handsome beaded sheath and a Colt 'Peacemaker', Model 1872, caliber .44/40. It was this revolver that the US Army Ordnance issued to the cavalry troops in 1873, and it is evident that this Cheyenne was fortunate to acquire it as battlefield booty. The effective range at which experts could achieve good results was 50 to 75 yards; however, it has been known to reach 300 yards in some cases.*

The long breechclout and wide buckskin fringed 'apron' gave the wearer a bit of distinction and would be easily noticed by his enemy either on horseback or dodging from rock to bush on foot. Clout ornamentation was done in paints or dyes in bold patterns, in stripes, squares or dots. There were also beaded clouts and later models with sequins appended. By the 1880s, most clouts were red or blue flannel blanket cloth instead of animal skins. A small, colorful beaded pouch in front held a special war medicine bundle of buffalo hair and birds' feet. This was especially prepared for him by the members of his family. His body paint is as follows: his face shows he is a member of a secret society; the upper half of his body painted yellow represents a vow he has taken during great danger.

PLATE 1

1   Plains Indian warrior, 1874–80

2   Central Plains Lakota Indian, 1874–80

3   Cheyenne Indian, 1874–80

Left: Sitting Bull, a Teton-Sioux, was born at a camp on Willow Creek, near the mouth of the Cheyenne River, and near old Fort George, about 1830. Cruel in nature, lazy and vicious, he never told the truth when a lie would serve better. As a Medicine Man, he had the squaws of his tribe abjectly subservient, and through them maintained control over all the bucks (author's collection).

Right: Curley, Crow Scout for Lt. Col. George A. Custer, 7th Cavalry, deserted the field of battle at the Little Big Horn, 25 June 1876. To save the honor of Curley, historians claim that Custer dismissed his Crow and Ree Scouts before the battle commenced. Years after he has been hailed as the only living survivor (author's collection).

fire'. Before the last camp fire was extinguished, an ember was placed inside a buffalo horn along with a piece of fungus punk and tightly sealed. This was slung over the shoulder of the brave chosen as 'Fire Keeper'. It was his role to make certain the ember kept lit and smoldered all through the journey to bring forth life and warmth once more to the new village.

Clothing generally worn by all Indians was a breech cloth, moccasins and a fringed jacket. Cloth became a trade item and later, when it was easier to obtain, clothing changed somewhat from deer-skin jackets and breeches to cloth in bright colors. Ornaments such as porcupine quills and embroidered, beaded geometric patterns were added to the garments to show the man's wealth. Other decorations might be white ermine tails, scalp locks, silver conchos, eagle feathers and colorful trade beads. It was possible to distinguish a Plains Indian from a Woodland Indian just by looking at his ornate clothing. Woodland Indians followed an angular geometric pattern in addition to flowery vine-like designs. Many of the designs represented subjects such as tepees, mountains, bones, trails, lightning and heavenly stars. The Plains Indian drew upon the circle form in many ways. Circle designs were very common. They were either sewn in colorful beads, porcupine quills, or painted on buckskin. Some designs were zig-zagged, diamond shaped, a pattern of stripes, animal figures, snakes, rainbows, eagles, hail, lightning, and a representation of the gods. The circle was believed to have certain ritual properties and was displayed on garments used in everyday wear – including religious ceremonies. They even lived in conical homes with circular bases which they arranged into camps in a ring formation.

Horse stealing and warfare were continuous affairs among the Plains Indian. When game became scarce in their immediate area, they would invade their neighbors' hunting grounds, causing a tribal feud. To punish the invaders, small raiding bands or 'revenge squads' were sent out. Their purpose was to scalp and steal horses.

Horse stealing was not always the result of revenge, it was a consuming passion with the Plains Indian. Acquiring horses by raiding other villages was a lot easier than tracking down wild horses and breaking them. Young warriors were brought up to believe that to steal the horse of a neighbor was a most challenging and commendable act. A clever technique of horse stealing was practised by the Pawnee who dressed in wolf skin disguises and crawled undetected on their hands and knees into an enemy camp at night. So quietly was the theft carried out that the loss was usually not discovered until the following day. During the Indian wars, when a pursuing Cavalry troop was encamped on the plains, many of their mounts were lost in this manner and the sentries swore they saw and heard nothing all night. This was also a way of knowing the strength of a Cavalry troop, by counting their mounts.

It was a pretty well established fact that if an Indian walked up behind you, you wouldn't know it until he tapped you on the shoulder. It probably was because of his soft moccasins. Each tribe had its own foot wear shape and decoration so that a well-trained Indian scout could generally tell an enemy tribe by glancing at a set of moccasin tracks. Some moccasins had long heavy fringes or animal tails at the heel to drag over the footprint and erase the track.

Plains Indian moccasins had hard, thick soles, giving them greater protection from cactus and hard prairie ground. Woodland Indians had a softer sole, as the ground offered pine needles and thick heavy grass to walk on. During cold winters and heavy wet snow, moccasins of another type had to be used. These were waterproofed to some degree by making soles and uppers from the well-smoked skin tops of old lodges. They were not perfectly waterproof, but they never became hard or cracked from constantly having been soaked. These cold weather moccasins also had high buckskin tops to protect ankles, with long leather thongs to fasten about the ankles tightly. There was no need to decorate this type of footwear, as it was designed for hard service. To keep the foot warm and comfortable, leaves, sagebrush bark and clipped buffalo hair was matted into insulation pads of various thicknesses.

Winter moccasins were either made with animal hair turned inward or cut extra large so heavy inner wrappings could be added. Moccasins intended for ceremonial and festival use had decorations covering the entire upper portion and moccasin tongues. Older styles were colorfully quilled.

Southern Cheyenne moccasins had broad scallops in a design while the Sioux often had the top quilled in long red and green triangles, with beads in white, red, blue and yellow and stepped edges. Crow beaded moccasins had a 'U' shaped beaded area on top, or green and red designs interweaving across the top. Both Comanche and Kiowa footwear had a pointed toe shape with strong diagonal lines in the beading.

The bow and arrow was the primary weapon for hunting and warfare, but there was also the lance, knife, club and hatchet, long before the White Man's guns were adopted by the Indians. White traders began furnishing firearms to Indians as early as the last part of the eighteenth century. The early types were matchlock and flintlock, muskets and pistols. Canada's Hudson Bay Company originated a short-barreled, lightweight, cheaply constructed musket, in a .60 caliber. The barrel was octagonal at the breech and had a smooth bore, while the stock was full, with a squared butt covered with a brass butt-plate, and a cast brass side-plate in the image of a scaled dragon on the left side. The trigger guard was large and bow-shaped so it could be fired with a winter glove cover-

Portraying a Blanket Indian, Basil White Eagle, a chief in his own right, and an actor on screen and television, explains the many uses of blanket language. He is of the Menominee tribe (author).

ing on the hand. Just recently a new fact came to light: another reason for such a huge trigger guard was that it was not designed initially for a winter glove, but for several fingers to pull the extremely hard trigger to ignite the charge.

The Indian was somewhat skeptical at first about these 'smoke sticks', as they called them, and at first refused to have anything to do with them. But once they became accustomed to the noise and the recoil, they recognized its great potential over the bow and arrow for distance and knock-down power. The Northwest Trade Gun (also called 'Fusees') became the Indians' preferred weapon.

Even though the percussion cap superseded the flintlock ignition system as early as 1816, it was not accepted by the American public until the mid-1820s, and by the time the mountain men introduced the half-stock 'plains (percussion) rifle' to the Plains

Indian, they refused to trade for anything other than their old 'stand-by', the flintlock. Flintlocks were not all that dependable, but they were cheap to operate and simple to use. If an Indian needed a fire, he charged the pan of his flintlock with powder and pulled the trigger, and from a shower of sparks ignited a handful of dry bark, leaves and grass, afterwards blowing the embers into a flame. Percussion caps, the newer innovation, weren't as easy to procure in the wilderness as flints were. But, before long, traders and wagon train immigrants would soon come along with a good supply to trade, or the Indian raided and took what he wanted. Loading a flintlock or a percussion cap and ball rifle was a meticulous, time-consuming task. Powder had to be measured, the ball had to be rammed down the barrel with a long rod, and the lock had to be primed with powder or capped. All this took about a minute. The Indian could in that time ride 300 yards and discharge 15 arrows.

After the Civil War, there were many experimental

weapons on hand. Since the percussion ignition seemed to work well during the war, only a handful of both rifles and pistols were chosen for another experimental changeover, the Rim-Fire cartridge. Most popular of the revolvers chosen by our government for the army were Colt, Remington and Smith and Wesson, all to be converted to handle a rim-fire cartridge. Rifles, such as Winchester, Springfield, Remington and Sharps were changed slightly in caliber, but to also take a rim-fire cartridge.

The Plains Indian was totally confused, and knowing nothing about these new cartridges attempted to load them at the muzzle, ramming the cartridge down the barrel similar to the percussion models instead of properly loading the cartridge at the breech. However, it didn't take long to catch on to the new system and they were back to pillaging once again with their new rifles. Weapons, mainly rifles, were acquired through trade, gift, capture or theft. The Indian became more expert with them, and used their firepower in an attempt to thwart the white

---

PLATE 2

4 Apache Indian scout, 1878

5 Apache Indian, 1878

6 Apache Indian, 1878

4. *In 1866 an Act of Congress was passed by General Order No. 56, enlisting a force of 1,000 Indians by the Quartermaster Department as scouts in the Territories and Indian country. They received the regular army pay of $13.00 a month and were equipped as cavalrymen, but regarded as soldiers only in a temporary or provisional sense. The government saw fit to issue the Indian scouts a nickel-plated Colt single action .45 caliber revolver with a 7½-inch barrel. The reason for the nickel plating was supposedly to keep the weapon free of rust as Indians often neglected their arms. The 'Indian Scout Colts' were issued between 1873 and 1891, with high serial numbers and stamped USID (United States Interior Department) and USIS (United States Indian Service). Although Army blue jackets were standard issue for Indian scouts, they were sometimes cast aside because of the intense heat in the southwest. Many returned to their usual dress of light fabrics and colors. Every so often they would streak their faces when going into battle out of sheer habit.*

5 and 6. *The word 'Apache' apparently stems from the Zuni name 'enemy'. They are a tribe of North American Indians of Athapascan stock. These nomadic tribes formerly ranged over south-eastern Arizona and south-western New Mexico. The chief divisions of the Apaches were the Arivaipa, Chiricahua, Coyotero, Faraone/Gileno, Llanero, Mescalero, Mimbreno, Magollon, Naisha, Tehikun, and Tchishi. They were a powerful, warlike tribe, with constant enmity against the whites. Their strength, endurance and stamina were a source of amazement to those whites who knew the Indians well. They were swift and*

tireless at climbing mountains or running ninety miles in thirteen hours. On the side of a mountain they could outrun a horse, and their lung power was remarkable. Physical pain and suffering could be borne to a great degree, and they were able to endure temperatures down to 25 or 40 below zero dressed only in a loin cloth. When mortally wounded or when escape was impossible they would fight until their death. A cruel race, the Apache, they could inflict heinous punishment on their captives by roasting their heads over slow fires, or cutting off, piecemeal, the less vital parts of their bodies and finally smashing in their heads. Liquor, or 'tiswin', was their own brew, when they couldn't steal whiskey from the white man. Bows and arrows seemed primitive, along with fifteen-foot lances, but they were sometimes more effective than our modern arms. When an Apache acquired a firearm he used it fully, but still retained his bow and arrows. At close quarters, when weapons ran out of ammunition, his primitive bow was especially reliable. Apaches were content with clothing of any variety, the more grotesque the better. The breechclout was about two yards long. It passed between the legs and hung over the waist belt in front and back, the rear part falling to the ground. Moccasins were similar to boots, reaching nearly to the knees. Each one was made of half a buckskin turned over in two or three folds allowing them to be drawn up as a protection to the thighs. The soles were made of undressed cowhide with the hairy side out and the toes turned up several inches for protection when running. Apaches designed this type of boot as a direct response to the environment of poisonous snakes and thorny brush. Wrapping their heads in a turban of lightweight cloth gave some relief from the sun's rays or could also be used as a bandage, to tie things with, to signal, and to carry food or other items.

PLATE 2

4 Indian scout, 1878

5 Apache Indian, 1878

6 Apache Indian, 1878

expansion. Although having a good supply of arms, the bow and arrow was his old standby, and was always readily available. In hunting, he became adept at killing buffalo at great speed from horseback, using his old percussion rifle. He had copied this rapid-fire stratagem from the white hunter, spitting a musket ball down the barrel (already primed with powder), from a supply of balls carried in his cheek. The trick was to fire the weapon as the muzzle was lowered, before the ball could roll out. If the weapon was fired as the ball rolled off the powder a little and down the barrel, the force of the ball would just penetrate the buffalo's skin without any severe damage or knock-down power. Should the ball hang up half-way because of accumulated residue from previous firings, the barrel might bubble or explode, creating serious injury to face and hands.

Maintaining his weapons after use was rarely thought of by the Indian. It was neglected through all elements of the weather and hard use. When the stock was badly cracked or broken, he mended the part with wet rawhide which, on drying, shrank to a strong and usually satisfactory repair. Various sizes of brass tacks in designs were driven into the stock to incite good medicine on many guns, and sometimes mirrors were embedded in the stock and used to signal other parties at great distances. How good a shot was

Close-up of three popular Indian weapons.
Top: *Northwest trade gun, flintlock, .60 caliber, with an enlarged trigger guard for a mitted hand.*
Middle: *Springfield trapdoor, .50 caliber cartridge. Brass tacks meant good medicine.*
Bottom: *Plains rifle, maker unknown, .50 caliber percussion half stock. Wrist mended with a brass sheet, probably by a white pioneer (Ron Bork – photo by author).*

the Indian? Studying government records and journals of the cavalry and foot soldier, the Indian wasn't much of a marksman. First of all, he could not afford to waste precious cartridges on rifle practice, since the rifle was mainly used. Second, the white man wanted more in trade for the cartridges than an Indian could afford, so he either stole or raided to acquire them or went without.

The application of war paint was a sacred ceremony for the Plains Indian warrior. He stripped himself of all clothing except for a loin cloth, cartridge belt and moccasins. Painting both face and body was a way of mental conditioning, as well as a personal protective display of courage in the face of the enemy. If there was a variety of colors to use and enough time to do it, he would very carefully choose the colors that appealed to him. Stripes and spots pleased his spirit-guided ideas taught to him by his tribe or from membership in a secret war society. War paint was not used to frighten the enemy, it was a symbol with a well-founded meaning, such as to seek vengeance for a wrong perpetrated by the enemy. As an example; a slash of white paint down each side of the face from cheek bone to chin represented: 'My relatives have been killed by the white man, I shall avenge them.' Several white or yellow bands across the nose meant: 'I have two sisters captured and held hostage, I plan to free them.' A red chin meant: 'I am going to destroy the intruders of my land.' Another example may show white dots running down from beneath the left eye: 'My heart is heavy for you have slain my family.'

Scalping has been attributed to the French, during the French and Indian wars, when a scalp brought a bounty—proving an Indian had been killed. However, a tuft from a long haired dog or a portion of the tail from a horse was· substituted many times as an Indian scalp until the scheme was uncovered. The French then employed Indians who, when coming into possession of a scalp, studied it and looked for lice or nits (eggs of the louse). If these were present, the bounty was granted.

The majority of Indians had a peculiar custom in taking scalps. Striking an enemy with a 'coup stick' after he was down meant he could demand the scalp trophy. This custom was attributed to the warrior's desire to be the first to strike an enemy so that he could claim to be in advance of all others in the battle and therefore the foremost and bravest. The manner of taking a scalp in battle was with a sharp butcher knife. The warrior would cut around the braid of the scalp lock a circle two or three inches in diameter and then with a jerk tear it from the skull. If there was plenty of time, and he wasn't exposed to any danger, the entire scalp was torn from the head. Some who were unfortunate enough to have this done to them during a battle recovered but suffered ever after from headaches, earaches, nervous prostration, and constant colds. The unprotected cranium subjected the victim to great inconvenience during every climatic change throughout his life span.

Scalps were displayed on top of tepees, on war shirts, scalp hoops, weapons and war shields. Long hair from women was usually the first choice and most of the time the whole scalp was taken, dividing it later into many smaller scalp locks. Every tribe had a different method of scalping. Some cut in triangular shapes, others in ovals and squares. So if a victim was found with a parcel of hair cut away in an oval or triangular shape, it was known which tribe had done the deed. Scalps, to the Indian, were the badges of distinction, as well as the evidence of his claim to greatness among his people. Many frontiersmen traveling alone on the prairies were generally warned by their seasoned fellow buckskinner with this parting phrase: 'Stay warm, and keep your top-knot' (meaning 'hair').

The Plains Indian took pride in riding his painted pony into battle. Symbols of heroic deeds were painted on both sides of his animal by the women of his family, while he cleansed himself in a ceremonial sweat bath. The same symbols that appeared on his horse were reproduced on his body by himself. The warrior even awarded his mount with high battle honors and painted red circles around old wounds. The famous red hand print painted upside down on the right shoulder was applied only to a pony who had taken his master into danger and returned him safely home. Personal battle awards might be a lucky amulet in its bridle, braided coup feathers in its tail and forelock, and painted symbols upon the horse's body showing ponies stolen and enemies slaughtered.

A long braided rope was secured to the lower jaw of his horse and left to drag behind. Although he could manipulate his mount with this rope when riding, it was also useful in case he fell off in battle, the rope being long enough to allow him to catch his horse again. Few trappings were used as the Indian rode bareback most of the time; the saddle was used very little. The warrior's pony was small and tough and could travel great distances without winding. When riding into battle and then retreating, the warrior might have taken along several other horses

One of the great Indian personalities in history, Chief Washakie, of the Wind River Reservation in Wyoming. Washakie standing with wide-brimmed hat in hand, his Shoshoni followers behind him (circa 1883) (Union Pacific Railroad Museum).

and staked them in some hidden thicket not too far off. If pursued by his enemy, he might switch mounts frequently so the ponies would not tire easily.

As many hunting parties passed each other on the Great Plains, spoken communication was almost impossible, so sign language was used to identify them-

A Cheyenne Indian returning from a battle with trophies from dead soldiers. Horses and weapons were much sought after (Artist: E. L. Reedstrom).

Warm Springs Apache Indian Scouts, Modoc War, 1873. One cannot help noticing the uniforms and weapons in this photo. The uniforms are from the government stock-piles of the Civil War. The old 'Hardee Hats' with obsolete brass decorations, adorn their noble heads. The old Cavalry stand-by is the 7 shot tubular Spencer carbine, shown in each of the Scouts' hands. Even though this weapon came equipped with the cartridge box containing 10 ready loaded magazines, they were issued only one magazine tube of 7 cartridges. The government's reason was to curb any probable retaliation they might harbor (National Archives).

selves and understand one another. To communicate by sign language required some skill, and a degree of ingenuity and forethought beyond that required in vocal or emotional language. Carrying on a conversation by hand signals was nearly universal among all Indian nations, and was handed down from a remote period. No one knows of its origin, and the Indians themselves did not know how they acquired it.

Sign language was very figurative. For instance, if an Indian desired to say that you were not truthful, he touched his tongue with one finger, and held up two

PLATE 3
7 'Curley', Crow Indian scout, 1880
8 Brule Sioux, 1880
9 Sitting Bull Jr., 1890s

7. *'Curley', Lt. Col. G. A. Custer's trusted Crow Indian scout. On June 25, 1876, the 7th Cavalry reached the Little Big Horn where they came across the huge Indian camp they had been seeking. All the scouts – Crow, Ree, and Arikara – were relieved of their duties as it was not their fight. Curley was one of those scouts. Many historians believed he was the last man to see Custer alive. Later, Curley was hailed as 'the last survivor of the "Battle of the Little Big Horn"', after he had fabricated a story that he partook in that battle and escaped with his life by hiding inside a horse's belly. Here Curley poses in a five-button Army blue tunic, his hair swept back Crow style, an 1872 issued woolen blanket wrapped around his torso, a quirt dangling from his left wrist, and partially leaning on a Springfield 45/70 carbine with little concern for the weapon. Ironic as it may seem, Curley did not speak any English. His language until his death in 1923 was that of the Crow tribe. Up until 1959 Curley was labeled as the only survivor of the 'Custer Massacre'. This author has since found additional material and proof of an eyewitness account of one D. R. Ridgeley, trapper, who, with two other captured white men, escaped from the Sioux encampment the night after the battle. (For further details see* Bugles, Banners and War Bonnets, *E. L. Reedstrom, Bonanza Books, 1986.)*

8. *With a feathered headdress, this Brule Sioux has adopted portions of the white man's wardrobe which was common for that*

period with Agency Indians. The term 'Blanket Indians' means reservation Indians who receive clothing, food, and blankets from government annuities with their promise to lay down their arms and follow the white man's ways. Blanket language was very important in council meetings with other chieftains or white men. The manner in which his 1861 Army blanket was draped around his body or carried indicated what he wanted to express. In this pose he is ready to address the head Chiefs of the tribe in a council meeting. His battle club, with two saber tip blades, accompanies him. He will illustrate that he will be peaceful forever by sinking the two blades into the ground. Eagle feathers behind his head are decorated with tufts of red-dyed horse hair showing that he was first to strike and kill the enemy.

9. *Sitting Bull Jr. wears a small headdress according to tribal rank which he has earned. He cradles the traditional peace pipe that white men so often smoked at peace parleys, later breaking their promises. Having shed all buckskins, he now adopts the white man's clothing, showing his good faith. He wears his blanket as a tribal councilman would, along with a long pipe bag made of tanned deer hide, sinew-sewn with rows of glass seed beads for decoration.*

Great Indian warriors sometimes earned enough honors to wear a double-tailed bonnet, so long that it would have dragged the ground. Ordinarily, these long tails were gathered up by the wearer and draped over an arm when walking, but on horseback they were dropped to fall free to dance in the wind while in motion.

PLATE 3

8   Brule Sioux, 1880

9   Sitting Bull Jnr., 1890s

7   'Curley', Crow Indian scout, 1880

E. L. REEDSTROM

fingers toward you, signifying that you were double-tongued, that is untruthful. If he wished to say that a given place was distant two, three or more days' journey, he twirled the fingers of both hands, one over the other, like a wheel rolling, then inclined the head as if asleep, and held up as many fingers as there were 'sleeps' meaning nights; thus indicating the number of days' travel necessary to reach the place in question. If he desired to refer to the past, he extended the right hand in front with the index finger pointed, and drew his arm back with a screw motion, meaning a long time back. If he intended to refer to the future, he placed his hand with the index finger extended at his back, pushing it forward with a screw motion, thus signifying a distant time in the future. If a man on horseback was to be described, he did so by putting the first and second fingers over the fingers of the left

The government enlisted white Scouts as civilians, employees of the Quartermaster's Department, but Indians were usually enlisted men, and recognized as part of the Army. Congress passed an Act in 1866 providing to enlist a force of Indians, not exceeding one thousand, who were to act as Scouts in Indian Territories, receiving a regular army pay of $13 a month and equipped as Cavalry men. They were only regarded as soldiers in a temporary or provisional sense (painting by the author).

A Sioux warrior with long braided hair typical of those belonging to secret societies. It is not unusual to see his bow and arrows carried in this manner (sculpture by Ron Bork).

hand, jerking the hands up and down either in a slow or fast pace. If he wished to state that he had a large quantity of anything, he made the sign of a heap with his two hands shaped like a funnel, then moving them upward from the ground to a point, in the form of the letter 'A'. If he desired to say that he had nothing, he simply opened the palm of his right hand, and in a sweeping-away motion, with a movement of the forearm to the right, indicated that the hand was empty. These are only a few of the many symbols of sign language, but it doesn't stop there. Mounted warriors often communicated in sign language by movements of their horses, whether in circles or some other deployable act. Other signals were a flashing mirror in the sun and waving a buffalo hide over their head in different motions, and another means was by fire and smoke. The latter was of great service while in the mountains, and to the Indians was perfectly intelligible. Even though smoke was hard to manage on a cold windy day, yet they made it serve their purpose well.

Sign language was practiced so often by both Indian and white man that the US Army published a lengthy book on the subject (*Indian Sign Language* by W. P. Clark), primarily for their frontier officers, to communicate with various chieftains in parleys and peace agreements.

As nearly as can be estimated, there were over one million Indians scattered throughout the land, as reported by early trappers and traders. Indians were superstitious of being counted and, as the white man was seldom permitted to enter villages, no real appraisal of their numbers could be made. There were more than 600 separate and distinct societies, and within each society were hundreds of small, separate, thinly scattered tribes and communities. Each of these small groups had its own language (there were over 250 languages and dialects), practiced its own style of dress, designed its own kind of housing, and had its individual customs and standards of living.

Over the years, many of the older people who could still remember rituals, customs and spiritual ceremonies died and carried their memories with them. There were no books written by American Indians to pass on the customs to their children's children, but only experiences painted on buffalo hides of the many hard winters and fierce battles they had to face. Today's Indian relies on the white man's records and ethnological studies for details that have been lost and forgotten by the head tribesman. The American Indian has much too long followed the white man's path. When he stepped out of his moccasins to walk in the white man's shoes, he left his past behind him.

The capture of Geronimo may well be said to mark the end of the Indian wars in the United States. It was, however, followed by one more incident which attracted widespread interest and some fear. The defeat of the Indians had placed them in a position of humiliation and submission, and possibly through accident they turned to the promises of a new religion to restore the prestige and glory of a departed day. The 'Messiah Craze' or the 'ghost dance religion' was to be the swan song of the American Indian. The Messiah craze swept the country in 1889 and 1890, and it was unlike any other that had been staged before. The craze coincided with a period of unrest among the Sioux, and the combination of dissatisfaction and prophetic frenzy brought both red man and white to

Apache renegade, bent on running the white man out of his territory. Cradling an 1876 Winchester .44/40 caliber lever action rifle, he is ready to do battle with anyone representing white supremacy. Dressed much like the reservation Indians, he slips across the guard post with ease and undetected (painting by the author, 1964).

a pitch of excitement where anything could erupt, and far too much did.

From over the Rockies came a story that a Piute medicine man had seen great visions. Wovoka or Jack Wilson, a young brave whose boyhood had been spent in the family of a white rancher, was much affected by an eclipse of the sun coinciding in time with a serious illness. In his delirium he visited the spirit world, bringing back with him the message of a coming day when the glory of the red man would revive. Old mighty leaders would return, as well as the vanished herds of buffalo, and troops of wild horses waiting only for the lariat.

To bring all this about, it was necessary for all to join with fervor in dancing for six days at each appearance of the new moon, making invocation for the

Bloody Knife, Custer's valiant Arikara Scout for the famed 7th Cavalry is far in advance of Major Reno's column. The Scout took a bullet in the skull at the Little Big Horn Battle, 25 June 1876. (Artist: E. L. Reedstrom).

return of the spirits. In due time the reward would present itself. News of the ghost dance spread out into Oklahoma and the Cheyenne and Arapaho tribes learned of it. They sent a delegation of inquiry to the Shoshoni, and after their return they were convinced of the emergence of the Messiah. The word spread Eastward, to the Sioux agency at Standing Rock and the camp on Grand River where Sitting Bull sat in sullen gloom, looking back at his diminished state and power.

Sitting Bull recognized this as an opportunity to regain his former prestige, but only his band was allowed to participate in the ghost dance. The greater number of the Sioux were slow to be infected. Nevertheless, the new craze made a strong appeal to the deepest instincts of the Indian heart. The white man watched the manifestation with growing apprehension.

The craze was at its height at Pine Ridge Indian Reservation, South Dakota. The Indian agent became alarmed and asked the Army to take charge. Newspapers all over the country began to fan the embers with colorful accounts of frenzied dancers, wild excitement and burning prophecies. All through the autumn of 1890 the situation grew more and more tense. It was soon rumored that a general uprising was at hand. The ghost dance was very strenuous, particularly since it was given three times a day. Both men and women were holding hands and dancing slowly in a circle, all wearing the 'ghost shirt'. This was a hunting shirt usually constructed of buckskin, but since leather was scarce cloth was used. It was to be worn in all religious ceremonies, representing symbolic customs of the past and manners to which the Indians were to return. Just before the bloody battle of Wounded Knee, South Dakota, Yellow Bird, a Sioux medicine man, told the Indians that the shirts were 'medicine' against the white man's bullets. This did not prove to be the case for when the fighting was over there were 150 dead Indians – men, women and children strewn everywhere. The US troops had 25 dead and 35 wounded. The troops sent in were of the Seventh Cavalry, Custer's old command. It has been said that they were thus the instrument of revenge for the defeat of 14 years before at the 'Little Big Horn'. Never again have the gallant Sioux gone on the warpath.

2 The Fringe People

Between the years of 1800 and 1840, hundreds of traders and trappers swarmed the immense under-developed wilderness of the great American West, the region between the Missouri River and the Pacific Ocean, approximately our northern and southern boundaries. They trapped mostly for beaver and occasionally other valuable fur-bearers, hunting big game for hides and meat, seeking out the widely scattered friendly Indian villages in which to trade manufactured commodities for furs and pelts. They called themselves 'Mountain Men' but others as well as the Indians called them the 'Fringe People'. The 'Mountain Man', as he is known to us today, did not come into and remain in the West in force until William H. Ashley took out his first trapping and trading expedition in 1822. That year seems to mark the definite beginning of a well-organized group attempting to penetrate every waterway in which beaver were found. The fur trade not only contributed much to the history of inland North America, it was also responsible for the discovery of much of the region. It not only remained for many years the major industry of the continent, but it produced a colorful class of men from these northern latitudes, men such as the voyageurs, engagés, free trappers, couriers de bois and the mangeurs de lard.

The *voyageurs* were a hardy class of men, trained from boyhood to the use of the paddle. Their canoes were marvels of durability. Made of thin but tough sheets of birch bark, securely gummed along the seams with pitch, they were so strong, and yet so light that the Indians thought them an object of wonder. Many of them were Iroquois Indians—pure or with a mixture of white blood. When they moved their camps, they brought their women and children, along with whatever they solely possessed. The whole supply system depended on these French-Canadian voyageurs who paddled their light canoes heavily laden with trade goods, provisions and sometimes important passengers. The *engagés* were men employed as trappers or hunters by a fur company, and were not prevented from taking a limited amount of trade goods on a trip to do a little private trading.

The Plains Indians were able to supply plenty of

Buffalo skinners working on a carcass. Four men could skin a buffalo in less time than one person can peel an orange (Artist: E. L. Reedstrom).

buffalo skins, but disliked trapping; hence the trading companies organized bands of engagés, trappers who spent most of their time in the Rocky Mountains or Black Hills, and returned yearly to a company post on the upper Platte or Missouri River, in order to turn in their furs and enjoy a week's riotous living on the proceeds. In their songs they expressed how hard they could live, sleep, and eat dogs; in short they could endure anything.

Peltry was also obtained from 'free trappers' who managed by prowess or diplomacy to obtain a certain immunity from the Indian. Supplies and trading goods were sent up-river from St Louis in the spring floods as far as possible by steamboat, and farther in rough 'bateaux' manned by French-Canadian voyageurs. Peltry and buffalo hides were sent down in the same way; or, if the year's taking surpassed the available tonnage, 'bull boats' made of buffalo hides stretched on a wicker frame, bound with buffalo sinews and sealed with buffalo tallow, were used.

The *'free trappers'* or French-Canadian trappers and traders were not connected with any fur companies. They outfitted themselves and worked alone or in parties, selling and trapping where they chose. They were a precarious breed living for themselves, traveling with their Indian wives and half-breed children.

The *couriers de bois* (woods runners) were a more

Left: *Don Good, of Hobart, Indiana, is an authentic buckskinner of this day and age. He belongs to a number of mountain men organizations that dedicate their weekends to shooting black powder rifles and eating dried venison. Don also travels the circuit lecturing at schools, on television and various other organizations. Here he demonstrates loading a rifle, first loading his charger with black powder (author).*

Centre: *A correct amount of powder is poured down the barrel. The rifle's butt is lightly tamped on the ground making certain all of the black powder has come together in bulk (author).*

Right: *A lead ball, same caliber as the rifle bore, and with either a little spit, or, better, lard, to act as a lubricant, is then wrapped in a round cloth patch and guided down the barrel with the aid of a wooden bullet starter (author).*

---

independent and daring body, living on game and dried buffalo meat. They were messengers, runners and packers.

At the very bottom of the heap were the '*mangeurs de lard*' or pork eaters; living on cured rations; they were the unskilled laborers, usually green hands or 'green horns'.

If you were living in St Louis, the gateway to the West, during the early 1800s, you would most likely see a Mountain Man. The very words ring with adventure and excitement. Whether he be tall or short, lean or stout, there would be no mistake in identifying his characteristics. His skin was burned to leather toughness by the sun, his long hair straggled about his shoulders and his keen eyes peered out from under a wide-brimmed hat or a beaver fur cap. His fringed buckskins were decorated in the style of his favorite Indian tribe, patched, tattered, spotted with animal blood, and smelt of burnt pine cones from the many

Two very well preserved beaver top hats of the day. A man of fashion in New York would happily pay $10 for a beaver hat. The Hudson Bay Company exported to England enough North American beaver pelts to make 576,000 hats (author's collection).

Left: *The ramrod plunges the cloth-wrapped ball down the barrel, seating it snugly on top of the black powder. Several tamps indicate a well seated ball (author).*

Centre: *The hammer is pulled back to the first cock, or safety cock, and a percussion cap is gently seated over the nipple (author).*

Right: *By pulling the hammer at full cock, the rifleman is ready to fire. This is in accordance to a rifle that has no 'set-trigger'.*

camp fires he had slept next to. Around his neck were strung his bullet pouch and powder horn. A second leather pouch may be his 'possibles' bag, where he kept almost any article not connected with his rifle. A strong leather belt around his middle holstered a large knife in a leather scabbard, and generally included a long barrel flintlock pistol. And, lastly, cradled in his arms was a .50 caliber Hawken half stock flintlock rifle.

That was a Mountain Man, fearless, alert, tough as a hickory nut and able to fend for himself in an unknown wilderness where everything was his enemy.

St Louis, a fast growing metropolis, was already becoming the center for fur trading. Though the permanent residents numbered more than 2,000, there was by far a larger floating population of French-Canadian voyageurs, Spaniards, merchants from the East, emigrant farmers, and Indians. Fur was the topic of conversation, usually the beaver pelt, whose glossy

coat of fine hair was supplied to manufacturers for the gentleman's top hat of the day. Beaver hats had been worn in Europe as far back as 1760, but they were not fashionable until 1770, and it was only a few years later that the tall, slender beaver hat became a gentleman's style of the day throughout the eastern United States. Further, the grey beaver hat was worn during the day, and the black hat during the evening hours, according to fashionable tradition.

The Hudson Bay Trading Company exported enough North American beaver pelts to England to make 600,000 hats, and it still could not keep up with the demand. In New York, a man of fashion would gladly pay the sum of $10 for a beaver hat, and without thinking twice. As the North American fur business enjoyed its growing market, manufacturers expanded into other products, accenting clothing with various other furs attached to men's and women's apparel in ornamental style. The beaver hat was not only comfortable and stylish, it was also waterproof. Unlike the earlier silk hat, which had to be made proof against water, the beaver hat held its shape and appearance in any type of weather. A quick brushing in the direction of the beaver hairs' growth brought out a glossy luster every time.

The two regular beaver trapping seasons covered the cool periods of the year during which the fur was rich in oil, much heavier and the skin thicker; late fall to early winter, late winter to early spring. Midsummer skins were worthless.

Beavers were found throughout the West, particularly along waterways lined with cottonwood, willow, birch, alder and aspen, which, in the main, constituted their food supply. They lived in mounds, with entrances several inches below the low-water mark.

One trapper was able to handle a string of about 50 traps, which he inspected daily. A good man could possibly handle 100 traps, but the question was how many traps could be carried. If he was going on a marsh, lake or river, where he could travel by boat, or into a region where he could carry his baggage by horse or wagon, he might take along all the traps he could tend, the more the better. But if he was going by overland routes into the rough, woody regions where most game abounds, and consequently must carry his baggage on his back, he would probably find that 50 small traps, or an equivalent weight of large and small ones, would be as much as he would like to carry.

In some cases, trappers preferred to work in small parties. At twilight, each member of a party set out with four to six heavy steel traps. A successful procedure was to place the trap in about four inches of water near the entrance to a burrow. The bait, a pleasantly scented secretion of the beaver's castor glands, was placed on a leaf suspended directly above the trap. So tantalizing was the scent that the beaver stood up on his hind legs and walked directly into the trap. When it sprang, he dived into the deep water and was usually drowned by the weight of the trap before he could gnaw off the imprisoned foot. At the break of dawn, the trappers would visit the area and check their traps. Beavers were usually skinned on the spot. A lengthwise incision was made down the belly and

Jake Hawken's 'Rocky Mountain' rifle barrel measures 34½ inches. A .53 caliber ball is backed with 130 grains of FFg black powder. Presently owned by John D. Baird, author of Hawken's Rifles, the Mountain Man's Choice (author).

PLATE 4

10 **Courier de Bois, 1800–40s**
11 **Engagé, 1800–40s**
12 **Voyageur, 1800–40s**

10. *Courier de bois (Cur-de-bwa). These hunters were French or half-breed Indians. Their jobs were to hunt, trade goods, act as messengers and pack goods in canoes. Their territory was the Northern and Western United States and Canada. Their clothing was colorful and composed mostly of woolen goods, silks, homespun and broadcloth. When they traveled in colonies, their women and children usually accompanied them. Any decorations from the natives would be 'Woodland Indian'.*

11. *Engagé (On-ga-shay), French. A hired trapper or an enlisted man. These men were employed hunters. They were furnished with an outfit by a company and so were bound to sell their furs to that company. Shown here with a low crown hat, fur-trimmed sack coat, cloth breeches with 'botas' or 'half-breeds' below the knees to protect their legs from snake bites and thorny brush.*

12. *Voyageur (Vwa-ya-zhu), French. A man, usually a French Canadian, who signed on with the early-day fur companies because he liked the wilderness and carefree life that his work afforded. Also, like 11 above, called Engagé (French) meaning 'traveler', was the French Creole boatman on the Mississippi River. The fancy garters tied below his knees were for color and decoration more than anything else.*

PLATE 4

10 Courier de Bois, 1800–40s

11 Engagé, 1800–40s

12 Voyageur, 1800–40s

four traverse cuts down the inside of the legs. At the camp, the pelt was stretched on a frame, scraped, and dried. Later it was folded up, the fur side in, for packing. Besides the fur, the tail, a camp delicacy, and the castor glands were saved.

Wild animals were taken for various reasons besides the value of their furs. Some were sought for food, others were destroyed as nuisances. The animals that were valuable for food could be run down by dogs, or shot by a rifle or fowling-piece. Nuisances might be destroyed by poison, but for the capture of fur-bearing animals, there was but one profitable method, namely by steel traps.

It was not unusual for a mountain man to lay his pelts before a fur-dealer and be asked, 'Are your furs shot or trapped?' If the answer was 'They were shot ...', he might find the dealer quite indifferent about buying them at any price. Steel traps did no injury to the fur ... and a good trapper knew this.

Within an approximate period of three months, a trapper who knew his business could earn several thousand dollars. A rule of thumb was seven dollars a day for a five weeks' trip. Good weather, good trapping grounds, good traps, good judgement, and good luck had to be combined to secure good profits.

When the mountain man was loafing between trapping seasons, he spent much of his time gambling, drinking, feasting, squatting on his buffalo robe and smoking his stained clay pipe. When an occasional visitor came into camp, there were many stories swapped back and forth; big talk of the hard winter, the many beaver pelts, fighting Indians or tangling with a huge grizzly. Some of the trapper's finest tales that came from his vivid imagination are now preserved in books and songs. But, at that time, a good story circulated from camp to camp, changing a little each time, until it was completely blown out of proportion. When it finally reached the trapper who originated it, he could hardly recognize it as his very own adventure.

Fighting Indians was nothing new to the mountain man. He was aware of the Indian's style, and he added a few refinements of his own. He often bragged that he could beat the Indian at his own game, and he did. Whether it was hand-to-hand combat, or fighting from tree to tree, it was generally the bloodiest of any combat ever to be witnessed. The trapper had to read signs, like that of an Indian. He had to follow trails, move about without being detected, sense danger, and plan a decisive sudden blow, catching Mr Low off guard. ('Mr Low' was an ancient mountain man's

Top: *J. & S. Hawken advertisement found in early St Louis newspapers.*

Centre: *J. P. Gemmer stencil found on all boxes that were shipped out of gun shop.*

Bottom: *A mountain man could trust a Hawken rifle because it was durable, trustworthy and accurate. It hardly ever needed any repairs whatsoever.*

favorite expression – refering to the wild Indian.) He knew that if he failed any of his own tactics or fell into the hands of the Indians, there would be no mercy; he'd lose his 'top-knot'.

Arrow wounds were most common among the mountain men, but not too many knew how to extract the arrow head, once lodged in a man's body. The Indian war arrow was an ingenious weapon of death. It came from nowhere, unbeknown to its victim. The swiftness of its velocity generally knocked the wind from a person and made it hard to catch his breath. It either lodged in a fleshy portion of the body or into a bone. The problem was to withdraw the arrow and point before the arrow glue and sinew dissolved from the warmth of the flesh around it. Generally, less than one half-hour after the arrow entered the man's body would be the extent of time before the arrow shaft would release itself from its arrow tip. With animals, it was much easier for the Indians to withdraw their own painted shafts and later add another arrow point. For a wounded man, time was a necessity. As soon as the man was hit with a barbed arrow, depending on how deep the arrow was lodged, it either had to be cut out or pushed on through the body. Most experienced mountain men had their own special way of extracting an arrow. One of the best means was the 'pincer pliers'. If the arrow tip was not too deep and not embedded into a bone, but only in the fleshy parts, the pincer pliers could be used to bend or crush the barbed points in order to withdraw the point without causing too much pain to the victim. Seven out of every ten who had been wounded with an arrow never survived. Some of the Indian tribes even poisoned their arrow tips with rattlesnake venom or the dead livers of lizards. Either one had gruesome consequences.

Every summer there was a big gathering of trappers, Indians and fur buyers, mixing together like a 'wild West' carnival. This meeting point was called the 'rendezvous'. Two great pleasure resorts were Taos, New Mexico, and Bent's Fort on the Arkansas River, with Sante Fe, New Mexico, and Independence, Missouri, as secondary meeting points. Caravans up from St Louis, Missouri, brought new traps, guns and powder and ball. Coffee, tobacco, needles and thread were among the choice supplies, along with bright beads, ribbons, mirrors and combs that the trapper could give as presents to the Indian girls. The choice pelts he had trapped during the past year were traded for items he needed out of necessity and for pleasure. Besides trading furs, here the trapper

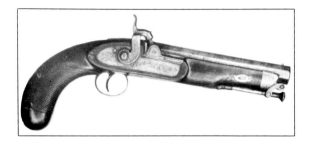

A Sam Hawken Percussion .41 caliber belt pistol with the Hawken name stamped on the top of the barrel. These pistols were sturdy and dependable, but not accurate at any lengthy distance. When the percussion system became available it was hard for the buckskinners to accept them over the old flintlock rifles (John Baird).

met all his old cronies, swapping tales of adventure, forming new partnerships, and competing in games of skill and chance. When the 'rendezvous' was over, he had the 'fixin's' for another year in the mountains.

When the trapper returned from the 'rendezvous', his young squaw and a parcel of half-breed children met him at his base camp. Gifts were usually handed

Tools of the trade are shown here from the personal collection of that celebrated Mountain Man, Mariano Modena. The Hawken rifle was purchased in St Louis in 1833. The patch-box is a rarity on Hawken rifles, and Modena may have requested one (Colorado State Historical Museum).

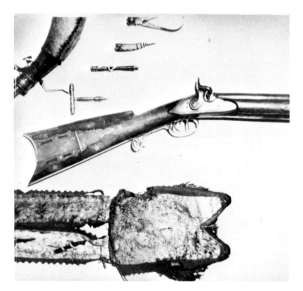

around to all, and much conversation along with questions about the great gathering continued well into the night. The mountain man's squaw was usually a good looking woman, able bodied, one who could dress out a large or small animal, treat skins, butcher the meat, make jerky, cook, sew, tend the stock and take good care of the children. She was 'keeper of the camp' while her man was gone for periods of weeks at a time. Mountain men were always generous, unselfish and loyal to friends. He shared his personal belongings, and lent a hand even if his life was endangered. In a tight spot, his assurance presented a secure feeling. The ingredients of coolness, self-confidence and resourcefulness were prime qualities commanding any situation.

The mountain man's jargon was certainly a language of its own. It was derived from the Missouri backwoods, Indian languages and dialects, Spanish, French and far Southern States lingo . . . with a little profanity mixed in. A dead man was a 'gone beaver', or he had 'gone under'. A man who met a violent death was 'rubbed out'. Women's fancy clothes and other accompaniments were 'fafarraw' or 'foofaraw', and any dance was a 'hop' or a 'fandango'. Tobacco was 'kinikinik', a buffalo skull was a 'kyack', and a large valley was a 'hole'. The two most potent liquors were 'Taos lightning' and 'Picketwire firewater'. When an Indian took a scalp, he 'lifted his hair', took

his 'top-knot', or 'tickled his fleece'. A prime beaver hide was a 'plew', and a rifle was a 'smoke pole', 'Ol' Betsy', or a 'long Tom'.

The English sporting rifles, which were circulating in the St Louis area, were shipped into this country by London gunsmiths. It was hard to market these rifles because they were so expensive, and a mountain man was lucky enough to place his name on the waiting list in order to acquire one. The Harpers Ferry, first made in 1800 and later improved, was too heavy for a saddle gun. Although many of the flintlocks were still favorites with the trappers, they too had their drawbacks. The percussion ignition system took some time to catch on, but while it was slowly becoming a favorite over the flint ignition, the Hawken gun shop had plenty of time to modify and perfect their rifles to meet the demands of the mountain men who drifted into St Louis for supplies, often stopping by the Hawken gun shop with some ideas to enhance future Hawken rifles.

The Hawken rifle was slowly becoming a favorite with the mountain men who swore by its sturdiness, simplicity and dependability in the field. Its accuracy and great power was a match for any big game that moved freely across the plains and mountain areas. A well placed, long range shot could drop a buffalo in his tracks or topple the mightiest of grizzlies. The Kentucky rifle was too fragile and not powerful enough to

---

PLATE 5
13, 14 Tenderfoot, 1820–25
15 Mountain Man, 1820–25

13. *In the early 1820s, during the fur trading days, many adventurers traveled into the mountains completely ignorant of what lay ahead of them. They wore everyday clothing which could not withstand either the heavy underbrush or constant wear. Boots wore out faster by walking on sharp, jagged-edged rocks and wading through ankle or knee-high mountain streams, which caused the boot leather to dry out quickly and split in a number of places. While preparing for the trip, weapons were hastily chosen. Some ventured into the mountains with only a large caliber belt pistol; in this case the new percussion system. It wasn't long before the tenderfoot learned that a heavy caliber rifle was the answer to survival in the wilderness. For both distant shooting and greater knock-down power it was much better than his small handgun.*

14. *After a few years in the mountains light linen shirts and buckskin breeches were common wear after everything else wore out. Cloth shirts were worn in the summer when the heat made skin shirts uncomfortable, and during the winter a cloth shirt was a welcome item beneath a buckskin shirt. Cloth shirts were brought west for trade. They were constructed from cotton, wool,*

linsey-woolsey, calico, muslin, pillow ticking and linen. These shirts were of various styles and colored designs, and most trappers had a number of these on hand. The large hat is hand-made from a skin, soaked in a prepared solution, pounded out to head size, cut to shape, and then smoked.

Garter-gaitors or knee-ties held up 'half-breeds', an added leg covering for cold weather, sharp brush, cactus and thorns or snake bites. His 'possibles bag' hung from the neck and held everything he needed to build a fire, hold food, and prime and load his .50 caliber Hawken rifle.

15. *As the Mountain Man began to adopt the Indians' way of life and dress, his complete attire was buckskin. Now and then he would decorate a new hat that he acquired by trade and adorn it with eagle or turkey feathers, much like an Indian would embellish his scalp lock in war games. His ornate possibles bag, powder horn and Bowie knife encircle his small frame and a percussion half-stock rifle is cradled in his arms. From his belt hangs a 'bacca' (tobacco) pouch with a mixture of 'Kinnikinnic', 'honeydew', or 'Ol' Virginny'. This was firmly packed down into the bowl, sometimes carved from an animal bone lit with an ember from the campfire. The leg-gaiters are colorful, but this time they have a reason – to keep ticks and other pesky insects from climbing up his legs.*

PLATE 5

13, 14   Tenderfoot, 1820–25

15   Mountain Man, 1820-25

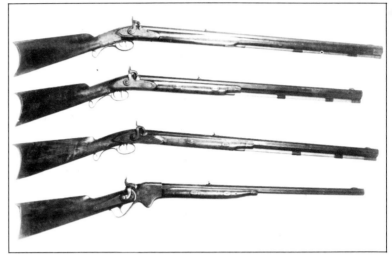

Above Left: *Sam Hawken, famed gun maker, as he appeared in retirement and only a few years before his death (Art from photo, E. L. Reedstrom).*

Above: *Full stock Hawken rifle of early type at top. Two center rifles are sturdy Sam Hawken half stock 'Mountain Rifles'. The Spencer (bottom) was fitted with a special barrel by the Hawken shop (Wm. C. Almquist Collection).*

cope with the hunting of large game. If dropped from the saddle by accident, the slim stock could crack in a number of places. The fine mechanism within the lock plate would also foul from the fall, causing the rifle to find its way to the bench of a gunsmith if one was nearby.

Many questions have come about as to the typical everyday dress of the mountain man. Naturally, the cut of the man's clothing depended upon his prosperity. His skins came from his own skills in trapping, decorations were either copied from a certain Indian tribe or to his own individual taste. Undergarments were never used by the mountain men. Only a breech clout was worn beneath a pair of buckskin leggings. These leggings were trousers without the seat. Along the outside seams of the leggings were long fringes that provided him with thongs and laces when needed. It is also believed that these fringes acted as rain drains, the rain dripping from the end of the fringe, rather than soaking and swelling the seams.

The upper part was also buckskin, either a coat type or pull over shirt. Fringes hung from the shoulder, chest, sleeves and sometimes outlined the pockets. If any type of buttons were used, they were made from leather woven into a ball shape, or cut ovals from the antlers of a deer. There may have been a storm cape attached to the shoulders, also of buckskin, and fringed. Moccasins with tough soles of rawhide called

'parfleche' were worn instead of shoes or boots. During extreme bitter weather, old pieces of blanket were wrapped around his feet to keep them from freezing. Over this costume, a heavy blanket or buffalo robe was worn loosely to combat the freezing winds.

For headgear, a light handkerchief wrapped around his forehead served that purpose during the summer months, or the usual broad brimmed black or brown beaver hat with a low crown. Most of these hats were made by the mountain men. A hole was dug into the ground as near as possible the shape and size of his head. A large, circular piece of rawhide, wet, soft and pliable, was spread over the hole. With a bunch of grass or buckskin, the center of the rawhide was pressed down into the hole until it assumed its size and shape. The surrounding circle of hide which was to be the rim was kept flat on the ground by constant patting of the hands all around it. When the hat was moulded, it was left in the sun to be completely dried. Then it was taken to a place where smoke and heat scorched it so that it was perfectly waterproof. Trimming the hat with strings and straps made it ready for use. For the winter, massive fur caps were worn. If the fur was wolf, as an example, the animal's head was preserved and displayed on the front.

This everyday wardrobe was enhanced in time of leisure by sashes, beads, fringes, braids, feathers and

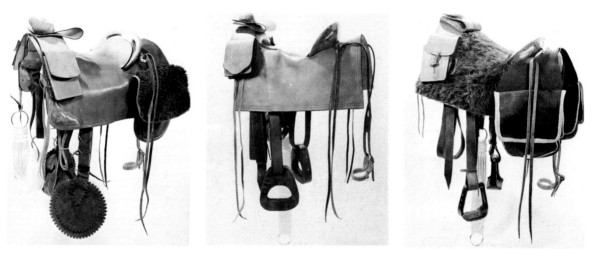

Above left: *Spanish saddle with a Mexican style horn, deep saddle bags, a rifle strap around horn, and front and back saddle thongs that are slightly longer for tying bed rolls and capotes. Spanish tapaderas cover the stirrups (Saddlemaker Bob Schmidt).*

Above Center: *Spanish saddle with a very early apple style horn. It has a 5-inch cantle which makes a deeper seat. The mochilla is of heavy saddle skirting and the stirrups made of sturdy cottonwood, edged with rawhide. Cruppers were generally used to keep the saddle in place in hilly or mountainous terrain (Saddlemaker Bob Schmidt).*

Above Right: *The Santa Fe saddle, duck bill horn, was used by American trappers as early as the mid-1820s, when crossing overland from Missouri direct to the central Rockies. Lewis and Clark journals reveal seeing this saddle in the hands of a Shoshoni Indian while crossing Montana territory in 1805 (Saddlemaker Bob Schmidt).*

Below: *This is what the ol' timers called a Prairie Chicken Snare Saddle, which appeared sometime after 1850. This is quite similar to the type of saddle that the Plains Indians used. It has suspended buffalo hide seat, rawhide rigging, with buffalo hide under each saddle bar for padding. Stirrups were wooden, covered with rawhide (Saddlemaker Bob Schmidt).*

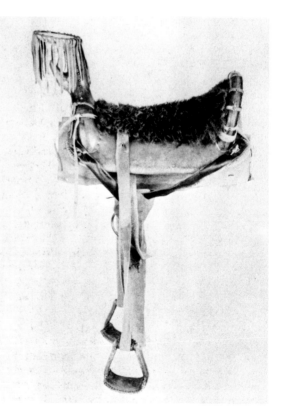

porcupine quills, adopted from their Indian neighbors. The brightest designs were to catch the eyes of the youngest and most desirable squaws, who were ever susceptible to the wiles of the mountain man. An Indian woman preferred a white companion to a red buck. She received more trinkets, gained more consideration from her white man, had an easier time of it, and acquired a little social prestige. On the whole, both trapper and squaw made excellent partners, and neither had much to complain about.

To tote all the paraphernalia the mountain man had to carry, he was wise to choose a sound, well broken Indian pony or a sturdy, active mule for a saddle and pack animal. Mules were mostly selected because they were termed 'sure-footed' on Rocky Mountain trails. The trappers swore that their mules could smell an 'Injun' a long way off, and signalled their masters by a certain switch of an ear ... with their head pointing in

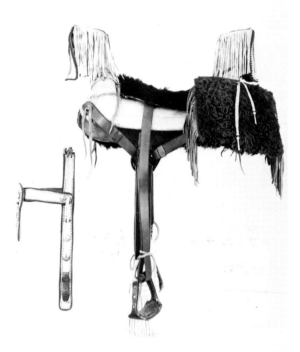

This is a squaw saddle, the style used by all Plains tribes. It was made of wood and covered with rawhide. Maximillian observed this type of saddle in use in 1833. He noted that both pommel and cantle 'frequently had leather fringe hanging from it'. This saddle had smoked brain tan leather covering the tree, suspended buffalo hide seat, buffalo hide pads for the saddle bars. The saddle was rigged with saddle skirting and mohair cinch. The stirrups are wooden with rawhide covering. The pommel and cantle flaps are brain tan leather with red trade cloth trim, blue and white real beads (or small pony beads) trim. The bags were buffalo hide with leather fringe, lined with pillow ticking. The headstall is brain tan, backed with split cowhide and trimmed with red trade cloth. Brass conchos are sometimes on the side of the headstall. It has brass buckles and saddle leather to hold the bit. The forehead piece is brain tan trimmed in red trade cloth with red cloth circle (Saddlemaker Bob Schmidt).

chances of relying upon his animals to survive in the great wilderness, a greater respect was bestowed on the animals by the trapper.

After 1835, there were five more 'rendezvous', each with the same highlights and delightful spectacles as seen before. But, after 1840, memories of the glorious days slowly died away. Many of the active mountain men either died or invested their hard earned money into eastern businesses. And, not being businessmen, they, too, came into poor returns. Some purchased farms in Oregon or Missouri, or served emigrants as guides and interpreters. Slowly, these adventurers disappeared, never to be heard from again. Had it not been for a man's fashionable beaver hat and fur trimmed collar, the mountain man may very well have never come into existence.

the direction of the disturbance. Lonely as it was in the mountains for one man, he could always talk to his animals as if they understood him. When drunk, his anger was sometimes taken out on the animals, either by whipping them or just plain cursing them out. However, when man had to balance out his

---

PLATE 6
16,17 Mountain Men, 1850s
18 Mariano Modena, 1850–70s

16 *and* **17.** *This Mountain Man's costume was designed not only to be comfortable in his daily wilderness chores but also to catch the eyes of the youngest, most desirable Indian squaws, who were ever susceptible to the wiles of the Mountain Men. Indian women preferred a white consort to a red one. In this respect she got more of the good things of mountain life, and an easier time of it. Headgear ranged from a light handkerchief in the summer to a massive fur cap during the winter. Year-round head coverings were usually a broad-brimmed brown beaver hat with a low crown.*

Underwear was unknown. He wore a breech clout and over that his buckskin leggings (trousers without a seat). Fringes hung from arms and leggings. They were woven into the buckskin seams and knotted on the inside. What remained outside were very long thongs, and when needed they were used for lacing

moccasins and other repairs. Most shirts of buckskin were pull-overs. Others were folded over in the manner of a double-breasted coat and tied in the middle. Storm capes were attached to the shoulders, and during winter a heavy blanket or capote (see center figure) was worn over the entire costume.

Moccasins with soles of tough rawhide called 'parfleche' were worn - and in cold weather he wrapped his feet with strips of old blankets.

Our first figure clutches a Hawken full stock percussion rifle, .58 caliber, while the middle man holds the famous Lancaster full stock percussion rifle, .50 caliber.

18. *Mariano Modena, a Mountain Man whose exploits of daring were extolled in 'The Rocky Mountain News' and other publications of the day. He would certainly take no prizes for sartorial elegance, but he was a hard man to beat when it came to shooting his famous Hawken rifle, the 'Big Fifty'. Later in life he was so badly plagued with rheumatism that he could not move his fingers or straighten up.*

PLATE 6

16, 17 Mountain Men, 1850s

18 Mariano Modena, 1850–70s

3 The Westward Trek

The only white men who penetrated the Far West region before 1830 were explorers, fur traders, and trappers. As soon as Lewis and Clark brought news of the untouched store of fur bearing animals in the core of the continent, commercial companies were organized to hunt them. The Plains Indians were able to supply plenty of buffalo skins, but they disliked trapping. Because of this, trading companies organized bands of engagés, trappers who spent most of their time in the Rocky Mountains or the Black Hills, returning yearly to a company post on the upper Platte or Missouri River. There they turned in their furs, and enjoyed a week of riotous living on the proceeds they received. Supplies and trading goods were sent up-river from St Louis in the spring floods, as far as possible by steamboat and farther in the rough 'bateaux' manned by French Canadian 'voyageurs'.

Every river, valley, mountain passage and water hole of the Far West was known to the trappers before 1830, and without their guidance and knowledge trans-continental emigrations would have been next to impossible.

In 1830, a party of trappers led by Jedediah Smith and William Sublette took the first covered wagons from the Missouri to the Rockies. Six years later,

Captain Bonneville, whose adventures provided literary material for Washington Irving, led the first wagons through the South Pass of the Rockies in Wyoming, and down the Snake Valley to the Columbia.

Many of the people involved were of French Canadian extraction. In Canada, Catholic Missionaries followed close on the heels of the traders, but the missionaries in this country were Protestant Yankees. In 1832, a group of Methodists joined a fur trading party on a long overland route and, by 1834, had established a mission in the valley of the Willamette River which flowed into the Columbia at the present site of Portland, Oregon. Two years later, a band of Presbyterians, including Dr Marcus Whitman and the first woman to cross the North American Continent, founded mission stations in the Walla Walla country, at the junction of the Snake and Columbia rivers.

Western Oregon was delightfully mild with an equable climate. The territory contained a mixture of open prairie with pine woods, rich soil, and natural meadows for grazing cattle. The missionaries published letters that spread the word of Oregon as a home and stressed the wilderness theme.

By 1842, the 'Oregon fever' struck the frontier folk of Iowa and Missouri, eager to resume their former pioneering experiences. Independence, Missouri, was the jumping-off place for the Oregon trail. Covered wagons converged there from the East in May when the plains grass was fresh and green.

Parties were organized, a captain appointed and an experienced trapper or fur trader engaged as pilot. Amid a great blowing of bugles and the sound of long whips cracking, the caravan of perhaps 100 wagons accompanied by hundreds of cattle on the hoof, moved off up the West bank of the Missouri River. At Fort Leavenworth, one of the bastions of the Indian frontier, emigrants enjoyed the protection of their

Wagon trains stayed close to waterways while travelling westward. The average distance was from 6 to 20 miles a day, depending on the type of animals used. Oxen or bull trains were slower than horses or mules; also considered was the weight, terrain and weather (Artist: E. L. Reedstrom).

country's army for the last time. Near Council Bluffs, where the Missouri River is joined by the Platte, the Oregon trail turned west to follow the latter river over the Great Plains. Not until ruts had been beaten into the sod to form a road was it less difficult to find the way. Numerous creeks and tributaries of the Platte, swollen and turbid in the spring, had to be forded, with a considerable amount of loss and damage to stores and baggage, not to mention lives.

Every night, the great caravans made a hollow circle of wagons around its fire of cottonwood or buffalo chips. Sentries stood guard to protect the hobbled horses and grazing cattle while humming to themselves old Appalachian Ballads, to help keep the herd calm.

As they pressed forward the trail became hilly and then mountainous. Beyond the South Pass came the worst part of the journey: a long, hard pull across the arid Wyoming basin, where the grass was scanty, and alkali deposits made the water unfit to drink. Between the Gros Ventre and Teton ranges of the Rockies, the emigrants found westward-flowing waters and took heart; but there was still 800 miles to go to the lower Columbia, following the meanderings of the Snake River. With fair luck an emigrant party that left Independence in May might expect to celebrate Thanksgiving Day in the Willamette valley. It was a lucky caravan indeed that arrived with the same number of souls that started out. Weaker parties slowly dropped out or just disappeared, whether by starvation after losing the trail, or at the hands of hostile Indians, no one knows.

After a route across the plains had been carefully chosen, and the exact number of families had arrived at the Eastern terminus, their first business was to organize themselves into a company and elect a Commander or Captain. The Company had to be of sufficient size to herd and guard the animals, as well as for protection against Indians. Fifty to seventy men, well armed and fully equipped to handle almost any circumstance, would be adequate. More than that could make their movement slow and cumbersome.

Selection of a Captain meant choosing someone who had good judgement, integrity of purpose and experience. His duty was to direct the march, select new campsites, order the starting and halting of marches, give orders to guards and control and supervise all movements of the Company. If need be, he was judge and jury, to some extent, administering punishment to any man or woman who stepped out of line of contract. This contract was drawn up before

When three enemies meet, 1873.

the march and signed by all members of the association binding each and every one to abide in all cases to the orders and decisions of the Captain in charge, aiding him in executing all his duties and making the individual interest of each member the common concern of the whole company. It was also necessary that each member of the company would watch over and protect the property of the others as well as his own. Punishments administered to individuals were similar to those prescribed in US Army manuals, which seemed fair when explained beforehand and was accepted by everyone.

Ruby Rivers and his family when they arrived in Carbon County, Wyoming, 1883. Taken by F. M. Baker on the flats between Elk Mountain P. O. and Mill Creek on the Overland Trail. Notice several women have cut a good 12 inches off the bottom of their dresses to make walking easier. They also sewed up pockets of lead shot within the hems to keep their skirts from flying over their heads during a good wind (Union Pacific Railroad Museum Collection).

Wagon train justice.

*Crossing the plains
with a hand-cart.*

On one Westward wagon trek, some two weeks on the windswept prairies; one member, a tall blonde-headed Swede, killed another man over a trivial game of cards. After a small select jury passed sentence to hang the man, another problem came about. There were no trees to hang the Swede from.

'There is one tree present ... a wagon tree' (the tongue of a wagon), someone remarked. It was a fine idea, and a wagon was selected, the wagon tree was uprighted and lashed securely. When the noose was dropped over the man's head and tightened about his neck, the hangman gave the doomed man his last rites and said: 'God knows how you'll wind up ... either in Heaven or Hell ... but I'll do one thing for you, I'm giving you a halfway start to Heaven by pointing you in that direction.'

Before the great adventure Westward, certain wagons had to be selected. They were to be of the simplest possible construction, strong, light and of well seasoned timber, especially the wheels, as the elevated and arid region over which they had to travel

was exceedingly dry during the summer months and, unless the woodwork was thoroughly seasoned, constant repairs were inevitable. Soaking wagon wheels in ravines and rivers, up to the hubs, helped immensely to keep the iron tires from coming off. The wooden wheels would swell up from the soaking and hold the iron tires on.

Wheels made of *bois-d'arc*, or orange wood, were the best for traveling on the plains, as they shrunk very little and seldom needed any repairing. This wood was hard to procure in the Northern States, and in its place well seasoned white oak was the best substitute. The rugged terrain caused many accidents, but most common to the sturdy wagons was the nuts coming off the numerous bolts that secured the running gear. To prevent this, all bolts had to be riveted at the ends, as it was seldom necessary to take them off. When it was required to remove a nut, the ends of the bolts were easily filed away.

On long journeys, wagons loaded down with a little over 2,000 pounds were pulled by six mules. (The allowance of provisions for each grown person, to make the journey from the Missouri River to California, should suffice for 110 days.) An additional 1,000 pounds may be taken providing it was grain and fed out to the team. Every wagon was furnished with

---

PLATE 7
19-24 Wagon train family, 1840s

The 1840s saw numerous wagon trains crossing the vast western prairies and climbing tall mountains. These canvas-capped wagons were the light weight Conestogas from the East and the Prairie schooner, superbly designed to transport pioneer families and their goods on the five-month-long, 2,000-mile journey to Oregon or California. The teams that pulled these wagons were oxen, mules and horses. Families tried to pack as much as they could – but, in order to lighten the load to traverse the muddy trails, furniture, potted plants, plows, iron stoves and huge grandfather clocks were discarded along the trail. This made it easier to conserve the strength of the animals for their long, tedious journey. A good supply of black powder was always on hand but hidden at the bottom of the wagon, as marauding Indians constantly plagued them. Their clothing was family 'hand-me-downs' for the purpose of their journey, and hardly ever did they dig down into trunks and bring out their Sunday clothes except for a dance, wedding or funeral.

Freezing winds, torrential rains, starvation, death and constant fear were with them daily. By the time they reached their destination, they could face almost anything that might arise. There will never be another epic such as the 'great white migration' to the West, with the courage and determination they displayed.

PLATE 7

19-24   Wagon train family, 1840s

Perils by Indians.

substantial bows and double osnaburg covers, to protect its contents from the elements. Osnaburg covers were heavy duck sheets used by traders; named for Osnaburg, Germany, where a similar fabric was made (*Western Words*, R. F. Adams). Government wagons were too heavy for six mules, since they were built to sustain a burden of 4,000 pounds, however they were seldom loaded with more than half that weight.

Mules were preferred over cows or oxen for hauling, as they traveled faster and seemed to endure the summer heat better. If the journey was not over 1,000 miles, and the grass abundant, mules were preferred. When the march extended to 1,500 or 2,000 miles, over rough, sandy or muddy roads, oxen endured better than mules as they stayed in better condition and performed the journey in an equal space of time. Besides, they were cheaper by far than mules. A team of six mules cost 600 dollars. Oxen were less likely to stampede if spooked by Indians, and could be overtaken easily by a horseman. Oxen traveling was not as disagreeable as one might expect. They could be made to proceed at a tolerably quick pace; for, though their walk was only about three miles an hour at an average, they could be made to perform double that distance in the same time. Lastly, when fresh meat was needed, the animal was used for beef.

When teaming together various animals out of necessity, it was found that oxen and cows worked comfortably yoked together for the duration of a day, and their steadiness and speed did not vary.

Supplies for a long journey were stored in secure and compact areas. Slab bacon was packed in strong sacks of 100 pounds each, and in very hot climates put in boxes and surrounded by bran. Pork was also packed like bacon, but was placed on the bottom of the wagon to keep it cool. Flour was packed in stout double canvas sacks well sewn, 100 pounds each. Butter was preserved by boiling it and skimming off the scum as it came to the top until it was clear like oil, then placed in a tin canister, and soldered up. In hot weather, the flavor and sweetness of butter was little impaired by this process and could keep for a great length of time. A good supply of eggs could be transported without breaking by placing them in a barrel of oats, some distance from one another with the feed acting as a cushion. Sugar was well stored in India rubber or gutta-percha sacks and placed somewhere as not to risk getting wet or moist.

Dried vegetables were put up in compact and portable forms so as to be easily gotten at any time while preparing a meal. They were prepared by cutting the fresh vegetables into thin slices and placing them into a powerful press. The press removed the juice leaving a solid cake, which when thoroughly dried in an oven became as hard as a rock. When boiled, the vegetables swelled to fill a dish sufficient for four men. Compressed vegetables were purchased from Challet and Company in Paris, by an agency located in New York, solely for our campaigning soldiers out West. It was the best preparation for prairie traveling during the late 1850s.

Pemmican was prepared in the following fashion: buffalo meat was cut into very thin slices and hung up to dry in the sun or before a slow fire. It was then pounded between two stones and reduced to powder, and placed in a bag made of the animal's hide, with the hair on the outside. Melted grease was poured into it and the bag sewn up. It would be eaten raw or mixed with a little flour and boiled, a wholesome and nutritious food, that would keep fresh for a good length of time.

The Prairie Traveler, written by Randolph B. Marcy, a handbook for overland expeditions, states: 'I would advise all persons who travel for any considerable time through a country where they can procure no vegetables to carry with them some antiscorbutics, and if they cannot transport desiccated or canned vegetables, citric acid answers a good purpose, and is very potable. When mixed with sugar and water, with a few drops of the essence of lemon, it is difficult to distinguish it from lemonade. Wild onions are excellent as antiscorbuties; also wild grapes and greens.

An infusion of hemlock leaves is also said to be an antidote to scurvy.'

'Cold Flour', a portable and simple preparation used extensively by Mexicans and Indians, was prepared by parching corn and pounding it in a mortar to the consistency of course meal. A little sugar and cinnamon added made it quite palatable. By adding a little of the flour into water, it could be drunk as a beverage.

The Captain always cautioned the members of his party to take along the chief articles of subsistence necessary for the trip, and to use them with economy. Many emigrants before them had exhausted their stocks before reaching their journey's end and had been obliged to pay exorbitant prices along the way to make up the deficiency.

Substitutes for salt, sugar, coffee and tobacco were derived from various sources that would never have occurred under ordinary circumstances.

A substitute for tobacco was found in the bark of the red willow, which grew along many of the mountain streams in the Rocky Mountains. The outer bark was first removed with a knife, after which the inner bark was scraped up into ridges around the sticks, and held in the fire until it was roasted thoroughly. When taken off the stick and pulverized in the palm of the hand, it was ready for smoking. The narcotic properties of tobacco were the same, and it was quite agreeable to taste and smell. 'Sumach' leaf was also used in the same way by Indians, and was similar in both taste and smell to the willow bark. A decoction of the dried wild 'horse mint', which was found abundantly under the snow, was an alternative for coffee. For want of salt, they burned the outside of mule steaks and sprinkled a little gunpowder upon them, which in their imagination replaced both salt and pepper. Horses and mules in a starved condition were butchered for food. The meat was not at all tender, juicy or nutritious, and when cooked or boiled the meat broke down leaving a stringy mush-like concoction.

Clothing for the prairie was important to health and comfort, and wool seemed to be the best material for constant movement of the body. Cotton or linen fabrics did not protect the body against the sun's rays nor the rains or sudden temperature changes. Coats were short and stout, shirts were of red or blue flannel, and trousers made of a thick and soft woolen material with reinforced seats and inner legs of soft buckskin, so as not to wear out with constant saddle riding. Woolen socks, and knee high leather boots, wide at the mouth to admit pant legs, served best for the horseman and guarded against rattlesnake bites. Moccasins were preferred to boots while traveling through deep snows during cold weather as they were more pliable and allowed a freer circulation of blood in the feet. Buckskin and elkskin pants were most effective in preventing the cold air from penetrating the skin and were also an excellent defense against 'cat claws', thorns and brush.

For snow blindness, green or blue glasses, a woman's dark colored see-through veil over the face and head, or darkening around the eyes and bridge of the nose with wet powdered charcoal, afforded great relief. Hunters or mountain men often crossed trails with the pioneers and offered suggestions to combat snow blindness. One of these was a pair of carved wooden goggles with long thin slits cut horizontally to see through. These were bound at each end by leather thongs and tied around the head, resting on the bridge of the nose after the manner of prescription glasses.

Some women dressed like men, but the more feminine women had an additional discomfort. They found their skirts blown over their heads during a windswept day. To solve this problem, buckshot was sewn into the bottom hem of their skirts saving them much embarrassment. Bedding for each person consisted of two blankets, a comforter, one pillow, a gutta-percha or gum painted canvas cloth to spread beneath the bedding upon the ground as well as to contain the complete bedding when rolled up.

Wrought iron pans for baking bread, kettles for boiling meat and making soup, huge coffee pots, tin cups, plates, knives, forks, spoons and sharp butcher knives made up the utensils for the open-air kitchen cook. The men saw to it that the necessary tools were packed and available at all times. Several axes, spades, picks and mallets for driving picket pins were stored conveniently and close at hand. Above all, 'matches' were carried in tightly corked bottles or tins with covers so as to exclude moisture. Should the matches become wet, a fire could be started by a flintlock pistol, or by a steel striker and flint, which was always kept on hand.

A little bluemass (a quinine derivative), quinine, opium, cathartic medicine and whiskey, put up in doses for adults, would suffice for the medicine chest.

Every wagon was provided with a covered tar bucket filled with a mixture of tar, resin and grease, two extra bows, six 'S' hooks, and six open links for repairing chains. Every set of six wagons carried an extra tongue, coupling pole, kingbolt, pair of hounds and one anvil with tools for shoeing. Each set of six mule team wagons were furnished with five pair of hames, two double trees, four whipple trees and two pairs of lead bars extra. Oil and lubricants were hard to come by. On one occasion a wagon family on their trek westward noticed that one of their wheel hub lubricants was depleted; quickly the wheel was removed and the bottom side of a bacon slab was cut away, and wrapped around the wheel hub axle. After the wheel had been replaced the difficulty had been solved.

Lariats made of hemp were needed for every horse and mule, with enough length to fabricate a rope corral for the animals. These were also useful for pulling wagons across deep ravines and rivers, and letting wagons down steep hills.

For repairing harnesses, saddles, bridles and numerous other purposes of daily necessity, buckskin and an awl was found in constant requisition. Every Captain or Wagon Master saw to it that each man possessed a rifle and side arm. Pushing into Indian country while enroute Westward was dangerous and every member of the company should have one of these weapons on his person, or at least not lose sight of them if not on march. A large majority of men favored the breech-loading weapon, but there were those who still believed in the old-fashioned muzzle loading rifle in preference to any of the modern ignitions. Experience in handling a breech-loading arm proved a greater advantage over the muzzle loader because it could be loaded and fired with much greater rapidity. After several days out on the prairie, the captain made certain everyone was capable of firing their weapons, including the women and children.

Because of the period, pioneers who traveled West had many ignition systems in firearms available to them, and some of them were experimental. Many men chose flintlock arms; others put their faith in the percussion ignition. The breech-loader was by far the newest and most dependable arm since the first black powder flintlock was invented, but the cost was generally beyond one's pocket.

Colt's new revolving pistol, of percussion cap ignition, offered six shots, and Colt's new patented revolving rifle offered the same, and the price wasn't that of the new breech-loaders. What was fascinating about this percussion rifle and revolver was its fire power. If several six shot cylinders were loaded and primed in advance, the odds would certainly be in one's favor by dropping a loaded cylinder into the arm in a matter of seconds instead of loading each chamber with powder and ball and capping it.

There were several drawbacks with this weapon. One was the possibility of simultaneous discharge from several chambers and the flash back of hot powder gases from the gap between barrel and cylinder; also, in the case of the rifle, the shooter's supporting arm was directly in front of the chamber and in the event of multiple discharge serious wounding could occur.

But to each his own. Weapons of all forms of ignitions were observed carried by pioneer families because they were better acquainted with their own personal weapon and avoid the additional expense of a new one.

An ox-train fully equipped for crossing the country consisted of 20 to 25 large ox-wagons, each drawn by 6 to 12 yoke of cattle, with a number of extra oxen to replace those that might become disabled. There was also an extra wagon to carry the outfit and provisions for the trainmen. These wagons extended a long distance over the prairie and along the mountain roads, and were easy prey for Indians lying in ambush to attack them. The trains made several stops each day; at each stop the wagons were formed into a pear-shaped corral, the pole of each wagon pointing outward, and the hub of the fore wheel of the next wagon

---

PLATE 8

25,26,27 Pioneer women, 1870s

25. *As the pioneers moved across the vast western prairies, wood became less a commodity as trees literally disappeared. Crossing the great herds of buffalo trails, they came upon many pieces of dried dung which they called 'buffalo chips', and these were collected in great quantities. In this illustration, a pioneer woman has gathered over 100 pounds of 'chips' which were used as fuel in their metal stoves or camp fires. Cattle dung also served the same way, but was not as plentiful as the buffalo's. When there were no 'chips' to harvest, women and children walked behind the wagons in clouds of dust, collecting weeds and sage brush.*

26 and 27. *A combination of sun, wind, hard soap and cold water could be painful to the pioneer women as they hand-washed their clothing. Their arms and hands became red, swollen black and painful as though scalded with boiling water. When high winds prevented any clothing from hanging onto lines or over obstacles, 'air-drying' became another problem. Clothing was then worn on a person so as their body heat could serve the purpose of drying each garment. (From* Woman's Diaries of the Westward Journey, *L. Schlissel, Schocken Books, NY 1982.)*

PLATE 8

25, 26, 27   Pioneer women, 1870s

A Mormon farmer (center, sitting) with his four wives, his mother and five children, in front of his log cabin with sod roof, late 1870s (A. J. Russell photo and Union Pacific Museum Collection).

set close to the hind wheel of the wagon just ahead of it.

The wagons were so placed as to form an enclosure which was large enough to hold the entire number of animals belonging to the train. Indians rarely attacked a train when in corral. It was a means of fortification that enabled the trainmen to defend themselves and their animals against great odds. When trains were attacked while moving, they immediately went into corral, and if the corral could be formed in time the Indians usually retired. Sometimes trains were kept in corral by an attacking party for days at a time. The entire number of animals for one of these large ox-trains, including extras, sometimes amounted to 300 to 350 cattle, and the number of trainmen required, sometimes from 40 to 50. The heavily-laden wagons were capable of making 12 to 15 miles a day. It required weeks and sometimes months for these slow trains to move between far distant points, across this immense territory.

Each wagon had its own ox-driver, or, as they were called, 'bull-whackers'. The whip used by the bull-whackers had a short staff not over 1½ or 2 feet in length; to this was fastened the lash, which was 15 to 25 feet in length, being very thick a few feet from the end of the staff and tapering down to a fine point. This was dragged behind them on the ground, at full length, and in the hands of a good driver it was a terrible instrument of punishment. The bull-whacker could take the staff in his two hands and, giving the lash one or two skilful twirls around his head, then with a blow strike an ox on any spot he aimed at, cutting the hide through as if with a knife.

An instance occurred on the Sweetwater River near the Devil's Gap, which will illustrate the bull-whacker's skill in the use of his whip. A train of ox-wagons while passing this point stopped as usual to rest. Some Indians who had been watching the train at a distance made up their minds to visit it. One loafer Indian, more inquisitive than he should have been, mounted the pole of the wagon, and, as usual, began taking things therefrom. At last he came to the bag that contained the ox-driver's outfit, and this the Indian proceeded to appropriate for his own use. The teamster, who had been watching him, concluded not to be robbed. Stepping back to the right distance the driver gave his whip two or three rapid twirls around his head and aimed a blow at the Indian's back. The Indian was naked, except for his breech cloth, and the end of the lash struck him just below the shoulder blade, cutting a gash 10–12 inches in length straight down his back. The whip cut entirely through the flesh to the bone for the whole length, and could not have been more neatly done than with a sharp knife. The Indian gave a howl, dropped the bag, jumped to the ground, and mad with pain and rage, prepared to attack the bull-whacker. The latter immediately placed his whip in position again, preparing to strike. Seeing this, and having a painful realization of what he had just received, the Indian retreated.

This act nearly cost the lives of the entire train. A Cavalry command happened to arrive shortly afterward, or there might have been serious trouble. There was great difficulty in making peace between the Indians and the trainmen, but it was done by presenting them such articles as the trainmen and military could spare.

Ox-teams were used in these trains because the animals were patient and faithful, could draw heavy loads, and readily subsist on the grasses along the route. Moreover, Indians could not stampede them and did not look upon them with such envious eyes as they did on the fine horses and mules that were afterward used in this service.

It required but a short time for the enterprising mining towns of the far West to discover that transportation by ox-teams was entirely too slow, and four and six-horse or mule teams superseded them. On these fine teams the red men made repeated attacks, often capturing the animals of the entire trains; nevertheless, horse and mule trains continued in this service until the completion of the Union Pacific Railroad.

Almost from its discovery until the present time, the country owes its advancement and improvement to trains drawn by animals. The slow but sure ox teams with their immense loads, the patient and faithful mule teams, the more rapid and tractable horse trains of wagons stretching miles across the treeless plains, or winding snake-like through interminable canyons or over rugged mountains carrying succor and supplies to distant mining camps, frontier towns and settlements.

The hardships and sufferings of the pioneers in those days may be learned from one of the pioneer women, Mrs Augusta Tabor. Miss Martha Hill, a relative, narrates the experience of Mrs Tabor as follows, as she heard it from Mrs Tabor herself (Thayer, W. M. Henry, private printing, 1887, NY pamphlet, author's collection).

My first acquaintance with Horace Austin Warner Tabor came about in this way: My father, a stone contractor, took the train one morning in August, 1853, for Boston, to hire stone-cutters. When about sixty miles from home two young men entered the train, one of them taking a seat by my father. In conversation it was developed that these men were stone-cutters, and looking for work. My father employed them. In two years from that time Mr. Tabor, who was one of the men, asked my hand in marriage. Another two years passed, and in January, 1857, we were married in the room where we first met. On the 25th of February we left my home in Augusta, Maine, for our new one in Kansas. We made our way to St. Louis, which was the terminus of the railroad, thence to Kansas City on a five-day boat. At Kansas City we purchased a yoke of oxen, a wagon, a few farming tools, some seed, took my trunks and started westward. My

Leaving the weak to die.

trip was not very pleasant, for the wind blew disagreeably, as it always does in Kansas.

We arrived at our destination on the 19th of April at 11 A.M. I shall never forget that morning. To add to the desolation of the place, the wind took a new start. The cabin stood solitary and alone upon an open prairie. It was built of black walnut logs, 12 × 16 feet; not a building, a stone, or stick in sight. We had brought two men with us, and how we could all live in that little place was a question I asked myself many times. The only furniture was a No. 7 cook stove, a dilapidated trunk, and a rough bedstead made of poles, on which was an old tick filled with prairie grass. I sat down upon the trunk and cried; I had not been deceived in coming to this place. I knew perfectly well that the country was new, that there were no saw-mills near, and no money in the territory.

But I was homesick, and could not conceal it from those about me. Mr. Tabor and the two men unloaded the wagon while I tried to clean up the cabin. I found a number of old *New York Tribunes* in the room, smoothed them out, made a paste of flour, and soon had the black, ugly logs covered, putting the newspapers right side up, that I might read them at my leisure, for I could see that reading matter was likely to be very scarce. Having covered the walls, I unpacked the boxes and made up a decent bed. I took out my table linen and silver, for I had not left home without the usual outfit, and then began to prepare my first meal. I cannot say that it was very inviting, but I did the best I could, and we were all blessed with good appetites. The two men took rooms near by and boarded with us, thus helping us to support the table. Mr. Tabor broke the land, put in the seed, and began farming in good earnest, exchanging day's labor with the neighbors to save hiring help. After doing my housework I also went into the fields to work.

No rain fell that summer, so that when harvest came we had nothing to gather. Mr. Tabor went to Fort Riley and worked at his trade, while I remained at home with my babe, and made a little money by raising chickens.

Indians and snakes were then numerous in Kansas, and I lived in constant dread of them both. I cannot tell which I feared the most. The rattlesnakes crawled into my cabin to get into the shade, and when I sat down it would be upon a three-legged stool with my feet under me.

The winter was warm and pleasant. When spring came we tried farming once more. An abundant crop resulted, but there was no market for it; eggs were three cents per dozen, and shelled corn twenty cents per bushel. I kept boarders and made some butter to sell. In February, 1859, Mr. Tabor heard of Pike's Peak, through some of Green Russell's party who was returning, and at once decided to try his luck in the new Eldorado. He told me I might go home to Maine, but I refused to leave him, and upon reflection he thought it would be more profitable to take me, as in that case the two men would go along and board with us, and the money they paid would keep us all. Mr. Tabor worked at the Fort through March and April, earning money for our outfit. The fifth day of April we gathered together our scanty means, bought supplies for a few months, yoked our oxen and cows, mounted our seats in the wagon, and left the town of Zeandale with the determination of returning in the Fall, or as soon as we had made money enough to pay for the one hundred and sixty acres of government land, and buy a little stock.

What I endured on this journey only the women who crossed the plains in 1859 can realize. There was no station until we arrived within eighty miles of Denver, via the Republican route; no road and a good part of the way no fuel.

We were obliged to gather buffalo chips, sometimes travelling miles to find enough to cook a meal with. This weary work fell to the women, for the men had enough to do in taking care of the teams, and in 'making' and 'breaking' the camp. The Indians followed us all the time, and were continually begging and stealing.

Every Sunday we rested, if rest it could be called. The men went hunting while I stayed to guard the camp, wash the soiled linen, and cook for the following week. Quite frequently the Indians gathered around my camp, so that I could do nothing all day. They wallowed in the water-sources from which our supplies were obtained, and were generally very filthy. My babe was teething and suffering from fever and ague, so that he required constant attention day and night. I was weak and feeble, having suffered all the

time that I lived in Kansas with ague. My weight was only ninety pounds.

We arrived in Denver about the middle of June, and as our cattle were footsore we were obliged to camp there until the first day of July. Then we went up Clear Creek where the town of Golden was being established. A miner came down from the mountains, from whom we inquired the way to Gregory diggings. Leaving me and my sick child in the 7 × 9 tent, that my hands had made, the men took a supply of provisions on their backs, a few blankets, and bidding me be good to myself, left on the morning of the glorious Fourth. How sadly I felt, none but God, in whom I then firmly trusted, knew. Twelve miles from human soul, save my babe. The only sound I heard was the lowing of the cattle, and they, poor things, seemed to feel the loneliness of our situation, and kept unusually quiet. Every morning and evening I had a 'round up' all to myself. There were no cowboys for me to cut, slash, and shoot; no disputing of brands or mavericks. Three long weary weeks I held the fort. At the expiration of that time they returned. On the 26th of July we again loaded the wagon and started into the mountains. The road was a mere trail; every few rods we were obliged to stop and widen it. Many times we unloaded the wagon, and, by pushing it, helped the cattle up the hills.

Going down hill was so much easier, that it was often necessary to fasten a full-grown pine tree to the back of the wagon for a hold-back or brake. Often night overtook us where it was impossible to find a level place to spread a blanket. Under such circumstances we drove stakes in the ground, rolled a log against them, and lay with our feet against the log. Sometimes the hill was so steep that we slept almost

---

PLATE 9
28,29 Pioneer women, 1880s
30 Bull whacker, 1880s

28. *The colorful prints in women's clothing soon disappeared from the many washings in both hard water and soap. Washdays were hated by pioneer women. When the soiled clothing was gathered up it was usually brought to a nearby creek or pond. Here they knelt over and literally hammered the clothing with a huge wooden paddle until they looked spotless. Naturally, this didn't help the clothing to stay in one piece. Jagged rocks ground into the wet cloth leaving tiny holes or tearing seams. When drying, the clothing was hung about, and if it wasn't for thieving Indians who lurked about helping themselves to various pieces of clothing, the prairie winds would claim a number of items.*

29. *Cabins were constantly swept out because of heavy gusts of wind that seemed to carry up almost anything not rooted down, including that ever-present dust which caught in corners like drifts*

of snow. Dust was endless. It came in small cracks of the walls, through closed doors and windows and forever caused discomfort in breathing to everyone.

30. *The 'bull whacker' (a stock driver) was the biggest show-off in the whole settlement. In his somewhat casual brutality with the animals he was constantly feared by both women and children. His long bull whip usually extended from 10 to 12 feet in length, tightly woven together with tough buckskin or elk hide. At the butt each lash, which was attached to the stick by a soft strip of buckskin, formed a loop, was frequently more than an inch thick, and graduated in thickness to the tip. As he swung his whip overhead in mid-air at a target nearby, the 'crack' could be heard at a great distance. Beside the deafening noise, it also could lay open a man's flesh half an inch deep. They were so accurate with these crude whips that a fly resting on the hip of an ox could be swatted without hurting the animal. This 6 foot 3 inch 'bull whacker' is merely showing off before two pioneer women who were taking a moment out to watch the spectacle.*

PLATE 9

28, 29   Pioneer women, 1880s   30   Bull whacker, 1880s

upright. We were nearly three weeks cutting our way through Russell's Gulch into Payne's Bar, now called Idaho Springs.

Ours was the first wagon through, and I was the first white woman there, if white I could be called, after camping out three months. The men cut logs and laid them up four feet high, then put the 7′ × 9′ tent on for a roof. Mr. Tabor went prospecting. I opened a 'bakery', made bread and pies to sell, gave meals, and sold milk from the cows we had brought.

Here one of our party, Mr. Maxey, had an attack of mountain fever, and for four weeks he lay very ill at the door of our tent, in a wagon bed, I acting as physician and nurse. A miner with a gunshot wound through his hand was also brought to my door for attention.

With the first snowstorm came an old miner to our camp, who told us dreadful stories of snowslides, and advised Mr. Tabor to take me out of the mountains immediately. Those who know anything of the surroundings of Idaho will smile at the idea of a snowslide there. But we, in our ignorance of mountains, believed all the old miner said, and left for Denver.

I had been very successful with my bakery in that camp, making enough to pay for the farm in Kansas and to keep us through the winter.

The 'dugout' was probably one of the first of the early one man-one room dwellings built by the homesteader on the Northern Plains. It was usually an area measuring 10 by 12 feet dug back into a hillside or bank along a stream, roofed over with cedar logs, willows and sod. Frequently, the front was completely laid up with square sod-cuts around the front door and sides.

A one-room 'soddy' was cool and comfortable during the summer and warm during the winter. Heating it was not difficult and the storage of wood fuel was viewed with little concern. Many unseasoned homesteaders faced the door South, thinking that on sunny days they could capture much of the sun's warm rays, not realizing that the snow could build man high drifts, entombing the occupant. As these dugouts usually had no windows and ventilation was never considered, many pioneers suffocated from smoke or the deadlier carbon monoxide that backed up from faulty stoves and chimneys.

Amongst the many other problems the homesteader had to face were the heavy rains. It was almost impossible to keep the water out once the earth was soaked. After having mud and water drop from the roof, along with insects, centipedes and other crawling things, the pioneer literally lived under his wagon

canvas until everything else dried out. Then the fleas and lice constantly plagued him, along with uninvited snakes and rodents.

If he provided a stove for himself, he was certain to build an adequate chimney made from a cylinder of mud-plastered sticks or mud-daubed barrels stacked one on top of the other. Last but not least, the only other danger, next to Indians and Range-Robbers, were the range cattle. It has been known that the grass on roofs of sod houses seem to flourish more, enticing a cow or cows to graze there. Their weight put stress on the weak roof, either partly destroying it or dropping them in for a short visit.

Half-dugouts were similar to basement apartment pits. They were waist high deep, or shoulder deep, with sod walls only a few feet high. Windows of either glass or oiled soaked paper were cut in the walls for ventilation and to keep the swift cold winds out.

A storm cellar was dug nearby, probably not too deep. Here provisions were stored along with hanging fresh meat, if there was any available. It might have a muddy floor with several inches of water, but it was cooler than the dugout. In severe weather when tornadoes were present, it was the safest place to hide.

Little wood was used to construct this dugout. Everything was built from two by three foot pieces of sod, except for the wooden beams supporting the roof and a wooden door and sill. Canvas, old shirts and gunny-sacks were pinned down to the floors of the dugout and acted as carpeting. Tearing apart the old wagon was the last thing a man thought of doing, should the need become necessary or if timber was needed for anything other than personal comforts.

After a certain period of 'homesteading', a man, usually lonely for a companion, married and began to raise a family, but before that he was ready to move out of his 'dugout' and into a four-wall 'sod house'. Of course, he would first have to build it before he could move his new bride into it.

The easiest way to begin cutting heavy prairie grass sod was to turn the soil over by plowing straight furrows at an even depth. This usually took over an acre. After turning over what was thought to be enough sod, the next step was to cut two by three foot slabs from the furrows with a spade, which was certainly a back-breaking chore. Then these slabs had to be hauled by a wheelbarrow or a flat bed wagon to where the building was to be erected.

For some strange reason, man has preferred to build his four-wall dwellings so they sit four-square to the points of the compass, much like the great pyramids of Egypt. After laying out a suitable size foundation with wooden pegs and squaring off the four corners, the homesteader began laying down the sod slabs. In between the slabs, he used a simple mud and water motar. Windows and door openings were laid out, and wood was used to frame them. The roof was made in a similar fashion to that of the first 'dugout'. Sometimes, flattened tin cans were used as shingles, overlaying one on top of the other, that is, if there were enough.[1]

For plastering the interior walls, a mixture of ashes and clay bound with a little water would even out the wall surface when applied with a brush or a wide flat putty knife. If a woman was handy, she would paper over this plaster with old newspapers, seal in the ceiling with cheese cloth and lay old canvas down on the floor to keep the dust settled. Doors were hung with raw hide or wooden hinges. Wood pins were hammered tightly into augered holes instead of using 'store-bought' nails. If the homesteaders were lucky enough to afford framed glass windows, you could be certain that curtains would follow suit.

After completing the building, a handsome set of deer antlers was placed above the front door, greeting any stranger to a house of good will ... and plenty. Shortly after the family had settled into their new sod house, those neighbors who had helped in its construction were invited to a grand 'old house warming', where everyone brought an abundance of food and later danced to a quick fiddler's tune. Cracking open a jug of new corn whiskey was as traditional as 'American Apple Pie'.

The prairie dog is not a 'dog' at all but rather a marmot or common ground squirrel. These fat, pot-bellied, reddish brown squirrels had an alarm call, a high pitched 'yek, yek, yek ...' that sounds much like the yapping of a small dog. Thus the popular name of 'prairie dog', but, originally, they were more accurately called 'prairie marmots'. These small animals inhabited the Plains states in great numbers before the turn of the century. At one time there may have been five billion inhabitants scattered from central Texas and western Arizona to northwestern Montana. In Texas alone in 1901, there were estimated to be over 800 million of these burrowing squirrels. Today, they have almost disappeared.

Timid and defenseless, the prairie dog sits up on his

California was too far for this family. The cost to travel there was beyond their pockets, and it took too long. They were satisfied with this area to homestead in the Loup Valley, Custer County, Nebraska, in the Spring of 1886, just in time to put in a corn field and erect a sod house before the first snow (Union Pacific Railroad Museum Collection).

haunches, a position he assumes much of the time, watching for an enemy. The mound surrounding his burrow entrance serves as a watchtower, and when an enemy is sighted, he can alarm the other prairie dogs with his 'yek, yek, yek', setting off a chorus of barks. With a certain amount of luck, a prairie dog could live as long as eight years. During winter months, the prairie dog does not hibernate, but comes out of his burrow to enjoy the warm sunshine, even when there is snow on the ground. Their food is simple in diet— any vegetable matter, alfalfa and garden crops. Insects, cutworms, grasshoppers and beetles are another choice. Stocking-up food for a long winter is unknown. The fat they have accumulated during the summer and fall season must be sufficient to endure the many weeks without food during the winter months. They get along well without water, but have been seen drinking from puddles after a rain and eating snow.

Early travelers of the Plains did not hesitate to eat them when food was scarce, but the job of hunting one and killing it was altogether another story. As the West began to settle, the prairie dog was regarded as a general nuisance to the people, but saloon keepers

---

[1]Although the canning industry received a healthy impetus from its sales to the Union Army, during the Civil War, the output of canned food was still at small sales to the general public.

Weapons were always loaded and kept handy, as the frontier produced some shady characters, besides the Indian. It was a general rule to 'Hel-lo' a homestead at some distance before coming any closer. After identifying yourself, business at hand could commence. However, the visitor may have had uncanny feelings that someone else nearby had a weapon trained on him, just in case his intentions were not honorable (author).

often raised them to sell to tourists as curiosities. The prairie dog was a mound-builder, building underground cities, connecting each other with tunnels. When horsemen crossed the plains, they generally avoided prairie dog villages. At a gallop, a horse could easily step into one of these openings in the ground and break a leg or become lame.

Prairie dogs almost put the homesteader out of business by destroying crops and obstructing irrigation ditches. As early as 1880, the ranchers were setting traps and blasting these rodents with shotguns and sometimes dynamite ... but this had little or no impact on the millions that populated the area. In order to bring the dog population of the plains under control, the United States Biological Survey began using poisoned grain and lethal gas, almost eliminating these yapping critters. Had it not been for the National Parks, the prairie dog population would be destined for eventual extinction.

The great blizzards and snow storms of the West were among the best agents the big land grabbers had in Montana, Wyoming and other Territories.

In Montana especially, the cattle of all brands were turned loose in the fall after the beef gathering had taken place and the fat cattle sent off to market. When the winter comes on, the herds drift together until there were perhaps 25,000 to 30,000 cattle bunched. Suddenly, there comes a snow storm and the bunch grass is covered up beneath two feet of snow. The storm is usually followed by a big fall in temperature. The mercury hits 30 degrees below zero. All the nutriment leaves the tall prairie grass on which the cattle have fed since the bunch grass was snowed under. The herd becomes crazed with hunger and a stampede follows.

The great body of starving cattle starts out, like an avalanche, heading straight for localities where homesteads have taken up in the greatest number. They bear down on the settlement and besiege the homesteaders, who vainly try to keep them back with their rifles. They shoot the hungry animals down by the hundreds and sometimes manage to hold them in check until their ammunition is exhausted. Then the fight must end. The cattle sweep down on the homesteads and not only eat up every vestige of hay the homesteaders have stored up for their own small herds, but tear down houses and outbuildings which the settlers built out of the prairie sod and devour the roots of the grass that remain succulent in the sod. Homesteads, hundreds at a time, are cleaned up by a herd of hungry cattle, quickly and thoroughly, on a single stampede.

When the herd continues on its way, taking the settler's herd of two or three hundred with it, it leaves him a homeless, ruined man. He may have had his homestead all clear of Government claim, but be in debt for cattle or supplies. When the creditor finally comes for his dues, the homesteader cannot pay him anything. He now loses his saddle, rifle or whatever he may have left. The homesteader is discouraged. The wake of the stampeding herd is quickly followed by the agent of a big land owner. He makes the discouraged settler an offer for his claim and the settler, nine times out of ten, is glad to accept the offer. The chances are that he will turn cowboy or hire out as a herder for some small cattle grower on a range. The agent of the land grabber may secure in this way immense areas of much-coveted land for his employer which he could get in no other way unless he paid a fair price, which he would not do. It is no infrequent thing for one of these agents to say: 'I wish there would come a good freeze out. We want more homesteads.'

That was one way in which rich cattle raisers obtained extensive tracts of the most available land.

The Pennsylvania Conestoga wagons were used for hauling farm products and freight in the East, and the larger wagons could carry up to 10 tons. Their boat-like shape and their white-cloth dust covers, which resembled billowing sails, gave them the name of 'Turn-pike Schooners.' Later, when they went West, they were re-labeled 'Prairie Schooners'. These cumbersome wagons creaked, squealed and tossed about violently during their trek Westward. The drivers of the wagons handled the reins on the left side of the rear horse. When passing another wagon, the driver would steer his wagon to the left of the wagon in front, and pass with as much swiftness as possible. Legend has it that it was this frontier driving habit which eventually made this nation into all left-sided auto drivers.

The Conestoga wagon was build during the 1700s, in Lancaster County, Pennsylvania, and was painted in colors used by the Pennsylvania wagon makers. The wagon bed was light blue, and everything beneath the bed, including wheels and tongue, were painted a rich red. Frame and flooring were oak, spokes hickory and axles of gumwood, which does not split under heavy loads. The tool box at the center was decorated with wrought-iron designs. A brakeman sat on the 'lazy board' extending out at the side. Usually, three teams of horses (totaling six) pulled this enormous wagon. The front team was the lead team, the middle pair the swing team, and at the rear there was the wheel team. Traveling time would be from 6 to 20 miles a day, depending on the types of animals used; oxen or a bull train were slower than horses. Of course, you also had to consider weight, terrain and weather. As these wagons rolled Westward, their sizes and shapes were altered to meet changing conditions. The prairie schooner, which was used on level plains and gradual mountain passes, had a flatter bed than the Eastern type. It was also smaller and lighter, and often was fitted up for family traveling on the 2,000-mile trek to California or Oregon. In emergencies it could serve as a fort or a boat.

For several decades prior to the Civil War, there had been constant demands from the West for free land, a demand opposed by the South, which did not wish to see the non-slave states grow too rapidly in population. In 1862, the Republicans, redeeming their

Ezra Meeker, with his young wife and child, made the hazardous journey over plains and mountains all the way from Iowa to Oregon by ox team in 1852. After 54 years an old 'Prairie Schooner' was rebuilt; he retraced the almost lost trail. It took him nearly two years to go from the State of Washington to Washington D.C. Monuments have now been placed along the greater part of the old pioneer way (Union Pacific Museum Collection).

campaign pledge of 1860, passed the Homestead Law, signed by Lincoln on 20 May, by which a settler could be granted free a quarter section of land, or 160 acres, provided he occupied and improved it, for five years. Fifteen thousand homesteads encompassing 2,500,000 acres were thus given away during the War. The dream of the West had indeed come true.

In the same year, 1862, the Morrill Act, sponsored since 1857 by Representative Justin H. Morrill of Vermont, became law. Under this act, designed to promote the establishment of agricultural colleges, the Federal Government donated to the states 30,000 acres of public lands for each Representative they had in Congress, for the purpose of providing funds from the land sales with which to found colleges. In addition to these two sources of free or low-priced land, there was yet another. Huge land grants had been made to the railroads to hasten their construction since 1850 and were to continue throughout and long after the War until they were to reach the unparalleled total of nearly 160,000,000 acres.

4 Gold Is Where You Find It...

On the wet, cold afternoon of January 24, 1848, two mill hands, Brown and Bigler, were working on a sawpit along a branch of the American River, where Captain John A. Sutter's Coloma mill stood. Suddenly they were hailed by an Indian running toward them with a message from their boss James W. Marshall who was working an upper tributary that day. A burned out 'tin' plate was needed at once. Nothing else was mentioned and nothing more was explained. At once the pan was secured from a log cabin by one of the men and given to the Indian. Not thinking twice about the incident, they returned to their work. Hours passed, and when it was time to quit for the day, Marshall walked in with a smile on his face running from ear to ear. In the palm of his hand he displayed several small gold nuggets and stated he had found a gold mine. To insure the fact that it was gold, they placed one nugget on a hard, smooth river stone and commenced hammering it with another stone. It was soft and yellow and didn't break, therefore it must be gold.

After more gold had been found and more tests were carried out, they concluded that the deposit was rich. After Sutter had been informed that gold was found beyond the 'tail race', he secured a three-year lease of the area around the mill from the local Indians. Then he tried to get title to the land from the military governor. The governor's messenger gave the game away to a miner who knew the region well while Sutter himself continued to announce the new find. As a handful of miners and prospectors entered the area, the Californian newspaper printed a small editorial of the episode. But no one paid too much attention to the news release, as San Francisco was but a small village of 800 people. In the past there had been too many prospectors who boasted of finding gold and exaggerated all out of proportion in reporting their finds. San Franciscans waited patiently to see what other news would come of it ... until Sam Brannan, an extrovert Mormon, rushed through the town waving a 'poke' full of gold advertising his new riches.

The stampede was on. By mid-June three quarters of the townsmen had left for the newly announced 'gold fields'. Many shops closed overnight. Their windows bore signs, 'Gone to the Diggings'.

Soldiers stationed at various posts, veterans of the Mexican War, deserted by the numbers. Between July 1848 and the end of 1849, some 715 soldiers out of 1,290 stationed in Northern California deserted, as well as the sailors in the Pacific Squadron. Sutter and Marshall did not benefit from this find. Marshall began drinking heavily, sold autographed cards and drifted from one place to another. Sutter tried desperately to hold his possessions together, and, after learning that the US Supreme Court decided that his

Sutter's Mill, California, 1849.

52

Some 150 southwest miners, and some family members, group for a company picture, just before the mine petered out. Circa 1898–1900 (G. A. Peterson Collection).

land grant from the Mexicans was invalid, he settled down in Pennsylvania. He died in 1880, just before Congress determined that their treatment of him was unworthy. Hence it has been said that the discovery of gold on the Pacific Slope ruined both the discoverer and the owner of the land on which gold was found.

No doubt there was much exaggeration in regard to the richness of the mines; at any rate, many adventurers risked their lives to reach the land of gold, expecting to fill their pockets daily with the precious metal. And yet, the real facts in the case were marvellous. Gold was found in such large quantities that the 5,000 seekers in '48 believed there was enough for every man who might come and dig the fields. Two ounces per day was an ordinary yield per man, but many did much better than that. As the value of gold was $12 an ounce in cash and $16 in trade, their hard labor was very remunerative. Colonel Mason, who made an examination of the mines for the government, confirmed, in his official report, their reputation for richness. He said that the leading store at Sutter's Fort in nine weeks received $36,000 in gold-dust, in exchange for goods; and that two men took

out $17,000 in seven days in a small ravine. He related that seven miners hired 50 Indians to work for them for seven weeks. At the end of that time, they had 273 pounds of pure gold, the cash value of which was nearly $52,416. Some men, on some days, made $100 each, and sometimes even more. A miner pulled up a bush that was in the way, and shook the earth from its roots into his miner's pan, as a farmer shakes a hill of potatoes, and the yield of gold from that bush was nearly $50. In 1850, a nugget of gold found in Nevada County valued at $312. It was not unusual for a piece of ground ten feet square to yield $10,000 from the surface dirt. Many facts of this kind proved that gold was indeed plentiful.

In December of 1849 there were 53,000 miners in the gold fields. It had been claimed that the rush of men to California, in five years after the discovery of gold, was so immense as to move the center of our country's population 81 miles west. Nearly $270 million was extracted from the mines.

A California newspaper stated: 'The summer of 1849 saw no less than 549 sea-going vessels in the port of San Francisco. In the month of August, 400 large ships were idly swinging at anchor, destitute of crews; for their sailors had deserted, swimming ashore and escaping to the gold mines. 35,000 men came by sea, and 42,000 by land, during the year. The Asian Coasts,

Australia, South America and Africa, all contributed a melting pot of individuals that thronged the roads to the placers.'

Prices were fabulous; a shirt cost $25; a comb, $6; a barrel of mess pork, $220; a dozen sardines, $35; 100 pounds of flour, $75; a candle, $3; tin pan, $9; shovel, $10; and a pick, $15. There was also a scarcity of women, and when one passed by everyone stopped whatever they were doing, removed their hats politely and only resumed their work when she was well out of sight.

Ten years later, the discovery of gold in what is now Colorado created another 'unparalleled excitement'. As Colorado was more accessible than California, the rush of prospectors was much larger. They poured into the gold fields by tens of thousands. Many even left the mines of California for richer ones, as they supposed, in Colorado. No amount of hardship and suffering could deter the tide of immigration. Many of the gold seekers were the most intelligent and substantial men of the Anglo-Saxon race from the East, West, and South. Unwittingly they came to lay the foundation of an empire. They were the modern Argonauts, who not only sought 'the golden fleece', but developed the richest, fairest, grandest country on earth.

Beginning at Cherry Creek, near the site of Denver, this army of prospectors scoured the 'Plains' and penetrated the Rocky Mountains, searching for gold. Clear Creek Canyon, Boulder, California Gulch, and a large number of other localities 'opened rich', augmenting the excitement with the increase of the gold product. Then followed the discovery of silver, which was as unexpected as it was fortunate, opening new fields of research, and bringing other thousands of enthusiastic toilers into the Territory.

At the same time, the prospector was abroad in Arizona, Nevada, Utah, New Mexico, Montana, Idaho, and, indeed, throughout the whole country between the Missouri River and the Pacific Ocean; and the news of rich mines in all these localities spread wildly over the land. Untold millions of metals were treasured in the Rocky Mountain region, and the key was found with which to open the vaults.

The exploratory expedition to the Black Hills was organized in pursuance of an order from the Lieutenant-General commanding at Fort Abraham Lincoln in the month of June, 1874. It consisted of ten companies of the Seventh Cavalry, two companies of Infantry, three Gatling guns, 61 Indian scouts, a number of army engineers and some scientists, newspaper men, two miners and a photographer. Lieutenant Colonel G. A. Custer was assigned to its command, and he was directed to proceed by such route as he should find most desirable to Bear Butte or a position on the Belle Fourche, and then push explorations in such directions

PLATE 10

31,32,33 Prospectors, 1848

31. *The California gold rush not only beckoned Easterners but foreign families as well. They were hard workers who wore unusual clothing and introduced new kinds of foods. Many could not speak English and were cheated, fleeced, and made fun of by the other miners. They were a melting pot of all European countries and religions, and they kept their old ways in a close relationship with their families. Introduced to California were some new European skills, such as wine-making from France, beer-making from Germany, and other industrial crafts and trades to help build the immediate area from the Spanish occupation. Though he tries to look neat from head to boot, unless this fellow makes enough gold dust to head to town for supplies his ragged trousers will have to wait a while longer before being replaced with new ones. On his head there is an odd-shaped cap that is foreign, but similar to the US Mounted Dragoons forage cap. His boot tops are turned down to allow more leg ventilation during warmer weather. He wears no pistol, but probably has a short-blade stiletto hidden at close hand.*

32. *A young man in summer attire befriends an old crony from one of the camps. With a turned-up-brim straw hat, he displays a brace of small caliber pistols holstered on his belt. His open vest, with wide fashionable lapels, reveals a soft display of ruffled material running up and down his chest. A silk bandana is neatly rolled and encircled several times around his neck under the shirt collar, and knotted. The shirt, made from an expensive fabric, has shoulder-puff sleeves after an early Victorian pattern. Wide-flapped pockets running almost horizontal give an unusual design against a vertical-striped background. Trousers are loosely tucked into wide-mouthed boot tops that have extra long mule ears.*

33. *This old miner was probably one of the earliest arrivals in the gold fields and looks as though he had put in more than his share of working the hills and streams. A battered, wide-brimmed hat shades neck and face, while two pairs of shirts comfort him in cool weather. Many prospectors adopted the custom of wearing holstered weapons, but this fellow finds it more convenient to stuff a revolver into his belt. Such revolvers were often of the percussion system that was manufactured by Colt firearms. Over his trousers are a pair of yellow-gummed leggings which hang from suspended belts attached to his waist belt. These were factory made and helped protect the knees and trouser seams from wearing out. In his hand he holds a small pick-ax. This is used to chip sample rocks from mountain walls during exploration of various areas. It also served as a weapon when his life was threatened.*

PLATE 10

31, 32, 33   Prospectors, 1848

Interior view of the Copper Queen Mine, Bisbee, Arizona.
Circa early 1900s (Arizona Historical Society).

as in his judgement would enable him to obtain the most information in regard to the character of the country and the possible routes of communication through it. He was directed to return to Fort Lincoln within 60 days from the time of his departure. The newspapers were happy with the notification of the expedition, for they had been preaching investigation of the Black Hills for years to improve and develop one of the richest and most fertile sections in America. Settlers and miners had no idea of what the expedition was really about. Officially it was a reconnaissance to obtain information about hostile trails through the hills and to explore them.

Lt Colonel Custer marched out of Fort Lincoln on the 1st of July, reaching the foot of the hills on the 22nd, and then pushing his command into the heart of the range. Custer found the region was rich in pasture land and, more significantly, he found gold. Before Custer had commenced his return march to Fort Lincoln, arriving there on the 30th, news of the discovery of gold had already been in print in the Chicago Inter-Ocean newspaper. Soon, the word spread like 'wild-fire' that there was gold 'from the grass roots down'.

Custer's trail was labeled 'Thieves Road' by the Sioux, and it was soon to be filled with miners, horses and wagons. Long before these events came about, gold had been found by the Sioux in the Black Hills of Dakota. At various times they displayed pieces at trading posts and were warned to keep quiet about their finds or else their land would be invaded by white prospectors. There were, however, a handful of prospectors who had visited the hills as early as the 1850s, and in returning home revealed their finds. Two Swedes found gold in 1856–66, and when they returned to the hills had disappeared. Various other civilian expeditions were organized, only to be turned back by the military.

The Black Hills were once dominated by the mighty Cheyennes, who had lost them to the Sioux. The earth was sacred to the Indians. It was their hunting ground and burial ground and where their gods lived. Because of Custer's respect for the Indians, he spoke freely to many delegations on the reservations, and many trusted his word. By doing this in advance, he was able to complete his expedition without bloodshed. Of course the newspaper correspondents who accompanied the command played up the gold discovery as America was recovering from the panic of 1873, and many unemployed welcomed the chance to change their life style.

On August 17, 1896, 'squaw man' George Washington Carmack found a gold nugget while hunting along Rabbit Creek, a tributary of Bonanza Creek which forks off the Klondike River. After clearing away some loose rock, he came across more gold lying thick between flaky slabs like cheese sandwiches. After panning the area, he extracted additional gold and staked his claim. He was not at all hesitant about relating his discovery to everyone he met, so the news spread like wild-fire, stirring the hearts of millions, and caused the name 'Klondike' to become famous throughout the world. There had already been smaller strikes in the Klondike region preceding Carmack's discovery, and there was ample evidence that the area was rich with gold, but the new strike began to unfold with unequaled drama and unsurpassed riches. Whenever the name 'Klondike' was heard the thoughts of men turned to the magical word 'gold'. Towns such as Dawson, Forty Mile, Sixty Mile and countless others sprang up as tent cities and thousands upon thousands of prospectors rushed pell-mell into the Klondike.

Southwestern figures such as Wyatt Earp turned up in Nome in 1899, where for two years he promoted prize fights and ran a saloon until the Nevada gold strike lured him southward once more. Frank Canton, Wyoming's former sheriff of Johnson County and chief detective for the Cattlemen's Association, followed the gold rush to the Klondike and served two years as a Deputy US Marshal in Alaska. John Clum, editor of the 'The Tombstone Epitaph', also traveled to Alaska where he accepted a job as postal inspector, traveling thousands of miles setting up more than a dozen Post Offices.

As far as women were concerned, Mattie Silks, with another kind of reputation, appeared in the Klondike, scaling White Pass with eight of her soiled doves and a set of gold scales, for one profitable season in Dawson in 1898. Down at Skagway, Jefferson Randolph 'Soapy' Smith, a soft spoken Georgian, made his appearance early in 1898. Smith came from Colorado where he attracted attention as a con man and organizer of rackets. Now in Skagway, he and his small gang were bent on wrapping up the town with a number of sham enterprises to which suckers could be usefully steered. He set up a Telegraph Office, a Cut Rate Ticket Office, Reliable Packers, an Information Bureau and Merchant's Exchange, not to mention his own saloon.

At the end of autumn, 1897, at least 100,000 prospectors stampeded their way to the Klondike. Many hikers, outfitted with huge packs on their backs, turned back after several tries up the precipitous White and Chilkoot passes. Even the few stragglers who dropped out of the line had to wait hours before they could get back in line. Local Indians charged 50 cents a pound to tote supplies to the top of the pass. Near the summit of Chilkoot pass was the customs station manned by the Northwest Mounted Police, who checked all prospectors to see that they had a year's provisions before permitting them into Canadian territory. White Pass trail paralleled the Chilkoot, and was another popular but dangerous pass to Dawson and the Yukon. White Pass trail continued north to Lake Bennett. These 40-odd miles often took a man one month to travel. Besides all the troubles these prospectors had to face, the Northwest Mounted Police began collecting a Canadian duty on all ore excavated. Soon only rich claims were worth the trouble. Portions of this trail to the lake had such insecure footing that more than 3,000 pack horses slipped and fell off the treacherous path down into the rocky pit nicknamed 'Dead Horse Gulch', while 'Dead Horse Trail' was littered with abandoned sleds and supplies. The gold fields lay within a small 25 by

Tools of a prospector during the early years. The portable scale in the foreground was used to weigh gold dust stored in leather pokes (author).

30 mile area, and the best locations had already been staked during the early rush.

The late stampeders that turned back made a meager living doing odd jobs or working someone else's diggings, or milling around Dawson's saloons awaiting the early summer months to leave the area as fast as they had arrived. The major problem in the Klondike was supplying Dawson's fast-growing population with food. Newcomers were warned that food was not sufficient to last the winter and the Northwest Mounted Police tried to get the prospectors to move to Fort Yukon in Alaska, but to no avail. Everyone was fearful of losing their claims by claim jumpers. Rumors of new strikes continued to spread as disappointed prospectors raced from one new area to another. It was 1,100 miles from Dawson to Nome on Alaska's West coast – if you had enough money for a ticket by boat.

In the late 1890s, the Klondike country flocked with gold seekers and adventurers, all hoping to locate a fortune or a new lease on life. Next to a good supply of ready cash, a man who had designs upon the placer fields in the Klondike region would need at least a one-year supply of food, clothing and working materials. This advice was given to all 'green-horns' by the men who had returned from the scene of the great gold strikes. These experienced miners and prospectors insisted that no man attempt the journey without a cash capital of at least $500 to $1,000. Many of those who rushed for the Klondike failed to take this advice, and as a consequence large numbers were turned back by the Northwest Mounted Police at the gateway.

An analysis of 20 so-called practical lists was made by experienced gold seekers who had spent up to ten years in the Klondike region. Their individual preferences varied as to the quantity and quality of certain kinds of rough and ready 'delicacies' desirable for that period of time. An adequate supply of food per day for one man varied from $4\frac{1}{2}$ to $5\frac{1}{2}$ pounds. This would bring the actual food supply for one year for each person to fully 1,600 pounds. Highly carbohydrate food was predominant; stimulants of alcoholic character were to be avoided. One pound of tea was equal to seven pounds of coffee, three-quarters of an ounce of saccharin (obtained from a druggist) was equal to 25 pounds of sugar, so that three ounces of saccharin was equal in sweetness to 100 pounds of sugar. Citric acid was a remedy for scurvy.

The list was as follows:

Bacon, pounds	150
Flour, pounds	400
Rolled oats, pounds	25
Beans, pounds	125
Tea, pounds	10
Coffee, pounds	10
Sugar, pounds	25
Dried potatoes, pounds	25
Dried onions, pounds	2
Salt, pounds	15
Pepper, pounds	1
Dried fruits, pounds	75
Baking powder, pounds	8
Soda, pounds	2
Evaporated vinegar, pounds	$\frac{1}{2}$
Compressed soup, ounces	12
Soap, cakes	9
Mustard, cans	1
Matches (for four men), tins	1

Stove for four men.
Gold pan for each.
Set granite buckets.
Large bucket.
Knife, fork, spoon, cup and plate.
Frying pan.
Coffee and tea pot.
Scythe stone.
Two picks and one shovel.
One whipsaw.
Pack strap.
Two axes for four men and one extra handle.
Six 8-inch files and two taper files for party.
Drawing knife, brace and bits, jack plane and hammer, for party.
200 feet $\frac{3}{8}$-inch rope.
8 pounds of pitch and five pounds of oakum for four men.
Nails, five pounds each of 6, 8, 10 and 12-penny, for four men.
Tent, 10 × 12 feet, for four.

PLATE 11

34, 35, 36 Prospectors, 1870–80

34. *The old prospector shows up with his reliable pack-animal, the 'Burro'. He is wearing everyday clothing of the period, which includes a Colt .44/40 revolver on his belt. His 'Big Neck Jenny', who follows him everywhere, totes over 150 pounds of tools, grub, water, bedding, tarpaulin, and sometimes high-grade ore hitched to her sawbuck saddle. 'Jenny' also serves as a night sentinel, alarming her overseer of any nearby impending danger. Now and then a general stranger wanders by, notices the camp fire, and drops in for a touch of 'Rio coffee' or maybe a plate of hot beans. A warm, friendly exchange of fresh news from town and a few amusing tales were always on the agenda after a hearty meal.*

35. *Standing above is partner number two. His business understanding with the other two prospectors is only a verbal agreement, which was common, but not a general rule. Such agreements lasted only as long as their mutual trust, which could* *suddenly, by a wrong word, explode into gunfire, turning businessmen into killers. Whenever gold presented itself, jealousy often followed. Some men would honor their verbal agreements only until they hit pay-dirt and then would break away on their own using their newly found riches as 'grub stakes' for another 'pot of gold' at the 'end of a rainbow'. It is hard to believe that superstitious gold hunters and prospectors plotted rainbows and followed their plunging colors to earth with thoughts and beliefs that an Eldorado lay at the end.*

36. *Partner number three looks as though he is going through a stage of perplexity. Gold is short and hard in coming, and he no longer believes his partners' futuristic plans. He is thinking about giving up and heading back to civilization to find gold in a hand of cards or table dice. He is down to his last pair of bib overalls, and a few more rock scrapes will leave him in his long-handle underwear. He complains that the profits made by his two partners went for cheap city booze and weekend funning.*

PLATE 11

34, 35, 36   Prospectors, 1870–80

E.L.REEDSTROM

Canvas for wrapping.

Two oil blankets to each boat.

5 yards mosquito netting for each man.

3 suits heavy underwear.

1 heavy mackinaw coat.

2 pairs heavy mackinaw trousers.

1 heavy rubber-lined coat.

1 dozen heavy wool socks.

½ dozen heavy wool mittens.

2 heavy overshirts.

2 pairs heavy snagproof rubber boots.

2 pairs shoes.

4 pairs blankets (for two men).

4 towels.

2 pairs overalls.

1 suit oil clothing.

Besides these things each man procures a small assortment of medicines, and each is provided with several changes of summer clothing. The foregoing outfit costs in round figures as follows:

Groceries	$40.00
Clothing.	50.00
Hardware	50.00
Total.	$140.00

The word 'Prospector' is defined in a dictionary as follows: 'a person engaged in exploring for valuable minerals or in testing areas supposed to be rich in content.' He was usually 'grubstaked' for an expedition into the mountains or desert with the understanding that the provider was to share in the profits. A time period was never discussed between the two partners, the prospector only returned when his provisions were gone or if his samples proved worthy of

A Grubstake from a Partner.

a second expedition. A simple handshake over a couple of drinks and a few words in verbal contract bound both men. Having been grubstaked, the prospector never gave a thought to hi-tailing it with all the tools and provisions into another sector to go it alone. He would surely be sought after and, when found, probably hung like a horse thief. As a general rule, prospectors didn't have much in life except their word, and that was golden.

Picture the old-time prospector with a wide-brimmed, oil soaked sombrero, several months' growth of hair on his face, patched clothing in some places almost worn through, and breeches stained with every imaginable color, tucked loosely into high topped leather boots that had seen better days. Just behind him stands his trusted friend, a big thick necked burro answering to the name of either 'Jocko' or 'Jenny', one of the most sure footed animals in the West when it came to mountain climbing. On the burro's back is a sawbuck saddle with grub boxes hanging on both sides to equalize the load, along with other miners' paraphernalia. A bed roll, large tarp, canteen filled with cool creek water and a small caliber lever action rifle tucked off to the side and handy if needed in a hurry was added. A short handled pick, shovel, single-jack hammer and a 12-inch gold pan adorned the top of the animal's pack, neatly tied down and package-wrapped with a tight diamond hitch. The prospector might have several burros, each tied to one another with a six-foot lead rope for leading the animals in single file. As late as the 1940s, these 'desert canaries' could be seen slowly treking across the Western bottom lands and into cool and shadowed mountain canyons. If a westerner didn't know your name, he made one up for you. Nicknames such as the forty-niner, desert rat, coffee cooler, pocket hunter, hill rat and sage rat were given the prospector as well as a host of others. He relied on no one except the man or men who grubstaked him. He was kindly to visitors who came upon his camp and was always the listener in conversations except when a certain hair-raising story came to his mind, causing his tongue to wag like a hound dog's tail. And speaking of dogs, you can be certain he had a couple of mutts traveling with him. These men were usually loners, and it was unusual to see more than two in a party. If someone asked one of these old duffers what he would do if he ever found that pot of gold at the end of the rainbow, that he had chased for so many years, you'd likely get this answer. 'I'd prob'bly do nuthin' much with it. Ya see, it's lookin' fer thet pot o' gold what keeps a feller on the

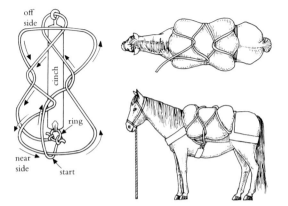

*Almost every packer had his own variation of the famous diamond hitch. This is the basic pattern (*Wildwood Wisdom *by Ellsworth Jaeger, The Macmillan Company).*

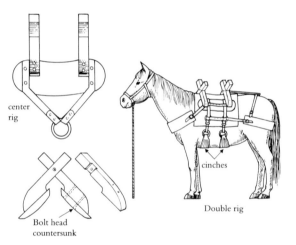

*Two types of sawbuck pack saddles, the center rig and the double rig, that are standard for pack horses and burros (*Wildwood Wisdom *by Ellsworth Jaeger, The Macmillan Company).*

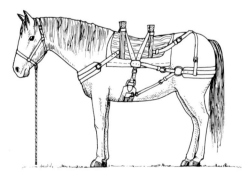

move. Efen I found it tomorrow, I'd still be up and after anotha' the nixt day.'

If anyone should know the feeling, this author does after having had the experience of seven years of prospecting the West. It's not so much the satisfaction of finding the gold as the adventure in searching for it.

Although the discovery of gold in California in 1848, and in Colorado, ten years later, was accidental, as miners say, these discoveries created this new class of workers, the 'prospectors'. He may be a native or foreigner; an ignorant adventurer or a Harvard graduate. He was a man who was out to make a 'lucky strike', or one who knew industry and perseverance would help him on his way to success. A great many of these gold hunters often found their level in poverty or the grave, leaving the field of exploration open for the more enterprising to occupy.

Now and then a map was brought to light, showing rivers, tributaries, mountains and peaks, a military trail, a wagon road and a near-by town that had petered out after a small strike. The problem was to decide which map was the 'real McCoy' and which was a phony. Many prospectors were suckered in by purchasing such maps, following them for years without any luck. And, then again, one out of a thousand maps might reveal gold bullion for the finder.

Placer mining (above ground) first enlisted the attention of gold-seekers because it was the easiest, most accessible, and made prompt returns. Mining consisted of washing the surface dirt. Thousands who invaded California in 1848–49 engaged at once in this sort of mining. When the process of washing the gold from the dirt was remunerative, the miner said 'it pans out well'. His pan furnished the figure.

As compared with lode mining (underground), there was no outlay to be made in the outset, and no risk to run. At the close of each day the miner knew just the amount he had earned. He might have been entirely ignorant of practical and scientific mining, but he knew enough to separate gold from the surface dirt. He might be poor as a church mouse, but his muscle and perseverance gave him as good a chance as his more well-to-do co-worker enjoyed. Poverty stands abreast with competency in this kind of work; poverty may sift dirt as fast, and perhaps faster, than competency.

Center rig sawbuck saddle. Hung on each side are boxes containing the prospector's tools, grub, etc. On top of all this goes his bed roll, tarp and anything else useful in his work.

Lode mining.

We have seen also that gold-seekers in Colorado, in 1858–59, devoted themselves to placer mining in Boulder, Gilpin, Park, Summit, Lake and other counties. Here they could work but five or six months of the year on account of the severity of the weather; but one million dollars a season was the average amount of gold secured for several years. Indeed, California Gulch alone, where three or four months of labor covered the working season, turned out one million each season for a series of years.

The gold gathered by placer mining had been washed down from the mountains, through past ages, into the creeks, rivers, and gulches. Much of it worked through the loose gravel down to the river bed, where miners found the richest deposits.

Of course there is a limit to placer mining. The gold is exhausted in time; and miners who are not prepared to engage in lode mining pack their trappings and start for other placers. This includes the class who have not the enterprise or capital to engage in lode mining; and it is a very large class too. Crowds of placer miners left Boulder, Gilpin, and other counties of Colorado just named in 1863, for other placers in the Rocky Mountains, or as far away as Montana and Idaho while some of the richest lodes were still being worked in the counties which they forsook. The Bobtail, Gregory, Winnebago, Burroughs, Kansas,

---

PLATE 12
37, 38 'Klondike' prospector and woman, 1896–98
39 Chinese prospector, 1896–98

37. *The gold fields in Alaska were cold, and nobody knew how to dress and what was needed in such weather. The three-quarter, double-breasted, lined Mackinaw flannel coat with a wide circular rolling collar sold for three dollars and fifty cents and was suitable for the cold air and chilling winds. The black, heavy, woolen-lined 'driving cap' with ear flaps tied up sold for 38 cents and was worth every penny. A flannel shirt with underwear beneath, topped off with a heavy cloth material, black and grey pin-striped, some-times called 'fishskins', were tucked into combination Arctic tie boots made of pure gum rubber. A heavy unkempt beard generally accompanied the complete wardrobe, whether for style or the Alaskan weather. On the ground behind the prospector is a 'rocker' used to separate gold ore from crushed rock or gravel.*

38. *Few women were found in the gold field region, but those who were, dressed warmly like men during the day. In the even-ing they changed femininely into their stylish satin striped taffeta skirts and dainty embroidered front waists. Portrayed here, the woman wears a blue-and-white striped cape with a sleeveless hand-knit sweater over the cape to keep the Arctic winds from*

blowing it over her head. The breeches are men's Hercules overalls, several sizes too big, made from full 9-ounce York denim, and held up by a pair of 1½-inch elastic suspenders. The hat is from Stetson and the boots are oil grain 'Plow Boots' with low heels. A man's red flannel 'handlebar' union suit wouldn't embarrass or redden her cheeks as much as the Arctic elements might . . . even if the men found out about it.

39. *Scorned for their unfamiliar ways and the color of their skin, the Chinese were hated for the diligence with which they worked old diggings long abandoned by whites. They also worked odd jobs for cheap labor, survived on little or nothing while working their claims in the hills and simply irritated the jealous white prospector. This Chinese prospector is prepared for a short pro-specting trip or survey, decked out in his summer clothing of a wide sombrero, cotton pull-over shirt, heavy corduroy breeches, woolen socks and Arctic gum boots. In his back pack he is carrying a 12-inch gold pan, short handle pick, food for several weeks, eating utensils, pot, frying pan, small bucket, oil canvas, blankets, five yards of mosquito netting, a small whipsaw, and an ax. If a white man ventured out for this short period, he'd have a mule with a sawbuck saddle loaded down with goods for several months, most of which would get lost or wasted.*

PLATE 12

39   Chinese prospector, 1896–98

37, 38   'Klondike' prospector and woman, 1896–98

Water barrel, rocker and sluice made up the majority of heavy equipment when working the side of a mountain or a dry creek bed (author).

and a score of other mines were yielding thousands of dollars every month; but the mass of stampeders had no love for this more difficult method of acquiring fortunes. Perhaps many of them really thought that the shortest cut to great wealth was through placer mining; and so placers they must have. The word 'placer' is from the Spanish, and means 'content', 'satisfaction'; and this class appeared to be 'content' with placers only.

Since the rising value of gold has produced a great deal of interest once again, perhaps the art of 'panning' should be studied seriously. The gold miner's 'pan' resembles a frying pan minus the handle. It is circular in form and 10 to 14 inches in diameter at the bottom, flaring out at the top to a diameter three or four inches wider. The sides are about five inches deep. Before ever using it, the owner must be sure to burn the inside of the pan out over a camp fire, insuring that all impurities are released from the bottom, including any grease.

Now to the method of using it. A quantity of the dirt to be washed, say two shovelfuls, is placed in the pan, but it should not be filled to more than two-thirds of its capacity. The pan with its contents is then immersed in water, either in a hole or in a stream of such depth that the would-be prospector can easily reach into it with his hand while it rests on the bottom. The mass in the pan is stirred up with both hands so that every particle of it may become thoroughly mixed with water. When the dirt has become soaked and softened so that it is a thin, pasty mass, the pan is taken in both hands, one on either side, and a little

inside of its greatest diameter, that is to say, about halfway up from the bottom. Then, without taking it from the water, it is held not quite level, but tipped somewhat away from the individual. When in this position it is shaken, to allow the water to disengage all the light earthy particles and carry them away. When this has been done properly, the pan will contain only gold particles, nuggets, heavy sand, a mixture of iron particles and sand, lumps of clay and gravel stone. The gravel stones generally accumulate on the surface and can be picked off by hand and thrown aside. The lumps of clay should be crumbled and reduced by rubbing and mashing so as to be carried off the next time the pan is placed in the water. This operation requires a little skill and practice. An oscillating motion will give a whirlpool effect to the muddy water, causing it to escape over the depressed edge of the pan without losing the lighter portions of gold. After much of the muddy water has been passed off, and only black sand and black iron remain along with the gold specks, revolve the pan so as to get rid of the sand and iron leaving only the gold in the crease of the pan. A magnet is sometimes used to remove the iron, but be certain to keep the gold in the pan separated from the sand and iron. A few times of doing it will give you all the experience you need. Bottle the gold and cork it well. You have just experienced what the old-time miners and prospectors had to do all day long.

Sometimes a pan would yield 50 cents to $2. At that time it was worth the effort. When this author prospected the West in the 1940s, I was lucky to pan $3 to $4 a day. Gold at that time was worth $32 an ounce.

A sluice was a long narrow open box, set on an incline on bedrock or in a ditch into which placer sand and gravel was shoveled. This material was transported along with its running waters separating the heavier minerals from lighter ones by the faster settling rate of the minerals of higher specific gravity. This separation was completed by the addition of many riffles or other devices such as bars or grooves that would afford an irregular surface behind which heavy minerals could lodge. Textured materials such as gunny sack or corduroy were laid on the bottom of the sluices and wooden riffles or slats added in a horizontal plane every 8 inches and nailed down over the material. These were easily picked up at the end of the work day and the soaked material, after being washed out in a separate tub was replaced again. This tub was worked by hand panning the next day, after allowing the heavier minerals to settle on the bottom over night. The material collected in the tub was referred to as 'the tailing piles' or just 'tailings'. This is also the name for any accumulated pilings once worked from a mine and heaped into a huge pile of filtered dirt and rock. Some miners who became desperate after their stakes had dwindled down to nothing worked these tailing dumps and were sometimes lucky enough to find some color. This particular procedure was still being used in the 1930s and 40s after smaller mines had closed down or 'gone bust'.

Usually a 'rocker' was at the far head of the sluice box, constantly worked by one man. Another shoveled dirt into it that had been carted back from the mine or open pit. 'Rockers' were sometimes referred to as 'cradles' because of the similarity to rocking an old fashioned baby crib or cradle by hand. Dirt and crushed rock were thrown into the open hopper as one man rocked the cradle back and forth, adding buckets of water to every other shovelful. Gravel and sand filtered through a course screen or a tin plate punctured with several hundred holes. This sent the finer sand and material through the bottom of the rocker and out into the sluice box, where it was re-duced to sand, iron ore, and gold if there was any to be found in the area. Whatever accumulated at the bottom of the tub and at the end of the sluice was again panned by hand.

The latter day prospector used a chamois or 'shammy' skin to separate gold from mercury, if a drop-step amalgamation process was being used. (The

The author, Lisle Reedstrom, works with some old miners' equipment in Arizona's Superstition Mountains, 1946. It was here that the young man became interested in the Old West, while his old cronies could still remember horse manure scattering the streets of Phoenix (author's Collection).

'drop-step' amalgamation process used mercury coated copper plates formed into steps. Then fine sand or gravel, traveling with water, glided over each plate with some force and any gold present would be caught up by the mercury. A squeegee was used to skim off the mercury on each copper plate into a vessel and then smaller amounts into a shammy.) This was done by squeezing the mercury through the pores of the skin, wrapping string around the top of the accumulated bulk. Gold would remain within the skin in a small ball and the mercury was caught in a container and used over again. The gold was again separated from the remaining mercury by melting it into a 'button' in an iron crucible over a hot campfire. An experienced miner knew only too well to stand clear of the fumes of heated mercury, no matter how small an amount there might be. A good whiff could cause serious after effects, and sometimes could be fatal.

At the end of each day, every coated copper plate was squeezed with a flat end rubber swatch and deposited into a jar or on the 'shammy' skin. The old-timers used another method called the 'potato method'. When the gold and mercury was gathered into a jar, a single potato was cut into two halves. In the center, a hole was carved out about the size of a quarter and the material of the two elements was dropped into the center of the potato. Over a hot campfire, a large piece of flat iron, like that from an old wood stove, was placed. The potato was turned upside down and, holding the contents within by placing a small tin can lid over the opening, was set on the metal plate. The potato actually soaked up the mercury leaving only a small charred cinder of gold. This was smelted down into a button of gold and cleaned with muratic acid to bring out its original metallic color. The potato saturated with the mercury was squeezed out and the mercury was used over and over again; the potato served a good purpose.

In 1862 placer mining began in Montana, and in 1867 Alder Gulch alone, 13 miles long, had yielded 60 million dollars. From 1862 to 1890 the placers of Montana had turned out over 150 million. We have said that gold is washed down from the mountains into gulches and ravines, where the hydraulic method of securing it is brought into requisition. By this method water is carried long distances, often by ditches and flumes, to wash gold from the dirt on a much larger scale.

Gold bearing dirt was carried into the flume and sluices by swiftly running water, where the presence

Prospecting outfit, early 1880s (Arizona Historical Society).

of mercury at the bottom of these boxes attracted and separated the gold from the dirt. Once or twice a day, as the circumstances may be, the water was shut off, the boxes opened and the gold secured. Sometimes a powerful stream of water was poured into the side of the gulch to wash out the earth into the flume in a large way. Hydraulic mining caused such immense damage in California by filling up rivers and covering farming lands with debris, that it was suppressed by legislation, thereby largely diminishing the gold product, and causing a depression in the business. It was claimed that the suppression of this mode of mining threw 20,000 men out of employment. Many persons believed that the damage by legislation would be greater than the damage by the accumulation of debris.

In hydraulic mining, flumes were often carried across deep valleys and gorges in the same manner the railroad and highway bridges were built. Exhaustible placer mining was followed by 'lode mining', which included silver mining. Here it was necessary to sink a shaft down into the bowels of the earth by drilling and blasting. This was accomplished by hard work and at great expense.

A windlass was erected at the opening of the shaft for the purpose of lowering and raising a bucket in which the dirt below was brought to the surface for processing. The men, or 'muckers' as they were called, suffered many injuries when a full bucket was being hauled up, rocks would jar loose from the walls as the bucket banged against the sides of the shaft while being toted upward. As the rocks fell, they found their mark upon the miner's head or shoulders.

A mine may have several drifts, according to its depth, and the drifts may be on both sides of the shaft. Often the drifts extended a long distance, and railway

tracks were laid, to convey the ore to the bottom of the shaft, where it was lifted to the surface. To help shore up the ceilings of tunnels or drifts, heavy timbers were used throughout to insure against any cave-ins. In this dark abode, artificial lighting was needed. First, in early mining, candles were used, then later carbide lamps were attached to miners' caps with reflectors to illuminate their underground work place.

Veins of gold or silver do not follow any particular pattern. They will run from a thick vein to a slender one, and even 'peter out' only to continue again several feet away. Veins can be worked above and beneath, as well as at the sides by the men in the drifts. A vein may extend to such a length as to make it practicable to sink several shafts and a number of drifts.

It would be fitting to list a host of famous mines of the West in conclusion to this chapter, with a capsule account of each, but due to the lack of space it would be impossible to list any more than the story of the famous 'Lost Dutchman Mine', of which this author knows well after searching for it for seven years.

Some 35 to 40 miles east of Phoenix, Arizona, lies the Superstition Mountain range with its wealth of stories of gold, silver and tungsten. From the period of 1880 to this present day, we have read many tales of riches taken from these mountains that have been publicized in newspapers, magazines and movies (*Lust for Gold*, starring Ida Lapino, Glen Ford, taken from Barry Storm's book *Thunder God's Gold*). The Superstition Mountains are an eerie jumble of cliffs and deep crevices, known to the prospector as the 'mountain of mysterious flying arrows'. This mountain range, 5,000 feet high, was once the stronghold of the mighty Apache Indians who, by knowing every path, trail and brush cover, escaped many times from the hands of the government troops. Somewhere within its interior lies the 'Lost Dutchmen Mine', a hidden bonanza and the most celebrated treasure trove of the Western world. About 25 miles east of Mesa, Arizona, near the junction of Highway 60 and Apache Trail, the Superstition Mountains are credited with holding every imaginable secret, and within their guarded walls lies the Lost Dutchman's hidden treasure worth $1 to $2 million dollars in pure gold.

Jacob Walzer, a German emigrant (the Dutchman), arrived in this country in the mid-1860s. It is not known how he found his way to Arizona, then a territory. He soon found employment at the Vulture Mine in Wickenburg, and after a short time was promoted to the job of loading mine wagons with ore. This gave him the opportunity to do a little 'high grading', or filling his pockets with high grade ore. While this was common among miners of that period, it cost Jacob his job. Very little is known of the German's activities after that, until he acquired a partner, another German by the name of Jacob Wiser. Later, both men were reported prospecting around the Superstitions, and they began to let their activities be known to their friends. In a small community of Florence, south of the mountain range, they bragged about a rich strike that they had uncovered, and they produced samples of ore for proof. The whole town was in an uproar. Walz (the name was soon shortened by his friends), professed that they had discovered an old Spanish mine, possibly one of the Peralta mines. (The name came from an early eighteenth-century Mexican family that discovered a number of gold mines.) After more than a year had passed, Walz announced to his friends that his partner, Wiser, had been killed by the roaming Apaches, then a constant threat to any one alone in the mountain or desert areas. The old 'Dutchman's' story was accepted and Jacob Wiser was soon forgotten. Snowbeard, another nickname of Walz, finally moved to Phoenix, where on a number of occasions he startled the residents there with his gold bearing ore. He would leave town at night returning after three days loaded with rich ore worth thousands of dollars. There were a number of attempts to follow the old Dutchman, but he would lose them in the desert that he knew so well.

All Walz wanted out of life was the pleasure of entertaining his friends at the nearest saloon, where he would while away the hours getting drunk, during which he would talk quite assuredly of his wealthy Spanish mine. When the 'Dutchman' grew too old to venture into the hills any more, he was pursued by many to draw a map and take on a new partner. But his mine was safe, and he alone knew its whereabouts, only to hint as its location from time to time, confusing all interested. After the great Phoenix flood of 1891, the 'Dutchman' caught pneumonia from the effects of exposure and died quietly at the home of Julia Thomas, a negro woman whom he had befriended. Just before he died it is said that he fashioned a crude map for the negro woman revealing the actual location of the mine. The map soon disappeared or was stolen, but the woman hunted for the 'Dutchman's' mine for many years relying upon her memory. It led

It took several men to operate this winch located in the heart of the Superstition Mountains, Arizona. It was called 'Dutchman No. 1'. Notice the opening in the Saguaro Cactus, then thought to be a Spanish map marked by gold seekers looking for the famous 'Lost Dutchman Mine' (author's Collection).

her into one blind canyon after another without any success. Trails to the 'Dutchman' treasure grew dimmer as years pass by, and the story is fashionable only when told around a camp fire in the open desert. It is said that any gold brought out of the hills was the gold fillings from a man's mouth. The legendary lost treasure trove has been written about more than any other gold mine in the West. Its history entails mystery, danger, adventure and perplexity. 'Gold is where you find it', is an old expression among prospectors, and many have spent their lives looking for it.

5 Hide-hunters and Buffalo

The extermination of the buffalo meant the decline of the Plains Indians. It also meant the decline of the buffalo hunters who were hired out by the army, railroads and private concerns ... to supply these institutions with meat and warm robes. Some of the more adventurous hunters continued to look for newer horizons, others brought their fortunes back to their hometowns, married and raised large families. But the trails ended for the older men; with what little savings and bad luck brought them, they generally ended up in an unfinished cabin on the outskirts of some western town. These old hunters were ignored and scorned by the townsfolk and as time passed they quietly died off by themselves, leaving a few trinkets of their past to a few close friends.

Those who knew of the great slaughter the buffalo hunters willingly had taken part in held contempt for these raw-boned buckskinners. Oddly enough, however, a certain interest was instilled in the younger generation as they gathered around the old hunter, eagerly listening to his many tales of a by-gone frontier. Once in a while the old hunter would disappear into his cabin only to return with a huge rifle cradled

Shooting buffalo from both the passenger cars and from the engine. Heavy betting was made on how many buffalo were brought down by one man. The onslaught sounded like a pitched Indian battle (Union Pacific Railroad Museum Collection).

in his arms, and on many occasions he displayed Indian trophies, some bearing a human scalp taken from a brave and fierce-fighting Indian. With all the colorful trappings, Indian artefacts and weapons displayed before glittering young eyes, the old hunter would then relax himself in the midst of the children and begin what was always an adventurous buffalo tale.

In the early seventies it was possible to travel through herd after herd and in one day see as many as 1 to 12 million buffalo moving in scattered bands. Unlike the white man, who killed the buffalo for sheer pleasure and business fortunes, the Indians maintained their survival from these great herds. After a kill, the hides were tanned and made into clothing, tepees, bedding and saddles. Sinew was used for bowstrings and made into thread for sewing. Shoulder bones were used as hoes for simple gardening, and rib bones served as runners for a dog sled. Buffalo horns yielded cups and bowls and much later were made into powder flasks. The animals' hoofs were boiled down for glue, and even the buffalo's tail served as a swatter for pesky flies and mosquitos. At the end, when the butchering was completed, hardly anything was left to show that a once noble buffalo had ever existed. The only evidence was buffalo litter, commonly known as 'buffalo chips' to the white man. When dried, this too would furnish the Indian fuel for his cooking fires.

A hunting-party might consist of any number more than two. It was usual to bring a wagon and team and to prepare to camp out for a week or two, carrying enough food and water for the adventure.

There were two buffalo ranges in the United States. The Southern range extended from 32° to 37°32′ north latitude, and from 99° to 104° west longitude; or, roughly speaking, from the Arkansas River on the north to the Rivers Brazos and Colorado on the south. The Western limit was the Rio Pecos; the eastern, the Witchia Mountains in Indian Territory. This vast tract included a part of Texas, Indian Territory, New Mexico, Kansas and Colorado, along with several Indian reservations. Within this part of the United States was a mangy infested group of white and colored thieves, outlaws and holdup men; however, much caution was advised to any party traveling through the area to observe and be well armed. The hunting ground was best traveled in from the North, going by rail to any of the smaller stations on the South Pacific or Atchison, Topeka, and Santa Fe railroads. The stations of Hays, Ellis and Kit Carson were most frequented by sportsmen.

The Northern buffalo range cannot be exactly defined. It extended from the Missouri River on the north and east to the Rocky Mountains on the west, and the south fork of the Big Cheyenne River on the south. This tract included parts of Montana, Wyoming and Dakota, and numerous Indian reservations. It was then most difficult to reach, but the Northern Pacific Railroad passed through the heart of this fine hunting ground making it easier to reach. Most hunting-parties then started out from Rawlins on the Union Pacific Railway. Some, however, went from Bismarck, the terminus of the Northern Pacific Railroad, and traveled along the stage road from that city to Helena, Montana, branching off along the Powder River Valley.

The abundance of buffalo may be judged by the fact that it was estimated that 4,500,000 were killed during the three years 1872–74, and in 1878 over 60,000 buffalo robes were shipped down the Yellowstone River. In the season of 1880, a professional robehunter killed 2,000 head of buffalo in Montana alone. Some remaining few thousands inhabited the country between the Arkansas and South Platte, and in 1874 large numbers crossed over to the flats between the North and South Platte. The fine pasture of the Republican (Pawnee River) was the most attractive to the remaining herds, and the sportsmen could generally find them in this area in some quantities every fall. The deep canyons of the Cimarron Valley also held many buffalo, and were more easily reached than the main herd on the 'Llano Estacado' or Staked Plains. In the Northern range, the valleys of the Yellowstone, Bighorn, Tongue, Powder, Sweetwater and Wind Rivers were the most favored localities for buffalo, as well as elk, deer, antelope, and other 'Injun Cattle'.

A variety of buffalo, known as the Rocky Mountain Buffalo, was found in the mountains of that name; it was smaller and shaggier than the Plain's

Phil Spangenburger, Guns & Ammo *magazine's Black Powder Editor, gallops after these Wyoming buffalo in the manner of the 1840s buffalo runners. He is wearing a buckskin coat with buffalo fur trim, buckskin fringed pants and Cheyenne moccasins. He wears a scarf around his head to keep his hair out of his eyes while running the herd. Phil is armed with a replica (Green River Rifle Works) .58 caliber Hawken-style plains rifle (percussion). His saddle is an original 1840–1860s era Texas stock saddle of the type often used by these early plainsmen (courtesy of* Guns & Ammo *Magazine. Leather and clothing by Red River Frontier Outfitters).*

Buffalo, and was far more difficult to stalk. It inhabited the 'deepest, darkest defiles, or the craggy, almost precipitous sides of mountains, inaccessible to any but the most practiced mountaineers'. Its size made it easily distinguishable from the ordinary buffalo, which, generally speaking, might be found on all of the eastern slopes of the Rockies.

To avoid overestimating, I have, in every case, taken the lowest figures in buffalos killed, and the result is as follows:

	AMOUNT
Buffalos killed by Indians –1872–73–74	1,215,000
Buffalos killed by Whites –1872–73–74	3,158,730
TOTAL	4,373,730

(Based on government, railroads' and Indian traders' reports.)

The white buffalo hunter followed the Indians' instinct and prepared to hunt the buffalo in September

While hunting the buffalo with bow and arrow, the Indian's thrust of his arrow was so powerful that it sometimes passed completely through the animal's body (drawing by the author).

when the cows were fat and the wool thick for warm robes. As the buffalo migrated to the northern plains in the spring, and south in the fall, it was a difficult task to pick up their trail, as no one could tell exactly where they might be. A hunter might have to travel anywhere from 150 to 600 miles before he found any signs of a great herd.

When the herd was sighted, a fairly good marksman would find a high-rise and take a prone or flat position ... generally some 200 yards away from the herd. The rifle was placed in position and loaded. If a man was a decent marksman he could probably down from 20 to 30 animals in a few short hours. Few men ever became successful buffalo killers, or ever acquired the knack or possessed the strength, patience, nerve and endurance that was required. Any hunter, for

PLATE 13

40 Woman scout, 1877
41 'Calamity Jane', 1877
42 'Buffalo Bill', 1877

40. *Surprisingly, there were a few young women who held a man's job, dressing in buckskins and tall boots with a belted weapon on their hip. Sometimes they could not be distinguished from men as they swore like troopers, spat tobacco juice with some accuracy, and handled a bull whip with a great amount of skill. The young lady shown here is dressed in a full suit of buckskins, her hair is gathered up and pushed into a soft, wide-brimmed felt hat. The boots were the famous California Kip with wooden pegged leather soles and made for hard wear. She sports the new Colt double-action, self-cocking, center fire, six-shot revolver tucked into a fancy leather holster. Defiantly, she tightly grips a Sharps .50 caliber cartridge carbine and looks like she is ready to use it. Because of their light and fair-complexioned skin, they were sometimes labeled with unusual nicknames such as 'Peaches', 'Cookie', 'Shorthorns', 'Cousin Jenny', 'Sage Hens', and 'Queenie'.*

41. *Martha Jane (Canarray) Canary, better known as 'Calamity Jane', wore men's clothing and enjoyed hanging around with the boys. Born in upper Missouri around 1848, she moved West during the height of the Civil War. Dressed in buckskins, she served as an army teamster and later as a scout for General George Crook. The armament that she displays is a Remington-Smoot revolver (in belt), .32 caliber, five-shot, rim fire, with a bird's head grip and the new spur trigger. Holstered is a Remington 1874, .44 caliber cartridge, six-shot (7.25 barrel) new model Army revolver. The fringe on her jacket is nothing more than decoration, considering its length at one time and the purpose it served the wearer. 'Calamity' is careful in showing her favorite*

Frank Wesson Pocket Rifle or Bicycle Rifle, .32 caliber, rim fire, single shot. The skeleton stock is a detachable metal stock. 'Calamity Jane' may have hung out with notorious and legendary outlaws, but she never took part in their activities. In Deadwood, 1878, she devotedly assisted the one doctor during the town's smallpox epidemic. Until her death in 1903 she was seen in dance halls and bar-rooms all over Montana, Wyoming, and South Dakota. Jesse James, several relations away, told her if he lived to be 100 years old he would turn himself in. In 1946, J. Frank Dalton, age 102 years, appeared in newspapers claiming he was the real Jesse James.

42. *A youthful William Frederick Cody ('Buffalo Bill') as he may have looked working for the Kansas Pacific Railroad in 1867 as a meat hunter for the section gangs. Here he holds a Henry lever action cartridge rifle, .44 caliber rim fire. He slaughtered over 3,000 buffalo in one season, and at 21 he earned his name 'Buffalo Bill'. Besides working for the Pony Express, he saw service with the 7th Kansas Cavalry, served as a representative to Nebraska's legislature and another hitch in the cavalry in 1876. Bill organized his Wild West show in 1883 and his first European tour took place in 1887. Ned Buntline was Cody's advance agent, building a great myth around the buffalo hunter. As late as 1891 Cody fought against the Sioux with the Nebraska National Guard. Cody lived up to everything he bragged about. His good nature and free spending brought him trouble from his creditors and most often in later life he was broke. Buffalo Bill's favorite weapons were the .44/40 caliber, lever action Winchester, Model 1873, and his old breech-loading Springfield .50 caliber which he nicknamed 'Lucretia Borgia'. Cody died in 1917, but his adventures and staged plays have since become part of America's tradition.*

70

PLATE 13

40 Woman scout, 1877

41 'Calamity Jane', 1877

42 Buffalo Bill', 1877

E. L. REEDSTROM

A typical buffalo skinner on a mule (drawing by the author).

that matter, could go out and stalk a herd, probably killing two or three before he frightened them into a stampede. But a careful hunter could keep a dozen 'skinners' at work by making a 'stand' with the herd, without scaring the remaining animals away. From long range, the hunter must pick off the 'heads of families' or bulls as the case may be, time his shots and guess the distance with some precision. Each shot must be placed a little below the center of the body, and about eight inches back of the shoulder. The bullet should strike the vitals, generally rendering another shot unnecessary.

There were several methods that were practised in buffalo hunting, running them from horseback, and stalking, or still-hunting. Running a buffalo on horseback required a sure-footed steed, tolerant, and not easily frightened. The buffalo cow, which is better meat than the bull, runs rapidly when pursued, and unless the horse is swift it would require a long and exhausting chase to overtake her. The buffalo has immense powers of endurance, and will run for many miles without any apparent effort or lessening of speed. A long chase is very severe labor upon a horse, and, unless there is a good deal of surplus horse-flesh, one would never expend it in running buffalo.

Still-hunting was equally successful and did not require the consumption of horse-flesh. Stalking on horseback was most successful using the cover of broken and hilly localities. The hunter could pass from one hill to the crest of another without detection. With the herd in sight, if it happened to be on

the lee side, the hunter would attempt to make a wide detour to get to the opposite side of the herd, as he would find it impossible to approach within rifle range with the wind. The sense of smell was exceedingly acute with these animals, permitting them to detect the hunter at as great a distance as a mile. If the surrounding area offered no cover, he then had to crawl on his hands and knees until he was within rifle range.

Tongues, humps and marrow-bones are generally the choice portions of the buffalo. Smoked tongue became a delicacy in Eastern restaurants; long slabs of choice hump served the 'end of track' gangs; and marrow, when roasted in bones over an open fire, was a buffalo man's delight. 'If there was ever a sweeter, finer morsel of flesh than those well marbled strips from the hump of a fat, barren cow, I have failed to find it', said one old hunter, reflecting on its appetizing flavor.

It was estimated that during one winter in 1882 a thousand hunters engaged in the business of slaughtering buffalo along the line of the Northern Pacific Railroad between Mandan and Livingston. An eagle-eyed hunter gave the following interesting details as to the 'modus operandi' in slaughtering great herds of buffalo.

When a hunter sees a herd of buffalo, he usually slips up within a convenient range, from 300 to 500 yards, and always selects a cow for his first victim. He does this for the reason that a cow is followed by both her yearling and two-year-old calves, and they will usually stand by her side to the last. But under no circumstances will the experienced hunter kill his buffalo outright. If he does, the herd will stampede at once. The policy is to wound fatally, but so that the animal will dash around in a circle before falling. This was always done, when mortally wounded, and after a few moments the animal lies down. The remainder of the herd are not alarmed at this, but continue to graze or look on. After his first shot, the hunter pauses until quiet is restored within the herd, and again fires at another cow, with similar results. He always aims to put his ball just behind the fore shoulder, which will cause death in five minutes at the furthest. When the cows have all been slain, he then turns his attention to the calves, and lastly to the bulls. The experienced hunter generally bags his entire herd unless he is so unfortunate as to drop his game immediately, when all the survivors stampede at once. The buffalo does not scare at the crack of a gun. He has decidedly more courage than discretion. It is only when the crack is followed by an immediate fall that he realizes its deadly nature and

By 1883 the vast herds of buffalo diminished in size. When the butchery was done, the hide-hunters left as quickly as they appeared (Union Pacific Railroad Museum Collection).

takes alarm. The policy of killing the cows first and then the calves has resulted in the extinction of the female buffalo. Herds of melancholy bulls were still occasionally seen, sometimes in bands of twenty or thirty, and often without a single cow.

The buffalo bull, after he passes his fourth year, loses his attractiveness to the opposite sex, and the aversion seems to be mutual. Gathering about him his bachelor friends of equal age, he sullenly retires into the wilderness, and forever avoids the female members of the herd, who mate with other and more luxurious masculines.

Bulls were about all that was left of the buffalo. They largely owed their liberty to the fact that their hides were less valuable than those of the cows, while at the same time they were far more difficult to kill. The hide of the bull was worth from $1.80 to $2.00, while that of the cow brought $3.25, and that of the two-year-old calf was worth from $1.00 to $1.50. Later, the old bulls were sought out not for the hides but for the enormous head. A well-preserved stuffed head of an aged bull, decked out with glass eyes and horns intact, brought $25.00 in the Eastern Markets (*Forest, Forge and Farm*, September 1883).

Like every other man who achieves distinction by superior excellence in some particular calling, the title of 'Buffalo Bill' is said to have been at issue in the celebrated buffalo shooting contest between William F. Cody and Bill Comstock. (This is not mentioned in Cody's autobiography; nor is the date. However, it is thought to have occurred in either 1866 or 1867).

Cody was surprised upon receiving a letter from a well known army officer offering to wager the sum of $500 that Bill Comstock could kill a greater number of buffalos in given time, under closely guarded conditions, than any other living man. This was indeed a challenge for Cody. Upon mentioning this to friends he found many who were willing to accept the wager in his behalf. It didn't take Cody long to assent,

Phil Spangenburger, Black Powder Editor for Guns & Ammo *magazine, poses in a comfortable sitting position while shooting buffalo with a heavy caliber Sharps carbine. An effective hitting range was from 200 to 250 yards (Peterson Publications; Gun leather and clothing by Red River).*

The great shooting match (1866 or 1867) between two great hunters created a stampede of curious Easterners who flocked to Fort Sheridan by stagecoach and rail. Half-way through the slaughter, a crowd of people were rushed upon by a furious bull buffalo, only for it to fall within a few feet before them, dead, a single bullet between the shoulder blades from Cody's rifle (author's collection).

could until four o'clock p.m., at the end of which time the one having killed the largest number was to be declared winner of the wager and also the 'champion buffalo killer' of America.

To determine the result of the hunt, a referee was to accompany each of the hunters on horseback and keep the score. At this time, buffalos were so plentiful that thousands could be found without too much difficulty, and a site for the trial was chosen, 20 miles east of Sheridan, Kansas. The country was prairie level and rendered the hunt easy by horseback and offered an excellent view for those who wished to witness the exciting contest. So much sensationalism was created by a general publication of this match that when the day arrived, several hundred local visitors were present, as well as another hundred who arrived from St Louis by special train. Comstock was well mounted on a strong, spirited horse, and carried a .44 caliber lever action Henry repeating rifle. Cody appeared on his famous Indian pony, 'Old Brigham', cradling in his arms a breech-loading Springfield rifle of .50 caliber, which he nicknamed 'Lucretia Borgia'. The party rode out on the prairie at an early hour in the morning, and soon discovered a herd of about 100 buffalos grazing on a beautiful stretch of ground just suited for the work in hand. Both hunters immediately rode rapidly toward the herd, accompanied by their referees, while the spectators followed 100 yards in the rear. At a given signal the two contestants dashed into the herd, dividing it so that Cody took the right half, and Comstock pursued the left.

The sport began in magnificent style, amid the

agreeing to the following conditions. After a herd of buffalo had been found, Cody and Comstock were to enter the drove at eight o'clock a.m., and employ their own tactics for killing as many buffalos as they

PLATE 14
43, 44 Buffalo hunters, 1880s
45 Buffalo skinner, 1880s

43. *This buffalo hunter calmly surveys the vast region before him for the mighty buffalo herds. His favorite rifle is the Sharps, caliber .45–120. Some of these rifles weighed 12–20 pounds. Big caliber Winchester, Remington and Springfield rifles were other favorites chosen by the hunters. His pistol, a Colt .44–40 caliber, is holstered on his hip along with a double row cartridge loop belt, basically to carry cartridges for both weapons. A pull-over woolen shirt, corduroy breeches and high western boots complete his outfit. (Posed by Phil Spangenburger, Black Powder Editor for Guns & Ammo magazine, courtesy of Red River Frontier Outfitters.)*

44. *A typical look at another 'hide hunter'. Over his shoulder is an 1874 Sharps, .40–90 which took the bottleneck shell. Thrust into a holster is the .44–40 long barrel Colt. He wears the favorite white duck 'duster' to protect his clothing from mud and dust.*

(Model - Jerry Crandall, famed Western artist, courtesy of Red River Frontier Outfitters.)

45. *The 'buffalo skinner' was kept busy skinning buffalos. He was hired by several hunters who went into a partnership, hiring a dozen men to take the hides, clean them and prepare them for shipment at the railroad terminal. He wears an odd-looking buckskin pull-over shirt, trimmed with fur and fringe. The odor it gave off came from his shirt sleeves, which were saturated with animal blood and pieces of flesh – this was from wiping his Green River knife blade upon them. The buffalo hides were so tough to cut free from the animal that a 'skinner' might go through some thirty to forty knife blades constantly sharpening them on a portable grindstone.*

Knee-high boots, made from genuine moose skin with the fur outside and tanned by Indians, had that particular toughness needed by hunters on the plains. His cartridge belt, with its US 'H' brass buckle, is the model 1883 pattern Mills manufactured woven cartridge belt.

PLATE 14

43, 44 Buffalo hunters, 1880s

45 Buffalo skinner, 1880s

E. L. REEDSTROM

18   Colonel W. F. Cody (Buffalo Bill)

'Buffalo Bill' in his theatrical costume while entertaining great crowds of people, both in Europe and America with his Wild West show and Congress of Rough Riders (author's collection).

'Buffalo Bill Cody' in his everyday buckskins, while working for the railroad supplying buffalo meat for the crew. His tools of trade are a Remington pistol and a Remington rolling black rifle .50 caliber (author).

cheers of the excited spectators, who rode as near the contestants as safety and non-interference permitted. Cody, after dropping the first half-dozen stragglers on the outskirts of the herd, began an exhibition of his skill of horsemanship and strategy. Old Brigham had a great advantage over Comstock's horse, for this sagacious animal knew all about the rider's style of hunting buffalos, and therefore needed no reining. By riding at the head of the herd and pressing the leaders hard toward the left, he soon had the drove circling, dropping those that were disposed to break off on a direct line. In a short time, witnesses of this novel contest saw Cody driving his portion of the herd in a rushing circle, and in less than a half hour's time he had all those in the bunch, numbering 38, sprawled out on the ground, kicking and twitching away what little life they had left in them. Comstock had accomplished some fine work, but, by attacking the rear of his herd, he had to ride directly away from the crowd of spectators. He succeeded in killing 23, which, however, lay irregularly over a space three miles in extent; and therefore he not only killed fewer than his rival, but, at the same time, manifested less skill, which, by contrast, showed most advantageously for Cody. All the party leaving returned to the apex of a beautiful knoll, a large number of champagne bottles were produced, and, amid volleys of flying corks, toasts were drunk to the buffalo heroes, Cody being especially lauded and now a decided favorite.

The ceremonies were soon interrupted by the appearance of another small herd of buffalo cows and calves over the horizon, at which time both contestants whirled their mounts about and charged in that direction. In this 'round' Cody scored 18, and Comstock succeeded in killing only 14. After another 'spot' of champagne all around, the cavalcade of spectators rode northward for a distance of three miles, when they discovered another larger herd of buffalos quietly browsing. Cody also spotted the herd, and, after dismounting and removing both saddle and bridle from Brigham, swung back on his trained horse's back and sped directly towards the herd, directing his steed solely by the motions of his hand and pressure from his knees. Reaching the herd by circling and coming down upon it from the windward quarter, the two rival hunters rushed upon the surprised buffalos and renewed the slaughter. After killing 13 of the animals, Cody drove one of the largest buffalos in the herd toward the party, whereby the ladies, seeing this oncoming wild beast approaching them at close quarters, became frightened and started to scream. But when the ponderous, shaggy-headed beast came within a few yards of the party, Cody shot it through the heart, dropping it in a huge dust cloud, thus giving a grand '*coup d'état*' to the day's sport, which closed with this magnificent exhibition of skill and daring.

The day having now been far spent and time called, it was found that the score stood thus: Cody 69, Comstock 46. The former was therefore declared the winner, and was entitled to the championship as the most skilful buffalo slayer in America. Thus the name 'Buffalo Bill' Cody was granted to him for life through this courageous competition.

A favorite rifle amongst the buffalo hunters was the 'Old Reliable' Sharps in calibers of .44–77, .45–70, .45–90, .45–120, and nearly all weighing between 12 and 20 pounds. The Sharps rifle may have been the favorite weapon chosen by buffalo hunters, but it did not exclude the fact that Winchester rifles were also sought in the .45–70 and .45–90 calibers. The Remington had their favorite calibers, .44–77 and .44–90; as well as the army's Springfield trap-door model

The old-time hide-hunters would often work in twos and threes. This allowed one rifle to be cleaned while the others were gathering hides. The hunter in the center has just cooled and cleaned his 1874 Sharps .45–100 caliber, and is waiting to return to the hunt. The hunters are, from left to right: Phil Spangenburger, Larry Demitter and Don Pennington (gun leather and clothing by Red River).

There were times when the soft copper shells expanded in the breech, jamming the rifle, after many firings. Phil Spangenburger of Guns & Ammo demonstrates the situation in period clothes. He also wears 'half breeds' or 'Bota' leggings to protect against cactus, brush or snake bite (Peterson Publications and Red River Frontier Outfitters).

.45–70. Nearly all the hide-hunters loaded their own ammunition, using the straight brass cases which did not need resizing, thus simplifying the reloading problem. With factory loaded shells at 25 cents apiece, the hunter in reloading kept his expenses down to a minimum.

A hide-hunter's camp varied in size. He either skinned his own kill or hired skinners or strippers, as they were sometimes called. A small party might include one hunter, two skinners, and a cook, while a larger party with a skilful hunter might hire on a half-dozen skinners. All through the complete hunt, the skinners might go through some 30 to 40 Green River or Wilson skinning knives, constantly sharpening these with a portable grindstone. The number of animals shot in one day would usually govern the number that could be skinned. Generally the quota for one day may be 25, with only two to three skinners in the group.

Everyone had his own unusual way of curing hides. The Indians used brains, liver and soapweed, mixed with grease and rubbed in on both sides. The hide-

A tired old buffalo hunter relaxes with a group of children in front of his shack, spinning yarns of days of old when Indians were as thick as buffalo. With his trusty .50 caliber Sharps across his lap, he relates battle after battle with Indians ... as the children stand awestruck (painting by E. L. Reedstrom – courtesy Pat and Gib Crontz, Cedar Lake, Indiana).

pounds for a small cow to 50 pounds for a large bull. Buffalo hides at one time brought $3.50 each but declined after a few years because of overproduction. As the price dropped the hunters were getting $1.50 to only 80 cents a hide; with too few buffalos left and too many hunters, hide-hunting became less profitable.

Buffalo hunting lasted only but a dozen years, 1871–83, yet it was long enough to slaughter the enormous herds that once over-shadowed the broad grazing lands in the West, bringing the species almost to extinction. When the butchery was done, the hide-hunters left as quickly as they appeared, leaving the prairies whitened with sun-bleached bones that pioneer farmers in need of several dollars would pick up and haul away to the nearest railroad terminal. (Bones were sent back East to be ground-up and used for fertilizer.) These grizzled and hardy buffalo hunters knew how to survive blizzards, sandstorms and attacking Indians, yet they didn't know how to avoid lice and other tiny crawlers which crept into their clothing, incubated from the hundreds of robes piled about their camp. Dirty, greasy, unshaven, the hide-hunter was most generally a rough-looking individual, his camp smelling a mile away, but if visited by an outsider the visitor could always count on being treated very hospitably. The hunter was always ready to help anyone in time of need.

If nothing else can be said of the hide-hunter, we can credit him for clearing the plains for the cattle-man; supplying the railroad crews with food and robes; providing the army with leather and buffalo coats; simplifying the Indian problem; and broadening research for finer weapons and ammunition.

hunters salted the hides and rolled them, keeping the skins piled on one another and in such a place that melting snows would not soak them. Another way was staking each hide flat to the Prairie ground, flesh side down, until the wagons picked them up for marketing. Of course loading the hides was no easy task, as a green bull hide might weigh 80 to 100 pounds. When dried, the average weight of a hide could be 20

PLATE 15
46, 47 Buffalo hunting, 1885
As explained in this chapter, buffalo hunting took a little more skill and knowledge than one might imagine. Windage, distance, timing and where to place that fatal shot into a standing buffalo at a great distance must be considered. To the left, on the ground is a small camp fire. A small pail of snow is being melted down to be used to dip the ends of cleaning rods, the tips wrapped with heavy cloth to swab the hot barrels. The man sitting and firing took a few moments from time to time to rest his rifle in a small snow bank beside him in order to cool the receiver and the full-length barrel. When the heavy caliber rifle was too hot to handle, after many rounds have gone through it, it was cooled using this method.

46. Standing, and firing off an 1880, double-rigged plains saddle, is hunter number one. He wore a bandana wrapped around his head to keep his long hair from interrupting a perfect shot. His horse was used to the heavy recoil and deafening roar of the rifle's report - and even though he staggered a bit, it didn't harm the well placed target. To protect the breeches, he wore a pair of short leather chaps to save wearing out his knees when he kneels.
47. Hunter number two sits aiming his trusty Sharps, the barrel resting on a sand bag in between two wooden dowels commonly known as a 'cross-stand' or 'cross-tree'. This device enabled the shooter to steady his aim and lightened the barrel's heavy weight. The small sand bag took up the recoil. The accumulated shells lying about were later retrieved and used over again to re-load, as they were too expensive per shell to purchase.

PLATE 15

46, 47   Buffalo hunting, 1885

6 American Frontier Soldier

It was a big territory, and it sprawled from the vast prairies of the north-east to the crags and peaks of the continental divide; from the parched desert to muddy river bottom, it encompassed some million square miles of wilderness. Antelope and elk grazed there and endless herds of buffalo foraged in the natural pastures that were yet unspoiled by fence or plow. It was the hunting ground, too, for bear and wolf, who grudgingly shared the domain with another hunter: the Plains Indian.

Another faction entered the picture during the nineteenth century, however; and the frontier would never again be the same. The enterprising white man saw this lush country and coveted it for himself. Between newcomer and native was a thin blue line: it was the dusty, workworn uniform of the United States Army. Its ranks were sparse; the entire complement never numbering more than 15,000 men, faced with the staggering task of patrolling this frontier. It translated into one soldier for every 66 square miles.

In 1860, there were five active military posts in this wilderness. By 1868, no more than 30; and many of these were relatively small garrisons with accommodations for no more than 100 to 200 men. A number of these were vulnerable, isolated outposts built by a riverside; and owing their construction to whatever clerks, cooks or cavalrymen were available to cut logs and poles and erect the walls.

Then there were the 'guard posts' which offered a modicum of protection to the overland telegraph lines. These were, for the most part, tiny, crudely constructed stockades that only housed ten or fifteen men. The wood (sometimes mud) buildings were inevitably cramped, and stowage for personal gear

Typical mounted Cavalry man, circa 1846–48, war with Mexico, nearside (drawing by the author).

Cavalry trooper with full field gear, 1846, Mexican War, off-side (courtesy Jim Nemeth—historical artist).

Veteran Civil War infantrymen, the backbone of the Federal Army. Midwesterners, wearing the complete assortment of slouch hats. True mudsloggers! Uniforms out West hardly changed for the Army foot soldier. Quarter-inch tintype (Bob McDonald).

was at a premium. The creature comforts in these so-called 'forts' was negligible and climatic conditions ranged from too hot to too cold, depending upon the season. Many of the older forts, however, including some built during the 1860s, were genuine bastions of security. They were walled with stout palisades of 12-inch logs sunk four feet into the earth. Few, if any, Indians were ever tempted to assault these strongholds.

The regular army of the frontier was an odd assortment at best; its number made up of Minnesota farm boys and New Jersey clerks, the ever-present toughs and drunkards, discredited teachers, misfit lawyers and men who'd deserted their wives and children. There were also the 'snow birds', whose tenure always began in the fall, but only lasted until the first payday after the crocus bloomed. They had had the relative security of army rations and 16 dollars a month for the winter; now it was time to desert in favor of the more carefree civilian life.

Army rations were seldom very palatable and – often as not – the portions were meager. There was little enticement here to the hearty eater. The menu for an average month might be salt pork or beef, dried fish, rice, beans, dried vegetables and hardtack, unless the post had a bakery to provide soft bread. The seasonings were vinegar and molasses; and there was that ubiquitous pot of 'Rio' coffee: that legendary beverage proclaimed to be 'strong enough to grow whiskers on a cannon ball'.

When the Civil War broke out, most of the regular army was recalled East to join the Army of the Potomac. It was a 'civilian' army that replaced them on the frontier; mostly volunteers from the western states and territories, except for such notable eastern troops

as the famous 11th Ohio Cavalry. Then there were the 'Galvanized Yankees', which was the name given those captured Confederate soldiers who hoped to join the Union Army, usually to fight Indians, rather than rotting in a Union prison.

It was only after the hostilities between North and South that the wilderness army acquired some of its more 'glamorous' recruits. Experienced warriors without a war came West to seek a new challenge; another chance to fight, another chance to command ... even another chance to die, since iron-tipped arrows were no respectors of rank. Nor, for that matter, were the bedbugs or the rattlesnakes, but hardship was nothing new to these veterans.

Promotions no longer came fast, either. A grey-haired first lieutenant in command of a forlorn, undermanned outpost might look forward to his Captaincy after perhaps 25 years of service. That he had been twice decorated during the Civil War and was missing three fingers from a wound sustained in battle meant nothing; especially since his shavetail adjutant may have been a Civil War Captain, his First Sergeant a Colonel in the Volunteers and his Chief Bugler a former Confederate Major. The First Lieutenant's pay was $125 a month, with his only expenses being to feed and clothe his family, buy his own uniforms, side arm, sabre, horse and saddle.

There were also many foreign-born troops who found their ways to the Indian Territory; men whose gallantry in the face of hostiles was equalled only by their love of a drunken brawl in the sutler's store.

Major General of Volunteers Martin T. McMahon with staff after the close of the Civil War, 1865 (McMahon seated, center) (Signal Corps, National Archives).

There was saddler Julius Stickoffer, for instance, who served with Company L of the 8th Cavalry. He came from Switzerland to win the Congressional Medal of Honor for his action near Cienega Springs, Utah. Another example was Irish-born Sergeant John H. Foley, whose heroic action on the Platte earned him the Nation's highest award.

These men and others like them were no strangers to the guard house, either, since 'innocent' pleasures were few on the frontier. A tiny sutler's store was frequently the only social center for 300 men; and most of the recreation had to be provided by the men themselves. Variety shows were staged and, if no women were present – usually the case – some of the men performed in women's roles. Horse racing was another form of entertainment and betting was usually heavy. Officers also participated in the races. Another sport, not as popular with the commanding officer, was hunting. It relieved the boredom, but all too often the hunter just kept on going in search of a more convivial atmosphere.

Special holidays called for more elaborate celebration, such as a banquet or picnic, where delicacies may have been ordered all the way from St Joseph or Salt Lake City. Fresh strawberries, lemons or canned oysters were a welcome change from the austere diet on the post. If there were women on the post, they might have a 'hop' (dance) and there was always someone in the ranks with a fiddle, banjo, mandolin or trumpet to provide the music.

No branch of the US Army was immune from service on the frontier. The plodding 'walk-a-heaps' (an Indian expression for infantry) were there, and so were the slow-moving wagons of the artillery; but probably the hardest and most dangerous of the tasks was that of the mounted troops, whose job it was to protect over 5000 miles of telegraph lines, mail and stagecoach routes, wagon roads and river bridges. Formed during the Civil War by 'marrying' the old Dragoons and the Mounted Riflemen, the young US Cavalry was only four years old and six regiments strong in 1865. The following year, the 7th, 8th, 9th and 10th regiments were added. The latter two were made up of negro troops; called 'Buffalo Soldiers' (because of their kinky hair) by the Indians.

Recruiting standards were slightly different for the cavalry, too. Where the regular army required only 'age 18 to 35, able bodied and of good character', the cavalry added 'between 5′5″ and 5′10″ in height and no more than 150 pounds in weight'. Horsemanship was not named as a requisite, however, but there was more to cavalry service than sitting a horse, anyway. Building bridges and roads, cutting wood and sawing ice or spending dreary hours on guard duty were more common. Even the time actually spent in the saddle was frequently as an escort for ox-drawn bull wagons or the equally slow immigrant wagon trains moving through to the west.

When assembly sounded, the wise old regulars checked their personal supplies of coffee, sugar and tobacco, and brought out their hand-made pouches containing parched corn for their horse, which they slung over their saddles. When the column moved out, to the tune of multitudinous familiar sounds, the squeak of leather, whinny of horses, the drum of hooves and the muted babble of the troops, it was

PLATE 16

48 Corporal, 1st US Dragoons, 1846–48 (Mexican War)

49 2nd Lieutenant, Infantry, 1846–48

50 Infantryman, 1846–48

48. *A corporal of the First US Dragoons is holding a Model 1843 Hall-North .52 caliber smoothbore carbine, which took paper cartridges with round ball loads. Hanging at his side is an 1833-model sabre and attached to the pommel of his saddle are two Model 1836 flintlock horse pistols, .54 caliber smoothbore. The saddle is a Grimsley, adopted by the army in 1847. (The saddle below the horse is a close-up of the Grimsley.)*

49. *Represented here is a Second Lieutenant Infantry officer on campaign wearing a dark blue, single-breasted frock coat and sky blue trousers with a 1½-inch white stripe running down the seams. He wears the same forage cap the men wear, used by all branches. A crimson silk sash, tied on the left, was worn while on duty with the troops. His sabre is the well-known foot officers'*

model of 1840, suspended from a white leather buff belt. Rank was indicated by shoulder scales edged in silver border lace. All buttons were white metal.

50. *The Infantryman wore a white buff belt over his shoulder which held his cartridge box and another buff belt around the waist, each fitted with a brass plate. His large cartridge box, suspended from the shoulder strap, was of black leather and held forty paper cartridges in tin dividers. On its large flap was an oval brass plate. If percussion caps were used they were carried in special cap pockets in the jackets. If he was armed with a flintlock rifle, a brass brush and pick were suspended from a button on the front of his jacket. Cotton haversacks were carried by both officers and men, and marked on the flaps in black were the company and regiment. Several rifles may have been used by the Infantrymen: the US Model 1817 'Common' Rifle, .54 caliber flintlock; the Model 1841 Hall Rifle, .52 caliber percussion; or the US Model 1842 Musket, .69 caliber. In this case illustrated here is a US Model 1835 Musket, .69 caliber flintlock.*

PLATE 16

50   Infantryman, 1846–48

48   Corporal, 1st US Dragoons, 1846–48   49   2nd Lieutenant, Infantry, 1846–48

often well into the night. Except for the main roads and rivers, there had been little charting done of the territory and no way to know the whereabouts of Indian positions, friendly or hostile.

To carry the fight to the enemy required civilian guides, such as Jim Bridger, Kit Carson, California Joe and others; trappers, traders, mountain men and half-breeds who knew the land and the Indian ways. Since the Plains Indian tribes were frequently warring among themselves, as well, it was also easy enough to find a friendly Indian who jumped at the opportunity to earn much food, a hundred dollars and a fine blue coat just to track an enemy and lead the cavalry there. The following was published for the information and guidance of commanders of Indian scouts and published in the *Army, Navy Journal*, August 29th, 1868, page 18.

> The general impression that Indians cannot be caught is erroneous, and the methods usually employed are faulty. Indians committing depredations, which is the vocation of all hostile ones, usually move in parties of from four to eight, and after a depredation move night and day with rapidity for the first seventy or eighty miles, when their animals become foot-sore and weary and themselves careless, believing they are safely beyond pursuit, as they usually are. To attempt overtaking them at once is folly and ruin of the command; but by moving on steadily, never, under any circumstances, giving up the trail, keeping the animals well shod, for if not they are eventually lost, using all of daylight in the pursuit, the Indians, nine cases out of ten, will be overtaken before the eighth day, and since you travel at about equal rates, only gaining on him by moving more hours, he will almost invariably be found halting without lookouts and his animals grazing. By charging at the instant without waiting for any charge formation, his animals are captured and some Indians killed. For this, the men should at all times be kept well in hand, and as you approach the Indians, which a vigilant officer can always know by the appearance of the trail, they should be cautioned to mount their animals, and put their arms in readiness for instant use.
>
> A trial of two footmen or a single horseman need never be lost unless washed out by rains, and then should not be difficult to find again by a practised guide who knows the country. The guide should be used as a trailer, and to give information of water and grass, and should never be permitted, in any other manner, to influence the scout. When reaching crests, or debouching from ravines or woods, the officer should go forward singly and scan closely ahead of him, and by having his entire mind and attention in his work, he will almost invariably discover the Indians before his party is seen. The trails always pass water, and, although suffering must be expected from want of it, one seldom travels twenty-four hours without finding it. Riding animals are indispensable at the moment of the charge, but are not useful at any other time, as men can march further in fifteen days than horses without forage. Great care must be taken in packing the mules, and they must not be burdened by blankets and trash, which will always be done if not prevented.
>
> To send out expeditions under officers who will not literally attend to all of the foregoing instructions, and much besides; who will not, without regard to hunger, thirst, and suffering, continue on their course, and who do not possess the faculty of creating expedients to overcome all the many obstacles liable to present themselves each day, is a waste of time and material.
>
> The foregoing is drawn from an unusual experience and invariable success in Indian service.
>
> Fresh trails are to be the first sought, and when found should be equivalent to finding the Indians who made them.

Jogging across the hostile land, the best-armed cavalryman was a target, and every horse and mule a prize, so it was worth a soldier's life to maintain his place in formation. A hard-riding column with its scouts, flankers and rear guard could average 40 miles a day, depending upon the lay of the land, fording places and distance between water holes. Near the end of the march, though, a soldier might walk his tired mount, perhaps gathering buffalo chips or twigs for the cook's fire. Finding a wild onion might be a prize, either as a treat for his horse or seasoning for his own meal. Circumstances permitting, some marksmen or foragers might be allowed to skirt the surrounding hills for fresh meat for the pot.

Setting up camp, especially in a Regimental size formation, required a bustle of activity, but the formula was an established one: tents in two rows to form a company street, headquarters guidon flapping; officers' tents and barricades at either end, with horses picketed in the middle, sinks and fire pits dug and more chips gathered for the cook's fire. It was all orchestrated and followed to the letter, just as the special care for the horses that followed: cooling out, rubbing with straw or grass, feeding and watering, checking eyes, ears, nose, mouths and hoof ... not just in case of the inspection that might follow, but because the horse, like his sidearm and carbine, might mean life or death on the frontier if it failed.

The post-war cavalry was a proving ground for many breech-loading carbines developed during the

Civil War. There were Ward Burtons, Sharps, Remingtons and Springfields, as well as various repeating rifles; and some of the men carried their own Spencer, Henry, or even its famous successor, the 1866 Winchester. These may have cost nearly a half-year's pay, and $35 to $60 apiece was a fortune to the common soldier. His Colt's revolver, if lost, would mean a fine of $40, according to Army Regulations of 1863.

Punishments other than fines were quite common in the wilderness territory. Many officers, especially those who had served in the Civil War, were partial to handing out physical pain to keep the men in line, although it actually increased the rate of desertions. As late as 1868, a private who deserted was brought before a General Court Martial, dishonorably discharged and obliged to forfeit all pay and allowances due him except the just dues owed the laundress and sutler. His head was shaved and his left hip branded with a hot iron, bearing the letter *D* for deserter, two inches in length, and he was then drummed out of camp.

This severe punishment was outmoded years later and 'indelible' ink which took many washings to erase was substituted for the branding iron. With this

What a group of troopers would look like in the 1880s, just before mounting. They are in position to 'stand to horse' (author's photo of 2nd Reactivated Cavalry, posed).

The fighting frontier soldier hardly ever carried a sabre. Orders throughout the regiment stated that all sabres were to be left behind. One can imagine the rattle a sabre could create. Officers made certain that all items that might produce sound should be tied down. On the western plains, sound often carried several miles, giving away their position, spoiling a surprise attack against the Indians (author's drawing).

change, the letter *D* was reduced in size. Although flogging was abolished in 1861 by the Army, it was still ordered by some older officers who believed in stern discipline. For stealing a gun, a soldier was awarded 25 lashes with a plaited thong. The next day, the man was bucked and gagged for an hour, in full view of his 'bunkies'. 'Spread-Eagle' meant a man was laid upon the ground in a spread-eagle fashion, and staked and lashed to the ground, face up. He was exposed to the hot radiant sun, for two hours. Ants, bugs and buffalo gnats crawling all over his hands and face placed him in horrible torment.

On the Kansas plains, Lt Col George A. Custer tried and convicted offenders and had them thrown in a deeply-dug hole. For 24 hours or more, depending on the severity of his crime and the conviction of the court, a man could sit and ponder his fate while serving out his sentence. A wide variety of insects, spiders, snakes, and whatever might crawl down into the hole with the prisoner, keeping him busy the full length of his sentence. Other smaller but embarrassing punishments were 'knapsack drill' – carrying heavy stones in a knapsack upon the back, and marching to the beat of a drummer guardsman for several hours around the encampment. Some underwent 'isolation on a platform', or were spread-eagled and tied to a

85

wagon wheel designed to revolve in any position the guard chose. Carrying a 25 or 30 pound log on one's shoulder for half a day would almost make one believe the log grew in size and weight after the first few hours. Careless saddling of a horse, causing sores on the animal's back, was punishable by carrying a fully-packed saddle about the parade grounds for several hours. Company punishment for being drunk with a bottle in one's possession meant digging a hole in the ground approximately 10 feet square by 10 feet deep and then burying the bottle. For a man who didn't drink or gamble, it wasn't hard to put something away each month, and at the end of his enlistment he would have a nice little nest egg. Those who partook in drinking and gambling usually ended up owing everyone in camp.

All clothing issued to the frontier troops were left-overs from Civil War stock piles. Government clothing contractors seemed to have had some queer ideas of the human form and its proportions, and the waist length, choke collared, dark blue shell jackets and baggy, light blue, wool trousers generally fitted very poorly. For casual headwear, the floppy-crowned kepi, or forage cap, was issued; with the stiff flat topped 'Hardee hat' for dress. Trousers were generally worn outside the 14-inch high, square-toed boots, and in warm weather the grey flannel shirts were not worn under the heavy wool jackets.

Fully rigged for inspection, the Cavalryman of 1866 – 67 was a strapped up, rigidly jacketed trooper hung with several belts, leather pouches, and arms. At his belt, on the left, hung the so-called light artillery sabre; brass hilted, heavy, over a yard long, and about as useful as a croquet mallet in the hit-and-run guerrilla warfare of the Indian campaigns. On the right side of his belt, he carried a holstered .44 calibre Colt or Remington percussion revolver, a somewhat heavy but highly efficient six-shooter sighted to hit man sized targets at about 70 paces. A small leather pouch on the sabre belt held the paper or skin 'envelope' cartridges and caps for the revolver; lead bullets with a small conical tube of paper or skin (very thin, like sausage casing) holding the powder charges within them.

Hung from a wide leather shoulder belt was the soldier's principal weapon, his seven-shot, .50 calibre repeating Spencer carbine. Early models of this chunky carbine had had some use during the Civil War. This was the new model of 1865, carrying seven stubby copper cased rimfire cartridges in the tube

---

PLATE 17

51 Company Quartermaster Sergeant, 1861–65 (Civil War)

52 Cavalryman, 1861–65

53 Infantryman, 1861–65

51. *A Company Quartermaster Sergeant in the Artillery in shell jacket and short top boots holding a Linstock. This device continued to be a standard item of equipment for every battery as emergency gear, designed for use when the new friction primers ran out. His chevrons are the newest issue, with the single top bar running horizontal and issued late in the war. His sabre is the 1840-pattern light artillery weapon and his side arm could either be a Colt percussion or a Remington, caliber .44, or any other pistol of his choice. On his left sleeve is a two-year enlistment service stripe.*

52. *This Cavalryman wears a 'hardy hat', his brim correctly pinned to the right side (for Cavalry) and ornamented with an ostrich plume. Brass company letter and crossed sabres and regiment number are attached to the hat. He has on a shell jacket piped in yellow, wide shoulder carbine sling, waist belt and cartridge pouch (usually an old issue percussion cap pouch). On his left is the Model 1861 light cavalry sabre, with a heavy black leather sabre knot. Tucked in the front of his shell jacket is a small spur-trigger pistol, unlike those issued. His carbine is the Smith breech loader, caliber .52, which fired a cartridge encased in a rubber shell, later altered to take the metallic shell. He seems*

assured *that his rifle will have no difficulties in firing, considering the condition in which he is displaying it. Regular issued high top boots with tops turned down complete his uniform.*

53. *The Infantryman of the Civil War was entangled with many straps of leather encircling his figure - and the added weight caused him to discard some of his equipment during hot, long marches. The floppy 'Bummer' cap did no good for him by sheltering his face and neck from the sun. When his already heavy 'great coat' was soaked with rain it weighed twice the usual amount. His backpack contained most of his personal equipment plus a rolled-up blanket and shelter half, which was shared with another soldier or 'bunky' in setting up a small 'A' tent.*

Suspended from his shoulder strap is the Model 1855 cartridge box for the .58 caliber conical bullets. It has two tin inserts which held 40 rounds of mini-ball paper cartridges. The box had double flaps with an implement pocket. On a huge flap is an oval brass 'US' plate.

His waist belt contained a small percussion cap pouch and a bayonet and scabbard. A canvas haversack, painted black, had another plain white canvas sack within which he carried hardtack, ground coffee, sugar, bacon, corn, plates and eating utensils. The rifle he is leaning on is the .58 caliber percussion Springfield musket, Model 1861. It was the principal weapon of the Civil War. Finally, a tin cup hung from his knapsack which, when constantly struck against his oval canteen while marching, gave a low din of fanfare among the troops.

PLATE 17

52　Cavalryman, 1861–65

51　Company Quartermaster Sergeant, 1861–65

53　Infantryman, 1861–65

magazine loaded through an aperture in the butt plate. A cartridge was ejected (after the gun had been fired) each time the trigger guard lever was pushed down; and a fresh round chambered each time the lever was pulled back into place. The large side hammer had to be cocked for each shot, but the Spencer could be fired very rapidly. Its rear sight leaf was graduated to 700 yards, but this was more of a fond hope than a guarantee of maximum effective range. Even though its heavy, slow moving, lead bullet's high trajectory limited accuracy at long range, the Spencer was a better weapon in its day than almost any possessed by hostile Indians. Its major drawbacks were mainly in its ammunition, which was often poorly made, resulting in erratic shooting, jamming of the soft copper cases, and more than a few misfires. Most of the troops continued to be armed with the Spencer until the early 1870s.

Weeks of subsisting on sub-standard field rations of hardtack, salt pork, coffee and a bit of coarse brown sugar sapped the strength of the men, leaving them weakened due to dietary deficiencies and with little stamina to ward off or escape the ravages of cholera, scurvy, and other diseases. Some of the hardtack eaten as field rations in 1867 had been packed in 1860 and was moldy and vermin-filled. In the field, each soldier usually prepared his own rations. The fat pork was frizzled over a fire, or, if panfried, the grease was used to fry the 4 by 4-inch hardtack crackers. Coffee was boiled in the trooper's large tin mess cup. None of the rations were very appetizing, and food spoilage was common in warm weather. Fresh buffalo meat was very welcome when obtainable, which was more often for the officers than for the rank and file.

Troop A, 6th US Cavalry, Geronimo campaign 1885 (National Archives).

As much as many sub-officers would have liked their men to have target practice, the commanding officers refused to authorize it for fear they would have to pay for the ammunition out of their own pocket. The budget-cutting, penny-pinching Regular Army preferred to save the cost of cartridges rather than have its men well trained and accustomed to their weapons.

It is easily understood why a great many people, after viewing Hollywood's impression of Indian Wars, believe that all battles in the West were fought on horseback. Like most legends it contains only partial truth. The Indian tribes east of the Mississippi were willing to meet the foot-soldier in hand-to-hand combat as they were on equal terms, but were constantly afraid of defeat by mounted men. The reverse of this was true with the Indian tribes west of the Mississippi. Here they preferred to match their own excellent horsemanship against that of other mounted men rather than face the deadly, withering volleys of the Infantry. The Infantry in the West was a hard-marching outfit. It was not expected to keep pace with the Cavalry when the two were in a mixed column, but instead the Infantry would leave the camp about two hours before the Cavalry. They were caught and passed by the Cavalry, but the doughboys were retired long before the Cavalrymen finished taking care of their mounts. On a long and arduous campaign they became '"charioteers" as the Cavalry called the wagon-riding doughboys'. On one occasion they even entered battle in these conveyances. Putting

Infantry into wagons and telling the teamsters to stick close to the Cavalry, they charged; down into the Indian village galloped the Cavalry with the wagons full of Infantrymen bouncing and clattering right behind. The Indians were completely baffled and overcome by this strange maneuver.

On shorter campaigns the process of stepping them out was in order. Actually they might be called 'foot cavalry'. They put distance behind them fast and covered an amazing amount of ground in a day. Through snow and mud they even surpassed the wagon trains.

On occasion, when there was a surplus of horses, the Infantry was mounted and thus became the Mounted Rifles of the West. This the Indian feared more than all else with the possible exception of artillery or 'wagon guns'. Here was a group of men that could keep pace with the Indian, but yet would never try to match horsemanship in a hand-to-hand engagement. They would instead dismount, form and commence a steady deadly fire that swept through the Indians like a scythe. It takes extremely durable and well-trained troops to withstand sustained fire from an emplaced enemy.

The main use of infantry was as riflemen, whose

Squadron of the 9th Cavalry at Fort Robinson, Nebraska, 1889 (National Archives).

The Cavalry's McClellan saddle took plenty of punishment, and at the same time was often neglected by the troopers. These rawhide saddles have split in several places, causing serious injuries to the horse and mounted trooper (author's collection).

long range weapons were well suited to the purpose of slaying the Indian. Their long range firing, if it did not destroy the Indians, at least softened them up by reducing the number of their fighting men to the point where hand-to-hand combat by mixed cavalry and infantry would not be quite so difficult. Naturally, this also meant a reduction in casualties for

the Army. Among the infantrymen were placed the sharp-shooters who assisted in pouring in volley after volley of deadly fire. Between these two classes of troops a most telling fusillade could be deployed to the best advantage.

Cavalry, on the other hand, was a very difficult arm to handle and control in the field, especially in rough terrain. It easily got out of control and was rapidly dispersed. Only when the terrain was favorable could it be used as a mounted force. Cavalry, in the strict sense of the word, was not suitable for defense systems and could only resist or repel an attack by making an anticipatory encounter. In addition, it was almost always dependent on the condition and well-being of its mounts. (If the horses were not in an efficient state, and if their shoes were not carefully looked to and sore backs guarded against, they were destroyed and the force becomes worthless.) Mobile farrier's forges accompanied some of the campaigns but always stayed with the supply train because the size and weight prevented them from keeping pace with the fast moving Cavalry column. With each Cavalryman having only

one mount, a disabled horse put a man out of action. Disease, always a factor in the West, placed a further reduction on the mounted force. Capable officers kept a watchful eye on the men's horses but they were not veterinarians and were unable to detect a disease quick enough to prevent disablement and eventual dismounting of the trooper. This disease, epizootic, caused the column to become almost entirely an infantry campaign, crippling horses and mules by the hundred. The field commands loaded blankets, rations, and extra ammunition on their own backs and plodded on.

By 1872, a new regulation uniform for the Army was introduced. This was a desirable change from the old patterns; however, the most serious objection to the new dress was that it was expensive. The change in the dress hat was by far an overall improvement over the old hat, which was ugly, uncomfortable and unsoldierly. For the Infantry there were the new shakos, and for mounted troops a helmet with a horse-hair plume. The old pattern 'forage cap' fell to the 'Kepi', almost a direct copy from the French army

---

PLATE 18

54 Confederate Infantryman, 1861–65 (Civil War)

55 Color Sergeant, 1861–65

56 Colonel John Singleton Mosby, 1861–65

54. *This Confederate Infantryman is a Line Sergeant with Stonewall Jackson's Corps. About the only things of actual army issue are his jacket, haversack, canteen, rifle and square tip shoes, the rest wore out in the field or were lost. In many instances, especially after a battle, men would strip the dead of their possessions in order to survive the rest of the campaign. The weapon he holds is a Union Springfield, Model 1861 musket which is somewhat altered. Because of the hot, humid weather in the South, the Confederate government chose grey-colored uniforms for the men as it was ten degrees cooler than the Union blue. After the war the North considered the grey color for the same reason, and dropped the navy blue color of our present uniforms. However, the opinion of certain government officials changed the War Department's views, as it was considered disgraceful to adopt an enemy's colors after our great victory over them.*

55. *A proud flag bearer, the Color Sergeant, displays the Stars and Bars as a symbol of honor in the regiment. Although he bears no stripes of his rank, his butternut homespun jacket may have been borrowed for this pose. Although the color-bearer wears a simple uniform with a haversack, canteen, belt and cap pouch, he may well have hidden a revolver or two on his person.*

Color-bearers were always under fire by Union troops, and their chances of surviving a total battle or charge was less than 50

per cent. If the colors would fall, someone near at hand would retrieve them and continue on. To lose the colors would be a disgrace, despite the outcome of the battle. Note this soldier's stockings – he has tucked the bottom of his trousers inside them. This prevents any stones, pebbles, dust or dirt of any great amount building up in his shoes.

56. *Best of the guerrilla leaders was Colonel John Singleton Mosby, 43rd Battalion, Virginia Cavalry, C.S.A. Guerrilla warfare tended to get out of hand, as most bands were semi-independent. They did the Confederacy more harm by draining able-bodied men away from the regular fighting forces. Mosby's men numbered from 45 to 1,000 at one time or another. He harassed Sheridan's supply lines, so that additional troops were kept on duty patrolling roads, back of the front.*

This pose of Mosby looks as if he's ready to report to his superior, Jeb Stuart, with news of his last successful raid. He has all the temerity of an experienced soldier and every bit of respect from his men, the partisans. The uniform is of the Confederacy, the accoutrements are captured 'booty' from his many raids. On his left is the heavily constructed early US Dragoon sabre, a Union belt and rectangular belt plate with German silver inlay; the field glasses are French manufactured, and issued by the North. Mosby's boots were freedom of choice and not regular issue. These were called 'cuirassier' boots and offered a great deal more protection from weather as well as brush and tree limbs. (Cuirassiers were a defense for the body, originally made in leather, and used in fourteenth-century Europe. They were first made of stuffed 'pourpointerie', or boiled leather.)

PLATE 18

56   Colonel John Singleton Mosby, 1861–65

54   Confederate Infantryman, 1861–65   55   Color Sergeant, 1861–65

Troop 'C' 5th Cavalry in the field with arrested 'Sooners and Squatters' prior to the opening of Oklahoma, 1880s (National Archives).

hat. The government defined this kepi as the 'Chasseur Pattern', or the fatigue hat, model 1872. This was issued to our troops with a slight modification in 1875, and worn as late as 1898. This was worn on post for fatigue, stable and guard duty.

In the coat, the change was principally in the matter of appearance. One of the first requisites in the army was a feeling of pride which was well summed up in the French *esprit de corps*. It was hoped that the new uniform look would increase enlistments and attract a better class of men. The old coat, a four button down, was too plain, uncomfortable, short in the sleeves with an over-all baggy look. The new regulation five button fatigue blouse of dark blue flannel with falling collar was handsome in appearance and soldierly, being so unlike the four button sack-coat it could be recognized at once as military. During the Civil War, the system of clothing measurements had been established in four sizes. Number 1 was from size 30 to 32; number 2 from 34 to 36; number 3 from 38 to 40; and number 4 from 42 to 44. These numbers were stamped inside one of the sleeves of a jacket or dress coat. During the postwar period, this number was

Sgt. John Bouck, Troop 'K', 1st US Cavalry and Cpl. Sampson killed in action with Crow Indians, 5 November 1887, at Crow Agency, Montana (National Archives).

increased to five, as larger sizes were demanded in order to permit soldiers to tailor their uniforms to their own measurements. In time, this exhausted the larger-sized garments, leaving an assortment of improper sizes at depots.

Army fatigue hats also came in four sizes, Number 3 being equivalent to a size 7½, and worn by both officers and enlisted men. Made of black felt to a standard pattern, it was to be worn on fatigue duty and on marches or campaigns. Constant use of this hat, along with the elements of time, proved that the hat could not withstand too much punishment. After a number of good drenchings, it soon took the appearance of a dishrag on top a soldier's head.

Trousers were generally a mixture of sky-blue jersey, the seats and inside legs customarily being reinforced with canvas for the Cavalry. The regulation

issue top-boot did not reach the knee, and often trouser legs were stuffed into boot tops or were allowed to hang full length over the boots.

Cartridge boxes containing ammunition for both revolver and carbine were to be worn on the waist belt. However, the distribution of these boxes filled with a number of shells made it difficult for the troopers to manipulate or function in a free manner. Experimental patterns such as Hagner's #2 cartridge pouch, containing 24 canvas loops to hold .50 cal. metallic cartridges, and Dyer's pouch, with the same amount of shells, only loosely carried in a fleece-lined interior, did not last long on frontier service. They were considered unsatisfactory because they would not retain cartridges when worn by Infantry or mounted men. The more efficient looped cartridge belt called 'Fair weather' belt or 'prairie' belt, improvised by professional soldiers with years of experience on the frontier, found its way into the ranks of the horse soldier. These belts, manufactured by either the company saddler or the men themselves, was finding favor among an increasing number of troopers during these years. General Anson Mills originated a method to manufacture a woven web ammunition carrier, which for a number of years was rejected by the army. Finally, in 1878, after years of pleading, Mills succeeded in getting the Army to accept his newly perfected woven belt which carried .45–70 cartridges. Government arsenals did not produce these belts; instead they were purchased from private contractors. Leather equipment throughout the world was soon to be replaced by web ammunition carriers and its accompanying web equipment.

In 1842, the US Army officially dropped the flintlock, converting the 1831 model muskets to the percussion ignition. The Jeff Davis Rifle, carried by a few regiments of our volunteers, reported that they performed creditably on occasion, and christened it the 'Mississippi Rifle'. It was equipped with a bayonet but was still too slow to load and quick to foul. The .69 caliber US percussion musket, model 1841, was first issued at the front during the Mexican War, and it is claimed that some of the soldiers refused these newer rifles, favoring their old flintlocks. The American Civil War was the first modern war that introduced repeating rifles, metallic cartridges, and telescopic sights. Northern arms manufacturers produced quantities of rifles besides pistols, carbines, howitzers and mortars. During the first days of the war, many Yankee troops marched into battle carrying flintlock muskets and an assortment of European rifles.

The US rifle musket 1861 was the result of dissatisfaction with the model 1855 tape lock musket, which in service would not perform as expected. The Maynard tape primer was unreliable for general use, and it was recommended by the Ordnance Board to return to the ordinary percussion cap method of ignition. With all the improvements and modifications

Right: *'Taps' Cavalry Bugler in full uniform (Sketch by Frederick Remington; National Archives).*

Far Right: *Cavalry Officer in campaign dress (sketch by Frederick Remington; National Archives).*

Officers of the 17th Infantry, US Army, Pine Ridge Indian Agency, South Dakota, January 1891 (National Archives).

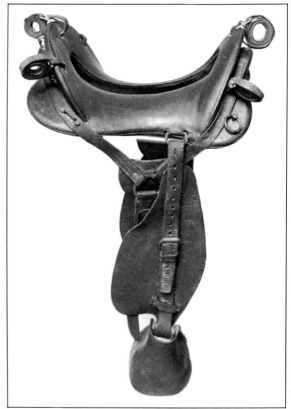

Off-side view of the model 1874 McClellan saddle (author).

on a number of rifles for Infantry use, a new issue evolved from the older models. The model 1863, .58 cal., Rifle Musket, type II, was simply a variation of the older 1861 and 1863 rifle muskets produced by Springfield Armory, as well as a host of other private contractors. It was the last standard issue Infantry arm carried by the troops during the Civil War.

A slightly improved version of the 1868 model rifle, the Springfield Model 1870, .50/70 caliber, was issued to the troops primarily as an experimental arm. Not too much longer after its issuance, the Army was dissatisfied with the performance of the model

PLATE 19
57 Cavalryman, 1867 (Indian Wars)
58 Lt. Colonel Custer, 1875
59 Frontier Soldier, 1885

57. *Dressed for winter, this Cavalryman is wearing his 'Great Coat' which came from the many stockpiles of government clothing left over from the Civil War. His full-length cape fell to his sleeve cuffs (unlike the Infantry capes which dropped only half way), and his coat displayed a double row of buttons (Infantry coats had a single row of buttons). The black muscrat gloves were experimental – and only a few regiments on the frontier were issued with them. The Army still issued full flap serviceable holsters from the Civil War for the Remington or Colt .44 caliber revolver (see E. L. Reedstrom's* Bugles, Banners and War Bonnets, *p.275, Bonanza Books 1986 – 'Summary Statements of Ord. and Ord. Stores in the Hands of Troops', Second Quarter, June 1867). A .50/70 caliber Springfield carbine is cradled in his arms, and a very early 'prairie belt' is worn around his middle – canvas thimbles to hold shells were sewn on leather belts. This original idea was adopted from Army Scouts, long on the frontier, who did not care for cartridge pouches because half of the*

contents were lost in 'prairie fighting'. His hat was the old 'hand-me-down' from the Civil War era, and after a few rains it wore like a limp rag on the soldier's head.

58. *Lt. Colonel George Armstrong Custer, 'Autie' to his friends and 'Jac' to his officers, sports a wide-brimmed civilian fur felt hat given him by his wife Elizabeth (Libby). A navy blue shirt with a wide falling collar and a red cravat started a new trend with the men in his regiment. A 'fair weather' cartridge belt began to catch on – sewing canvas loops to leather belts to hold cartridges. Buckskin breeches with an added reinforced seat, field glasses and his favorite .50/70 modified breech loading Springfield rifle completed his frontier garb.*

59. *The frontier soldier was beginning to be better prepared to fight Indians. His .45/70 Springfield rifle was an accurate weapon. He carried all his needs, including the new Anson Mills canvas cartridge web belt and the new Model 1880 'hunting knife', his knapsack, cup, bedding, and a new, tan, wide-brimmed hat. His only dilemma was his boots, which he often complained about. Why couldn't he have a set of boots higher up to help protect his legs from snakes, harsh brush and severe chafing from constant marching?*

PLATE 19

59   Frontier Soldier, 1885

58   Lt. Colonel Custer, 1875

57   Cavalryman, 1867

E.L. REEPSTROM

1870 and its .50/70 caliber cartridge. In 1872, the Ordnance Board considered the .45/70, ballistically a great improvement over the .50/70, and developed the new Springfield 'trapdoor', model 1873. Three models succeeded the Springfield model '73 in the .45/70 cal., models 1879, 1884, and 1889, and were used until the adoption of the Krag-Jorgenson in 1892.

The US magazine rifle, model 1892, Krag Jorgenson, caliber .30 (30/40 Krag), bolt action, was issued with a knife bayonet and with a magazine containing five cartridges. It was the first rifle to use smokeless powder and a reduced caliber cartridge.

As the western frontiersman pressed Westward, the War Department and Interior Department negotiated treaties with bribed chiefs for the relinquishment of their lands in exchange for some other lands farther west. After the War between the States, the railroads' and homesteaders' demand for land grew to such proportions that the War and Interior Departments were forced to compress the Indian nations even further. When some of the younger warriors, whose honor was only to be sustained in battle, refused to abide by the older chieftains' decrees of peace, the last phase of the Indian campaign came into being. Many soldiers, officers and enlisted men did not particularly relish the idea of fighting the Indian, but their oaths held them to the call of duty. One soldier said it thus: 'It is hard to go out and fight against those you know to be in the right.'

Typical Cavalry trooper, 1883, in field uniform. His weapons are: Colt pistol, .45 caliber, and Springfield (trap-door) .45–70 caliber carbine (Herb Peck).

Company of the 5th Infantry at Fort Keogh, Montana. Winter 1877 (National Archives).

7 Gambling Dens, Gamblers and Soiled Doves

Probably of all the towns west of St Louis, only San Francisco, Denver and Kansas City reached the status of first-class gambling centers for any considerable length of time. Ten years after the discovery of gold on a fork of the American River in 1848, gambling resorts of San Francisco seldom closed their doors. Suckers crowded the gaming tables, sometimes three and four deep, waiting their turn to stake their money on the turn of a wheel, a fast roll of dice or even try their hand at a game of paste-boards.

One of the first renowned gambling dens to be established in San Francisco after the gold stampede was the 'El Dorado', which opened in the spring of 1848, in a canvas tent, 15 by 25 feet in length. Later, a larger square building of rough boards replaced the canvas tent, at a rental price of $40,000 a year. This was not at all a fantastic sum for such quarters, considering that a boiled egg or an apple cost from one to five dollars and tea or coffee four to five dollars a pound. Whiskey, a very important item, cost 30 dollars a bottle.

The 'El Dorado' held a brief monopoly as a first-class gambling house, but shortly thereafter faced stiff competition. Countless other places quickly opened as adventurers and miners began to return from their 'diggings', with their pokes filled with gold dust. Most of San Francisco's gambling resorts were periodically destroyed by fires which devastated the town more than a dozen times between 1849 and 1850. But after each blaze the simple structures rose again over night.

It has been said that later San Francisco's gambling saloons were the most splendid in the world, and that the saloons of London, Havana, New York and New Orleans were far inferior in splendor of decoration and the quantity and quality of entertainment.

The principal gambling games in San Francisco were Three-Card Monte, Faro, Roulette, Chuck-a-Luck, Vingt-et-Un ('Twenty-One') and Rouge-et-Noir ('Red-and-Black'). Other houses had added attractions to titillate the visiting customers such as band music at the 'Portsmouth Square'. There were a variety of musical shows, special musical numbers by harpists and violinists, fiddling for hours at the 'Alhambra' each evening, and ballad singers at the 'Bella Union'.

Denver's period of importance as a gambling center began ten years after the California gold rush. The town's population consisted of fewer than 1,000 men and half a dozen women, all housed in 300 pine log buildings. Only a handful of structures had glass windows or floor boards; all other comforts of living were virtually unknown. Most of the structures were covered with hand split shingles, or roofed with logs and thatched with prairie grass and sod. Hearths and fireplaces were of adobe, and chimneys were made up of a framework of sticks plastered with mud or several barrels, one on top of another, also plastered with mud. The men who frequented these most forlorn and drab-looking buildings were Americans from every part of the Union, and included Mexicans, Indians, half-breeds, trappers, speculators, gamblers, desperados, and broken down politicians, also a few good and honest men. Their attire on arrival in town was the simple frontier regalia: wide slouch hats of every color, tattered woolen pull-over shirts tucked into buckskin pantaloons, and boots or occasionally moccasins. Holstered knives and huge revolvers of every caliber were suspended from their belts. They had no manners and their behavior was disgusting.

After the discovery of gold on Clear Creek and elsewhere in the Pike's Peak region, Denver took a change for the better. Frame and brick buildings began to be constructed, replacing the old mud-roofed log cabins, and the population improved both in number and character. 'False-fronts' on most buildings began to be displayed around 1868–70. One-story log cabins or board shanties were shielded by these 'false-fronts' to give the impression of a two-storey building. It was within character to these Westerners to brag a little and make the town look a little bigger than it actually was.

The Denver House was probably one of the first and most famous of pioneer hotels and gambling houses. It was a one-storey log building, 130 feet long and 36 feet wide, with glassless windows and a dirt floor, sprinkled frequently with water or coal oil to keep the dust down. In a short time, it took on a new look through its gambling proceeds, being later heralded as 'the greatest drinking and gambling saloon' in town. Among its crowded clientele were smartly dressed men, colorfully and fully armed, whose most common amusement was aggravating the bartender by shooting at him. In one documented story, a traveler stopped over in Denver to try his hand at cards and to rest up for a couple of days before he would continue on again. He took up lodging on the second floor, just above the gambling hall, and, after settling in, took supper and later that evening found an opening in a card game. After losing a great amount of money, he retired to his room where he dropped into bed completely exhausted. Early that morning a fight ensued in the gambling hall downstairs and a pistol shot rang out. Later that day, when the traveler did not answer his morning call, the proprietor, somewhat disturbed, had the door opened with a pass key, only to find the man dead in his bed. He had been shot in the back while he lay asleep. The early morning shooting had been responsible for the bullet passing through the floor boards and through the bed mattress, killing the overnight boarder. It was

later stated that that particular room was not occupied for some time, due to the incident.

Money was not always available at the gambling tables. Gold watches with fancy gold chains were brought out of hidden pockets and plunked down as legal currency. Ivory handled pistols were accepted, as was anything that could be evaluated and quickly turned into gold dust or cash. One newspaper account revealed a probate judge of the county lost 30 Denver lots in less than ten minutes, and afterwards observed the county Sheriff pawning his revolver for 20 dollars to spend in betting at Faro.

During the balmy days of the sharper in Denver the city seldom harbored fewer than a score of tough skinning houses. Such notorious houses were known as the Palace, the Bucket of Blood, the Morgue, the Chicken Coop, and Murphy's Exchange, better known as the Slaughter House, where shootings became a daily occurrence more than anywhere else in Denver. Denver retained many of its frontier characteristics for more than half a century, and, except for a few brief periods of suppression, was a wide-open gambling town until the early 1920s.

PLATE 20

60 Gambler, 1854–60s

61 Woman, 1854–60s

62 Gambler, 1854–60s

60. *For informal wear, the 'sack coat', with its small lapels, was boxy in outline and the sleeves had increased in girth. Trousers were somewhat baggy at the knees; however, they were long enough to reach the heels of shoes. For daytime and informal occasions, checks and plaids were favorites. Shirts were of handkerchief linen with eight-inch ruffles stitched on in vertical lines. Most collars were stiff standing. Disposable collars made of linen bonded to paper with stamped imitation stitching became available. Neckwear had a greater choice. Ties were narrow, colorful bows and at times sloppy in appearance. Vests were sometimes loud in color and plain, except for a double row of buttons in front. Footwear included square-toed, bowed pumps, half boots and laced shoes. (Buttoned shoes were introduced in the 1860s.) Straw hats became popular after the Mexican War. In raising his arm, our gambler reveals a holstered pistol.*

61. *The steel-ringed 'crinoline' was necessary to swell women's skirts to balloon-like proportions. Puffed or bell-like sleeves were the rage. Colors were crude, patterns were startling and bonnets were hideous. Materials were crêpe de Chine, organdie muslins, tarlatan, and satin. It was necessary, owing to the number of skirts, to walk in a special way to attain a graceful effect. Skirts were made with many flounces. Generally the first skirt, or lower one, which touched the ground, was changed often because of becoming dirty. Women who followed their men across wind-*

swept prairies sewed small-size buckshot into the hem of their lower skirt to keep the skirt from blowing over their heads. Hair styles for younger girls were the usual long flowing natural look. Women wore their hair mid-parted, smooth on top, bun at the back, side clusters; girls' long braids were wound about the ears. Wreaths were for evening wear.

62. *This cigar-smoking gentleman gambler wears a dark frock coat which came into fashion around 1816. Of military origin, it was derived from the great coat, but the body was always fitted. The frock coat was usually worn as undress; however, by 1850 it came into use for formal wear. The trousers or breeches were cut narrow with loud stripe designs; bottom straps or gaiter bottoms were still used, but abandoned by mid-century. He wears a ruffled shirt, stiff collar with hand knotted tie and a fancy embroidered, single-breasted, five-button vest. Hats were silk toppers, white, grey or black; in this case, however, a black beaver. Hair style was side whiskers, moustache, Imperial beard with thick bushy hair. Boots were commonly elastic-sided, square tipped toes, black with low heels. Jewelry was a heavy gold watch chain and fob.*

If anyone can admire our true American Western gambler, then you must consider his admiration for women of the night, his boldness in the face of danger, his 'big heartedness' as an easy touch, his table manners while manipulating gimmicks in cheating at a game of cards. His straightforward, true companionship for a friend was never-ending. He was bonded by his word—and let no man condemn him in the face of honor.

PLATE 20

60 Gambler, 1854–60s

61 Woman, 1854–60s

62 Gambler, 1854–60s

REEDSTROM

Roulette wheel.

Kansas City's bawdy houses were in existence principally in the 1870s and early 1880s, when the town's 30 or 40 gambling houses included such places as C. Maltbys, G. F. Fraziers and Galboughs Sporting Place. Also included were two of the finest halls in the West – the 'Main Street' resort of Major Albert Showers and probably the most luxurious house in the history of Kansas City – 'Potee's'.

Bob Potee's 'Faro Number Three' game house was located in Kansas City's red-light district on Missouri Street, just off of Main Street, and named 'The Marble Hall'. Situated over Streins Restaurant and Saloon, it had thick rich carpeting, carved mahogany furniture, lace curtains and gold bric-à-brac. Life size statues of nude maidens adorned the softly lit halls. On a warm night, Potee's honesty was challenged by a hot-headed dandy who lost a great deal of money at Potee's faro table as well as his composure. Displaying a pistol, the man pushed the muzzle against Potee's forehead and accused him of double dealing. Potee

tried to calm the man down and asked him to sit down. The tinhorn refused and cocked the hammer on his revolver. All at once, as spectators were trying to clear away from the table, several shots were fired, and smoke enveloped the dimly-lit room. When the smoke cleared, the dandy was spread across the Faro table lifeless, a bullet through his heart and in his hand his unfired pistol, still cocked. Bob Potee sat motionless in his chair, his hands flat on the faro table as before the shooting. His immediate remark was: 'Gentlemen, we'll begin with a fresh deck just as soon as the layout is cleared.'

Cheyenne, Wyoming, was probably the most notorious of the 'end of track towns', when the Union Pacific reached there in 1867. For two to three years the town was so tough that it was generally known to everyone in the West as 'Hell on Wheels'.

San Antonio, Texas, boasted of having a number of outstanding gambling emporiums in the early 1860s. Some of these early establishments included the Comanche Club, the Buckhorn, the Crystal, the Jockey Club, the University Club and the Black Elephant. Jack Harris took over the site of the Bull's Head Saloon to open his famous Vaudeville Theater and Gambling Saloon in 1869, at the intersection of Commerce and Soledad Streets. For years it was known as 'The Fatal Corner' because of shooting

The sleeve holdout. This apparatus consists of a leather band (A) fastened around the right arm beneath the coat sleeve, near the elbow, to which is attached a spring, pressure upon which works a rod which connects to a plate (B). Cards 'held out' are placed beneath the plate (B), which holds them in position. When player wishes to draw from his sleeve, he presses his arm against his body, thus setting in operation the spring which works the rod and throws forward the concealed cards from the plate. There were several other holdouts including a vest holdout and a table holdout.

Ring holdout was made to fit any ring and could be put on or taken off in a second.

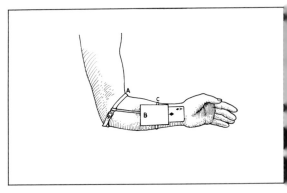

Top: *The 'Evans improved tapping dice'. Tap them once – percentage dice; tap them again – fair dice.*

Bottom: *Different types of dice.*

incidents where many men, including Jack Harris, King Fisher and Ben Thompson, received mortal wounds in gun battles. Other fine houses included the Silver King, the Globe, which featured classical concerts, the White Elephant and Scholtz's Palm Garden. The latter establishment was housed in a three-storey building with numerous bars, billiard rooms, gaming tables, and dining halls overlooking a tropical garden.

In 1874, Deadwood, South Dakota, was just as turbulent as Dodge City. The early days in Deadwood had more saloons than all other businesses combined. The bigger saloons were the only buildings of substance and dugouts and lean-tos of canvas served their 'rot-gut' to miners and citizens who couldn't afford anything else. Deadwood's chief claim to fame was the shooting of Wild Bill Hickok at Carl Mann's #10 Saloon on the main thoroughfare.

On August 2, 1876, Bill was playing poker with three friends, Charley Rich, Carl Mann and Captain Massey. For the first time in his gambling career, he sat with his back to the door. Late that afternoon, 'Broken Nose' Jack McCall, the assassin, entered the saloon in a careless manner. He sauntered nonchalantly around the room and then stopped directly behind Bill. He removed his hat, paused a moment and withdrew his .45 caliber Colt. The wide-brimmed hat hid much of the movement of the weapon being drawn, and no one gave McCall a second glance. Wild Bill had just drawn cards and was busily arranging his hand when McCall fired his weapon. The bullet entered the back of Bill's head, passing through and coming out below his right eye. The bullet also pierced Captain Massay's left arm, as he sat directly across from Bill. As the famous gunfighter lay motionless on the wooden floor, next to him lay the four cards he drew before his life came abruptly to an end. They were 'Aces and Eights'. Since that time poker players have known those two pairs as 'dead man's hand'.

Between 1867 and 1885, the towns of Newton, Abilene, Wichita, Ellsworth and Dodge City all claimed the title of 'Queen of Cattle Towns'. The saloon buildings in these towns might very well look familiar to the passing visitor or cowboy, for they were often loaded on flatcars, with all their whiskey barrels stored at the rear, ready at a drop of a hat to move to the next town when business dropped off. The names of saloons, gambling dens and dance halls changed so frequently in each succeeding town that the name 'Alamo' or 'Lone Star Saloon' may have been confused with another saloon ten miles down the trail. There was a Bull's Head saloon in Abilene and another in Newton, the Gold Rooms in Newton and again in Wichita and so on. Most saloons in cattle towns had every available game open to the sucker who could still jingle a few coins in his pockets.

On the night of August 19, 1871, during the cattle drive season, Newton, Texas, erupted like the 4th of July. All hell broke loose in Perry Tuttle's saloon when a Faro dealer was accused of cheating and was immediately confronted by a cowboy who attacked him. When the smoke cleared, five men were dead or dying and many others, innocent in the cannonade, were seriously wounded. This shows what a dangerous place a gaming table could be in a frontier town peopled with short-fused, gun-toting, unpredictable characters. Shootings were most common in saloons where games of chance were played each day.

In the final analysis, it would be much too lengthy to include the name of every famous frontier saloon that boasted of its every day mayhem with a brief thumbnail sketch of each. However, with adequate sources and references mentioned herewith, we will leave that up to the reader to seek out the one most interesting to him.

For the moment, let our thoughts drift back in time to a dimly lit bar room with a brass foot rail and recall the manners and protocol, the character and atmosphere of the early American western saloon. They were designated with an assortment of names such as dives, joints, skid row, inn, beer halls, groggeries, also including the quiet neighborhood *Bierstube* of Milwaukee and St Louis, which had a European flavor and family entertainment. Served in these establishments were wine, spirits and malt liquors, all of which were regarded as 'The good creatures of God', the 'hair of the dog', and 'the devil's brew'.

Successive waves of Irish and German immigrants came to this country with a good percentage of them being accustomed to hard beverages in many forms. The thirst of the newcomers expanded the liquor industry and staffed the bars with fully moustached barkeepers who pulled faucets of beer, and kept the whiskey flowing. Whiskey carried titles such as 'Joy Juice', 'Red Dynamite' (guaranteed to blow off your head), 'Rot Gut', 'Dust Cutter', 'Taos Lighting' (struck a man on the spot), 'Brave Maker', 'Panther Piss' (spit it out and hear it hiss), 'Firewater', 'Tarantula Juice', 'Bumble Bee Whiskey' (a drink with a sting). Others were 'Tangle Foot', 'Snake Poison', 'Mountain Dew', 'Nose Paint', 'Gut Warmer' and 'Coffin Varnish'. On these numerous concoctions, a man got pickled, whiskey-soaked or went booze-blind. The next morning he felt as if he had breakfast with a coyote – then he 'aired his paunch' – by vomiting all over himself. Early drinks were raw and specially brewed, or homemade. One concoction, one of the most famous of early western drinks, was 'Taos Lighting', made near Taos, New Mexico as early as 1820. It was a variety of aguardiente or burning water, made most often from corn or wheat. It was as good as any but it lacked color and age. There was a famous Montana drink called Shelby Lemonade, made from a mixture of alkali water, alcohol, tobacco juice and a dash of strychnine, to keep a person's 'ticker' pumping. Many of these virile and robust liquids were well above 100 proof mainly because the Westerner liked his booze strong.

The Westerner drank 'cowboy cocktails', which were nothing more than straight rye or bourbon. Scotch was unknown until the end of the century. Before a tent city or frontier town was completed, the main establishment to be erected was a huge saloon. Cowboys often rode 30 miles to 'belly-up' on pay day or play cards and down Old Crow at a nickel a shot. If a saloon or a hotel bar was fashionable, there might be a wine room in the back filled with willing and available women who steered a lonesome cowhand to an upstairs private room for a $2 'quicky'. A barber shop

often set up in a corner of the bar-room so that a 'gent' could enjoy his early morning bracer and get a shave or haircut at the same time. Local news was learned and gossiped here and often business transactions that played a great part in the town's growth took place here.

Bartending in a frontier saloon was not without its dangers. Most of these light hearted barkeeps retired with a sizeable nest egg and died peacefully in bed. However, some other areas were tough and rugged, with a shooting almost every day. In those days everyone went about carrying some sort of weapon, and the bartender would usually keep two revolvers 'capped and cocked' at all times under the bar. A short double barrel shotgun was also near at hand. Sometimes saloons were sandbagged and bullet proofed in order for the bartender and his customers to survive the day. After many scrapes, shootings and other disasters, customers were soon asked to hang up their hardware, receiving a token 'good for one free drink'. Saloons seldom ever shut down. When they did it wasn't because they had to, but because of lack of supplies.

A saloon could get a bad reputation if it kept the same dangerous customers each day. Notorious roaming gangs sometimes took over a saloon, spending money from a heist, or train robbery, not hiding out from the law – but taking complete control and staying there for days at a time, drinking and raising hell. To bring in extra trade, some saloonists maintained letter boxes so that steady customers could drink and receive their mail. Other bars lured patrons with racks of out-of-state newspapers. On many walls hung mounted long horns, deer heads, the butt end of a buffalo, old weapons, Mexican spurs and almost every imaginable piece of gear connected with the cattle trade. Of greater importance was that much-favored, most-looked-at painting of a nude woman sprawled out on a lavish sofa. Many a young cowboy carried that image with him on long trail drives, resolving to revisit and toast every drink to her on his return trip. Hanging kerosene lamps were always the target for some gun frisky cowboy or miner who was hell bent in treeing the town for one night. Many saloons purchased hanging lamps in great quantities and bought lamp chimneys by the barrel.

Around the bar's base ran a brass foot rail on which a man could comfortably hook his boot heels. Historians say that this was contrived so that a 'shorthorn' could erect himself on it to get his drink. Spittoons, cuspidors, or gaboons, one for every four gents, were placed alongside the brass rail for tobacco chewers, snuffers and smokers. Sawdust was sprinkled thickly around these huge brass cuspidors in order to absorb the accumulated saliva when 'baccer chawing' fanatics missed the vessel.

When a new saloon opened up proper, you were assured a rare look at a beautifully carved walnut bar which had taken its share of bruises riding around Cape Horn, lashed to the deck of a ship. The Saloonist was very proud of his walnut bar, even hanging freshly laundered hand towels every eight feet to assure the patron clean hands for a free lunch.

For the male population, the Western saloon was a refuge from toil, dreariness, and loneliness. Its many names came from the conversations of the elbow-to-elbow drinking characters who occasionally stopped by the 'bug house, cantina, jughouse, gin mill, doggery, watering trough, whiskey mill, and whoop up'. No matter what name a favorite saloon was called it began to disappear from the West. Barbed wire ended the cowboy's lawlessness. It suppressed him and limited him to his own range; his revolver became merely an ornament. The Western saloon days were over, but it was remembered as a place where he could go to amuse himself and lounge an evening away with a potion of devil's brew, while listening to law defying, re-told tales of the vast Western Frontier of days gone by. To the hardened Westerner, the saloon was his social club. He could dance with a pretty queen, rub elbows with gunfighters, and learn news from back 'stateside'. It has been said that a man took his life in his hands when he entered one of these 'road ranches', but, then again, it must have been worth it.

The sport of gambling reached its peak with the rise of frontier cattle towns, mining camps and the building of the transcontinental railroads which gamblers followed practising their skills and taking the suckers' money in any game they chose. In 1873, during the construction of the Union Pacific, at least 300 'sharpers', as they were called, were operating along the line of this road, with their ropers, cappers and other stand-bys, all of whom were engaged in conducting games of chance. By 1876, the entire Western country, from the Mississippi to the Pacific Ocean, and from the Rio Grande to the Canadian border, had an abundance of Faro artists, Monte dealers, and short card cheats, many of them gunmen and outlaws who infested tent cities, saloons and bawdy houses. The lure of the contest and prosperity suckered individuals of all calibers.

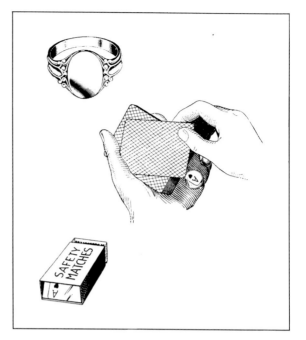

Ring Shiner. With this ring, all cards can be read when dealing. The reflector surface was turned inside the palm while the ring was worn on the little finger. The Match Box Shiner was laid on the table, permitting the dealer to read the cards as they were passed out.

Gambling was the amusement, the grand occupation of many classes, and it apparently became the life and soul of nearly every sucker that elbowed his way to a gambling table. By the late 1850s, an overwhelming majority of the 25,000 inhabitants of Frisco were men under 40. A woman was so rare that the sight of one would cause a gambling table to shut down.

San Francisco harbored around 1,000 regularly established gambling resorts, in addition every saloon and hotel bar-room contained two or more tables of Faro, Monte and Chuck-a-Luck. In the muddy streets roamed a horde of free lance Thimble-Riggers and Three-Card Monte throwers. Many of these were mere children from 13 to 15, who refused to pitch cardboard for a bet of less than $100.

The professional gambler was always a man with a good appearance, well dressed, and well informed on practically any subject matter. He conversed with intellect and was good natured and easy going, a man of good judgement with nerves of steel. Always jovial and possessing an untold limit of pluck and energy, his game usually continued into the night and far into the next day, and his conversation and naughty jokes were as fresh as the village market. He was always generous to a fault, and if you should meet him in a social way you would never guess his profession.

Most professional gamblers tested their ability before a huge mirror. Seated before his own image, he practiced his false shuffle and false cut, at the same time watching his reflection in the mirror. In this way he was able to see himself as others saw him, and estimate the chance that another man would detect his cheating.

While working their games of chance, most gamblers were armed with every imaginable weapon. They were well versed in the use of firearms and knives and handled both with the same proficiency and dexterity used in stacking a deck of painted pasteboards. Loaded short barreled pistols were as much an advantage as playing with loaded dice. It was a foolish man who accused a gambler of cheating at cards or making threats against his physical well being. Generally the customer cashed in his chips and quietly withdrew from the game without voicing any complaint.

Professional gamesters required pistols that were adequate to meet their special requirements. A cross section of manufactured weapons used showed a preference for short barrels and big bores, sometimes referred to as 'belly-guns'. The reason for the short barrels was for quick and easy clearance from waistbands, pockets and holsters. At close range these belly guns were just as mean and dangerous as they appeared and often reflected the personalities of their owners. It was not uncommon for a gambler to have hidden on his person a number of weapons, both pistols and knives. There were boot guns, shoulder holstered pistols, Bowie knives, belt buckle weapons (with three short barrels protruding out and aimed at a man's breadbasket), vest pocket Derringers and palm pistols. These weapons were never displayed or drawn unless forced and then the gambler would kill a man as mercilessly as he would brush a fly from his coat sleeve. The speed and efficiency with which the gambler dispensed this lethal dose gave him a fearsome reputation in many frontier and border towns.

Poker was virtually unknown during the gold rush days, and was not played to any great extent until the late 1850s. It did not become greatly popular until 1870, but since that time it has been the favorite game of San Francisco. All varieties of Poker, from Show-Down to Spit-in-the-Ocean, were played, but Draw-Poker was most popular around the 1880s, when Stud also had a great popularity.

Gambling in the West was very primitive in most cases, and with the exception of San Francisco, Denver and Kansas City there was an absence of the luxury and elegance with which first class gambling was surrounded in the East. There were scarcely any houses in which gambling was the sole or even the principal business; the typical gambling resort of the frontier was operated as an addition to the more important saloon or dance hall, or both. Sometimes a hall would operate no more than a Faro layout, a Monte bank, a Poker table and a Roulette wheel, and occasionally a Chuck-a-Luck cage, a table of Vingt-et-Un, and a Three-Card Monte pitch, all in the same room with a bar and a dance floor. These facilities, as meager as they might be, required at least a few good gamblers to run them. Generally it took three to handle a Faro game; a dealer, a lookout and a case-keeper, who sat at the table with an abacus-like device to keep track of the cards being played. Saloon keepers hired their own professionals to keep the card tables running, or invited independent gamblers to set up business in their establishments.

No records can be found to estimate the total daily or annual take at the frontier gambling tables. Individual stakes were small. The no-limit games at Tombstone in the early 1880s, and at Leadville, were exceptions rather than the rule, as were the big Poker sessions that continued far into the night. Poker games were usually one to two dollar limit, while bets at Faro and Monte ranged from 25 cents to a dollar. It was unusual to hear about a bet of $100 at Faro, or when a sucker who felt 'lucky' risked $1,000 on a single turn. This always attracted a considerable crowd, and afterwards was the talk of the town for many weeks. Ten cent chips at Roulette were common and a gambler could play dice for as little as a nickel a throw.

Gamblers as a rule made fine profits, although not playing for huge stakes, in the usual manner of frontier legend. Their winnings generally came from a large volume of business rather than from the size of the bets.

Women freelance gamblers in gaming resorts of the West did not show the superior skill of the men and few of them ever became really expert at manipulating a deck of cards or turning a Roulette wheel. Women were scarce on the frontier, and a sharper who was fortunate enough to have a mistress at his gaming tables attracted crowds and aroused much

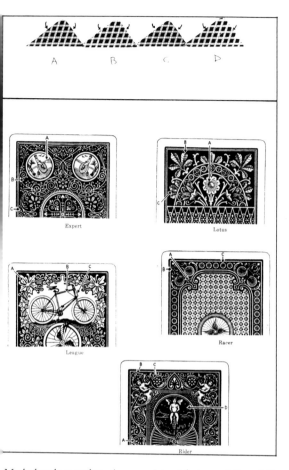

Marked cards or readers. Arrows point out design variations: 'A' could be a King, 'B' a black card, 'C' a red card or 'D' a heart, diamond, spade or club card.

Other favorite readers that were marked.

comment. Frontiersmen fought for the honor of losing their money to a lady gambler, and rather than call her a common cheat she was regarded as a lady trickster or a cunning little rascal.

Among a few well known lady gamblers were Poker Face Alice, who finally settled in Deadwood, Kitty the Schemer, who claimed to be Queen of the Gamblers on the Barbary Coast in the 1870s, Buckskin Alice of Leadville, Madame Moustache, and Minnie the Gambler. One of Madame Moustache's girls was a 15-year-old redhead named Martha Jane Canary, later known as Calamity Jane. Occasionally Jane would manipulate a poker game and the Faro

box, but she was much more adept at another business even more ancient than gambling.

No game was immune from cheating, and sometimes it was obvious that the gambler was up to some tricks. Frontier towns and tent cities were flooded with sleight-of-hand shell game artists, itinerant Faro cheats, poker sharks with marked decks and back alley street dice. There were ingenious devices for concealing an extra card in order to complete a winning hand. This device was called a 'Card Holdout' machine or 'Sleeve Holdout'. It consisted of a leather band fastened around the right arm, beneath the coat sleeve near the elbow, to which is attached a spring pressure upon which works a rod which connects with a plate. The cards which are 'held out' are placed beneath the plate which holds them in position. When the player wishes to draw from his sleeve, he presses his arm against his body, thus setting in operation the spring which works the rod and throws forward the concealed cards from behind the plate.

The Vest Hold-out was a much more preferred contrivance than any other gimmick because it permitted the holding-out of an entire hand if the player so desired. A piece of catgut was attached to that part of the apparatus concealed beneath the vest, and ran down underneath the clothing to the heel, where it was fastened either to the shoe or the clothing. The cards selected to be held-out were placed inside the clamp underneath the vest. When the player stretched out his leg along which ran the catgut, the plate inside the vest came forward and the cards could be easily withdrawn; when the heel was drawn back beneath the chair, the tension on the catgut decreased, and the clamp returned beneath the vest.

Other devices were known as Poker Check Mirrors, Triangle Reducing Glass and a popular item, the Pipe Reflector. All three had reflectors made of the finest imported Swiss flint glass, and were so arranged that the glass could show many ways of securing knowledge of what the other fellow held in his hand.

Another popular item was the Ring Shiner, an elaborate stylish ring that could easily be turned palm inward so the dealer can view each card dealt out by observing the reflective surface. The Ring Holdout was made to fit any ring and could be put on or taken off in a second. This item held a palmed card independent of being held by the fingers.

These are but a few of the many cheating devices, and in this chapter several more are illustrated that may be of some interest.

Perhaps the most famous expression in gambling

PLATE 21 (see Frontispiece)
63–67 Gambling, 1868

In simple evening's attire while sitting in on a game of pasteboards are three elderly gentlemen who expect a quiet and lucky night. The bartender is praying to himself that his expensive 'back-drop mirror' will last another night without being shattered by stray bullets. His only defense to curb any violence is a double-barrel cut-down shotgun hidden under the bar and close by. Also hidden on the lower game table shelf is an over-and-under .44 caliber Remington Derringer (a bellie-gun), and a stand-by just in case there's a 'one-eyed-man' in the game. The younger man, in a derby, and standing, is contemplating getting involved in the game. The white-haired gambler who is displaying a single Ace, holding it high, without any means of chips before him, is going to sucker the other two players in building the pot up more before he produces the other Aces.

PLATE 22 (opposite)
68, 69, 70 'Hurty-Gurty Gals', 1870–80

The early West's chief evil was the saloon, commonly known as 'thirst parlors' or 'road ranches'. Women of easy virtue mixed with large numbers of cowboys, miners, sodbusters, gamblers and plain whiskey soaks, all bellied up to the bar for a few jolts of frontier rotgut. These 'fallen angels' or hurty-gurty gals were just as much a part of a Western saloon as the colorful nude paintings hanging behind the bar. They drank watered-down tea with anyone who could afford their company and who wished to hop or skip over the floor with a partner for a buck a dance. Girls that worked for the saloonists were often called fallen angels, soiled doves, hurty gals, pretty waiter girls, bloomer girls, honky-tonk gals, beer-jerkers, box rustlers, easy women, fast women, fair belles, sportin' gals, owls and crib women.

A popular gal would average forty to fifty dollars in one night, besides commissions on drinks that she induced the men to buy.

Not all 'fallen angels' were pretty. One out of twenty was a beauty that later became a favorite with the big spenders. Most 'hurdies' were run-aways from farm families and broken homes. Many were not prostitutes as one might think. Owls, nightwalkers, or crib women were the lowest type. They operated in a curtained box in back of the saloon. Such fast women lasted only a year because they wore out easily.

Nester gals were usually the homely type, and some of them had faces like horses. When a cowboy asked one of these dance hall girls the question, 'How did you come by this profession?', she may have answered, '. . . It sure beats pickin' 'buffler' chips by a mile.'

The costumes that these hurties wore varied considerably. It was usually up to the management to prescribe a certain outfit for a certain hurty, depending upon how popular she was. Then again, the French styles from Europe with silks, fashionable ostrich feathers, and fancy hats, invited the management to adopt these fashions; only they shortened the hems and lowered the necklines to expose more of the woman's legs and bosoms.

At the 1876 Philadelphia Centennial Exposition the first tailor-made cigarette was displayed and promoted. As the cigarette companies grew, they included gaudy picture cards of women in daring costumes, showing more of their legs than anything else. More exposed bosoms were also explored in these racy, colored, picture cards that were traded by men who smoked that brand of cigarettes. The Duke Cigarette Company, which promoted these gaudy cards, called the colorful pictures 'Sporting Girls'. Each girl, in a unique costume, portrayed some activity in the sports line. But one card was as daring as the other. 'The cheesecake was more decorative than daring', said one saloonist in a Phoenix 'thirst parlor'.

Some of these girls soon drifted away, married and lived a proper life, raising children and attending church, while others died after a quick and simple life, remembered only by cowboys, sod-busters, or miners. Their names were insignificant, but for a lonely man on the frontier a painted face was never forgotten. At the end of an evening with them he was either in love . . . broke, or physically satisfied.

PLATE 22

68, 69, 70   'Hurty-Gurty Gals', 1870–80

history is this line, 'There's a one-eyed man in the game ...' which means literally to any poker player 'Look out for a cheat'. The following is a true incident which occured in Omaha where among the participants was a one-eyed man trying to palm a card in a little game of draw. One of the players who spotted this removed his revolver from his belt and laid it on the top of the table, saying: 'I'm not making any insinuations or bringing any charges, gentlemen, but if I catch any son-of-a-bitch cheating ... I will shoot his other eye out.'

Edmond Hoyle was perhaps the first technical writer on card games. His writings on the laws of Whist gave rise to the common phrase 'according to Hoyle', signifying full compliance with universally accepted rules and customs.

Hoyle's life before 1741 is unknown, although he is said to have been called to the bar. For the use of the pupils to whom he began teaching Whist that year, he prepared *A Short Treatise on the Whist* (1742), which went through numerous editions. His revised laws of 1760 remained authoritative until 1864, when the Arlington and Portland Whist clubs in London adopted a new code. French and German translations of the *Short Treatise* first appeared in 1764 and 1768, respectively.

The Hoyle Codification of the Laws and Strategy of Backgammon (1743) is still largely in force. He also wrote *Treatises on Chess* (1761) and on other games. Familiar with the laws of probability, he appended to one of his books a life table for annuities. He died at the age of 97.

8 Outlaw Days

Someone once wrote that 'war breeds crime and criminals'; and the American war between the states did not differ from any other war in this respect. There were two types of Western outlaws, the genuine imitation of a 'bad man' and the genuine 'bad man'. They were as different as night and day. Countless numbers of people held them in high esteem, overlooking the despicable deeds they performed.

To exemplify further, throughout the West there are two sorts of wolves, the coyote or prairie wolf and the gray or timber wolf. Either will kill, and both have a voracious appetite. One is a coward at heart and the other is courageous and daring. Both are cunning, and in appearance they sometimes resemble each other so closely that it is hard to determine the species. The gray wolf is fearless and bold. The coyote is sneaky and craven and throughout the West its very name brings to mind a skulking, slinking creature.

Here are a number of examples of outlaws better known in the American West with a brief history on each. It would be impossible to mention every one of them in one chapter, but the ones referred to here are better known for their daring deeds as outlaws and bandits.

William Clarke Quantrill would fall into the category of the coyote, bloodthirsty and with a heartless vengeance against all Kansas. He led his followers on their first raid against Olathe, Kansas, which he burned to the ground after carrying away jewelry, silver and gold. More than a dozen unarmed citizens were ordered to be shot to death at his command. His reason for seeking revenge was supposedly because of the death of an older brother at the hands of Kansas lawmen. This later proved to be false. Hated by the Union soldiers of Missouri and Kansas, Quantrill was loathsome to all who wore blue uniforms.

At the outbreak of the Civil War he gained a reputation as a hero to the slave traders, and he had no trouble enlisting a number of men to his pro-Confederate guerrilla tactics. Arch-murderers such as 'Bloody Bill' Anderson, Fletcher Taylor, and George Todd pledged their allegiance to him. Frank James and Cole Younger enlisted later, but Jesse James was too young for his older brother Frank to allow him to

Historian and Black Powder editor for Guns & Ammo *magazine Phil Spangenburger demonstrates the art of fancy shooting. At a safe distance from an opponent, by drawing a pistol a little slower and aiming for the mid-section, the odds were greater in hitting a man. Drawing fast, even at close range, could mean a wild shot, a total miss or a minor flesh wound (Red River Frontier Outfitters).*

join up with the band. It wasn't until 1864 that Jesse finally got his wish and became a member of the raiders.

Quantrill's gain was for himself alone. He had no official connection with the Confederacy. Murder, arson and robberies were carried out under the guise of fighting for the South. On August 21, 1863, Quantrill set out for Lawrence, Kansas, with a band of 450 men. They succeeded in raiding and killing, without mercy, 140 citizens and wounding 24. Property damage exceeded $1,500,000. The raid at Lawrence proved to be Quantrill's high point. From Kansas, his group followed him to Texas, where he advanced upon and assaulted a number of defenseless immigrant wagon trains and murdered dozens of travelers. In November, 1863, Quantrill and his gang were accosted by a Union officer, Captain George Todd, and his command. Quantrill lost most of his raiders in the escape attempt. On returning home with a few of his men, Quantrill was ambushed by Union soldiers at Smiley, Kentucky, and mortally wounded, being struck by a ball in the back which shattered his spine. He died June 6, 1865, at Louisville, after embracing the Roman Catholic Faith. He was buried in the Catholic cemetery there and later his remains were removed to Canal Dover, where he was born, for reburial.

The Reno brothers, John, Simeon, Bill and Frank, were not Western outlaws, but robbed and murdered throughout Southern Indiana and pillaged towns in Iowa and Missouri for more than two years. What gave them a place in America's criminal history was the fact that by robbing the Ohio and Mississippi Railroad on March 22, 1866, they were marked for distinction as the 'first train robbers'. It was just outside of Seymour, Indiana, that the gang, led by John Reno, forced a startled messenger to open the Adam's Express Car, relieving the safe of $16,000 in gold, silver and paper money. John and Simeon, along with Frank Sparks, were arrested, but were released on bond as the evidence against them was not substantial.

An epidemic of train robberies began as other hold-up bands sprang out of nowhere. Allen Pinkerton, representing the Adams Express Company, who were the principal losers in these raids, and who had determined to disband this holdup band, undertook the difficult task of tracking down the thieves. While the Reno brothers relaxed in their homes in Seymour, Indiana, they gambled and practically gave away their loot in huge sums. This was observed by other young men in the neighborhood and naturally they desired to likewise acquire these illegal and ill-gotten gains, and soon joined the Renos and their confederates. Robbery after robbery followed, and arrests were numerous, but powerful influences and intimidations of witnesses by the criminals made convictions practically impossible. Farmers who were hostile to the band were terrorized by having their livestock poisoned or maimed and their homes and barns burned until a reign of terror existed all over Southern Indiana.

The Renos met their Waterloo during the winter of 1867 and 1868. John Reno had robbed the County Treasurer's office at Gallatin, Missouri, of $20,000 and returned to Seymour, Indiana, the gang's base of operations. Here, John was decoyed and arrested by the awaiting Pinkertons at the Seymour depot and was tried and sentenced to 20 years in the Missouri Penitentiary at Jefferson City. He served every day of his sentence.

All during the winter of 1868, a series of safe robberies in county treasurers' offices took place throughout Western Iowa. The last was staged at Glenwood, Mills Co, Iowa, where $20,000 was taken. Pinkerton investigating teams found the criminals to be Frank Reno, Al Sparks, Miles Ogle and Mike

---

PLATE 23

71 Jesse James, 1870s
72 Frank James, 1870s
73 One of the James' gang, 1870s

71 and 72. *The bandit career of the James boys, Jesse and Frank, was encouraged during the Civil War when they both fought in Confederate guerrilla bands whose hit and run raids on Union troops terrorized citizens in the border zone of Kansas and Missouri. After the war, the two rebels organized ex-guerrillas, ranging from four to a dozen men. They struck trains and banks swiftly, sometimes paralyzing an entire community. Then, as quickly as they appeared, they would vanish into the countryside.*

Jesse holds an 1873 Winchester .44–40 and has two holstered pistols – a Colt and a Smith and Wesson, both of .44 caliber. Frank (center) also cradles an 1873 Winchester and a Remington pistol, .44–40.

Jesse and Frank led their gang members for fifteen years, from *1866 to 1881, executing twenty-six challenging robberies in and about Missouri, with a net take of close to $500,000 dollars. At the height of their career, other outlaw gangs imitated them, but only for a few precarious years, until they themselves met a bloody end. Late in March, 1882, Bob Ford ended Jesse's outlaw days by shooting the desperado in the back of the head with his pearl-handled, .44 caliber Colt. After that, Frank James decided to surrender to the Missouri authorities, where he stood trial and was acquitted. Frank decided to lead a straight life and finally settled down in Western Missouri. After a few years he appeared in a traveling tent show, telling stories of his adventures with his brother Jesse. On February 18, 1915, he died, still bragging of his outlaw days.*

73. *The right-hand figure represents a true picture of one of the James' gang. His pistol is the Remington Army percussion . . . and he wears a 'gunny-sack' over his head with cut-outs for eyes and mouth.*

PLATE 23

71   Jesse James, 1870s

72   Frank James, 1870s

73   One of the James' gang, 1870s

Rogers, a wealthy land owner of Council Bluffs, Iowa.

Following a robbery at Harrisonville, Missouri, the Pinkertons had traced the robbers to Council Bluffs, where a watch on the home of one of the gang members resulted in the capture of the criminals while they were trying to burn the loot. All were jailed at Glenwood, Iowa, but on April 1, 1868, they broke jail and William and Simeon fled with Frank to Windsor, Canada. Frank became associated with Charles Anderson, a clever burglar and an all-round criminal, and returned with him to Seymour. Shortly after the Glenwood robbery, Walker Hammond and Mike Colleran, of Seymour, held up an express messenger on a Jefferson railroad train, taking $15,000, only to be themselves held up by the Reno brothers and relieved of their plunder. Hammond and Colleran were convicted and sentenced to long terms and imprisoned in the Indiana State Penitentiary. Subsequently Frank, Sim and Billy Reno, with Miles Ogle and Charles Anderson, held up a train near Seymour, robbing the Adams Express Company's safe of $90,000. For this crime, Anderson and Frank Reno were arrested at Windsor, Canada, after a chase which lasted all summer, were remanded for extradition and later placed in the charge of Pinkerton detectives who transported them to the New Albany, Indiana, jail. Sim and Billy Reno were finally apprehended in Indianapolis, Indiana, and were also lodged in the same jail.

Henry Moore, Gerrold and Sparks, and an unknown man who held up and robbed the J. M. & I. R. R., had been arrested at Seymour, and while en route to the Brownstone jail were forcibly lynched by enraged citizens.

On the morning of December 12, 1868, about three hours before daybreak, a single coach train rolled quietly into New Albany. A masked mob, a Vigilance Committee, believed to be from Seymour, made its way to the jail where they battered in the door and overpowered the guards forcing Sheriff Fullenlove to release the prisoners into their charge, after which the robbers, Frank, Sim and Billy Reno and Anderson, were all hanged in the jail corridor. Notices were also posted in public places about the town of Seymour, naming 25 people alleged to be associated with the Renos, warning them that if any house, property or cattle was destroyed the Committee would meet once more and exterminate the known individuals. This ended a reign of terror and train robberies in Southern Indiana. The identity of the Vigilantes who

participated in curbing these robberies is a closely guarded secret. As for the originator of train hold-ups, John Reno served his time and was then released, never more to be heard of.

Jesse Woodson (Dingus) James, was born in Clay County, Missouri, September 5, 1847. Among the Kentuckians who settled in Clay County before the Civil War were Doctor and Mrs. Zerelda Cole James (Samuels), and their sons Frank and Jesse, sons of Mrs. Samuels previous marriage. The family were Southern sympathizers and were constantly harrassed by the Missouri Enrolled Militia, but only after Frank James had joined with Quantrill. The Civil War was more than half over when Jesse joined the guerrilla band, soon gaining a reputation for bravery, daring and excellent pistol shooting.

After the war, the James boys, under the leadership of Bill Anderson and operating with Cole, Jim, John and Bob Younger, Clell and John Miller, Charley Pitts, and the Tompkins brothers, Jim Cummings, Dick Liddell, and other members of Quantrill's band, began prowling through the West and Southwest Missouri and Eastern Kansas. They were looking for what spoils they could get and for years committed a series of the most despicable crimes of that period in Missouri, Kentucky and Minnesota. They held up banks in the day time, and robbed trains at night. They murdered respectable citizens who resisted them and killed law officers who attempted their arrest.

The published reports of the exploits of this band had more to do with the making of Western bad men than anything which occurred before they began to

$25,000 Reward Jesse James dead or alive.

operate. When the war was over, Jesse tried to surrender to the authorities and was shot by an overanxious band of Union soldiers. Envious enemies strove to brand him as an outlaw after a series of robberies which followed in 1865.

A number of statements, not documented, had come about that neither Frank nor Jesse had ever been captured and arrested by officers, State or Federal. Judge Philander Lucas of Liberty, Missouri, stated that sometime during 1865–66, around eleven o'clock one morning, the James boys, with Clell Miller, Jim Poole and George White, rode into Liberty, firing off their revolvers and acting like a bunch of Indians. Then they entered Muffert's Saloon, had drinks, and, as they left, Sheriff Rickards arrested and disarmed them, marching the troup into the Court House, and arraigned them before the judge who committed them to the County jail. As a matter of fact, there were no charges against them, and they were subsequently released.

After the Gallatin, Missouri, bank was robbed on December 7, 1869, Jesse James' horse was captured and identified. From that point on, the name Jesse James was connected with every robbery committed in Missouri and elsewhere, some justly so.

As a rule, after each crime the James boys and their partners would return to their home in Clay County, Missouri, where they were virtually immune from arrest, either through fear of them by the respectable citizens or through the aid they received from their friends and admirers. On June 3, 1871 the James and Younger brothers rode into Corydon, Iowa, intending to rob the county treasurer's office of recently collected taxes. When Jesse offered a $100 bill for change, it was found that the county treasurer was attending a meeting at the site for a new school house and it was he who held the combination to the locked safe. The gang was stymied for a moment. However the terrified clerk mentioned that the new bank across the square had one half of its capital on hand. Jesse consulted with his associates and the robbery of the new bank was agreed upon. On entering the bank, Jesse offered the cashier a $100 bill asking for change. When the cashier responded by opening the safe, he turned to face the muzzles of two cocked revolvers. Jesse's companions, who meanwhile had slipped into the bank, forced the President and cashier into the back room. They proceeded to empty the safe of around $15,000 and jammed the filled sacks into their saddle bags. Mounting their horses, they fled from town, passing the public meeting on the outskirts of

Riding away from a robbery, the gang would 'wrist-snap' their pistols in the air, creating an ear-shattering racket as they rode out of town (courtesy Carl Breihan's Collection).

town, where the new school site was being discussed, and where the county treasurer's attendance saved his safe from being plundered. As the bandits rode by, they fired their rifles and pistols into the air at the same time informing the gathering of the robbery.

On July 20, 1873, the James brothers committed their first train robbery on the Chicago, Rock Island & Pacific Railroad, wrecking the train 15 miles east of Council Bluffs, Iowa. They murdered the unarmed engineer, wounded the fireman, robbed and injured many passengers besides relieving the express car of a large amount of money.

On January 31, 1874, Jesse and Frank, accompanied by the Younger brothers, Clell Miller and Jim Cummings, committed their second train holdup, on the Iron Mountain Railroad at Gadshill, Mo., by flagging the train to a standstill. The purse was $10,000.

While investigating this robbery on March 10, 1874, Joe W. Witcher, one of Pinkerton's detectives from Chicago, was overpowered and bound with ropes and put on a horse. Clell Miller and Jesse James took him from their home in Missouri, to Independence, Missouri, where they killed him, leaving his body at the crossing of the Deerington and Independence Railroad where the Iowa Sheriff had left Robert Pinkerton three years before.

It was on March 16, 1874, that Louis Lull, a former Captain of Police in Chicago, but later with the Pinkerton's, and an ex-Deputy Sheriff, a man named Daniels, met John and Jim Younger on a road near Montegaw Springs, St. Clair County, Missouri. While arresting them, Lull killed John Younger, but was himself mortally wounded, dying six weeks later. Daniels was also killed and Jim Younger was seriously wounded.

The Jesse and Frank James band continued their depredations. Their next robbery was on the Union Pacific Railroad at Munsey, Kansas, in December, 1875, securing $55,000. The Missouri Pacific Railroad was robbed next at Otterville, Missouri, July 8, 1876, securing $17,000, after which McDaniels, one of the band, was killed resisting arrest while attempting to escape with part of the loot. The next serious crime committed was in September, 1876, when they endeavored to rob a bank at Northfield, Minnesota, and killed the cashier, J. L. Haywood. Citizens of the town opened up with gun fire, killing Bill Chadwell, Clell Miller and Charley Pitts. Bob and Jim Younger and Jesse James were wounded but escaped. Cole Younger picked up Bob and carried him away on his horse under a hail of bullets. A few days later, Cole, Jim and Bob Younger were surrounded in a swamp and were captured. Frank James managed to get Jesse into Dakota territory and from there to the Missouri River, where they stole a skiff and made their get-

away. Cole, Jim and Bob Younger were sentenced to long terms of imprisonment in the Stillwater, Minnesota, State Prison. On September 16, 1899, Bob Younger died in prison and on July 10, 1901, Cole and Jim Younger were pardoned by Minnesota State Board of Pardons. On October 18, 1902, Jim Younger committed suicide at St Paul, Minnesota. (Cole Younger, born in Jackson County, Missouri, January 15, 1844, had his own little band. He and his brothers, Jim, John and Bob, were first cousins to the James boys.)

On April 3, 1882, Charles and Bob Ford, friends of the James boys, for a reward of $10,000 offered by Governor Crittendon of Missouri for Jesse's body dead or alive, shot Jesse in the back of the head while he was hanging a picture in his front room at St. Joseph, Missouri. Bob and Charley surrendered themselves, were tried, convicted and sentenced to death but pardoned by Governor Crittendon and paid the $10,000. Thus to Governor Crittendon is due the final disbanding of the James brothers band of outlaws and in this he was aided by Sheriff Timberlake of Clay County and Commissioner of Police Craig of Kansas City.

PLATE 24
74 'Billy the Kid', 1879
75 Bob Dalton, 1892
76 Cole Younger, 1897

74. 'Billy the Kid' (William H. Bonney), born in New York City on 23 November 1859, finally landed in Silver City, New Mexico, with his mother and step-father. At the age of twelve, he killed a man in a saloon row with a pocket knife. Some say that the man insulted his mother, who worked on the side as a wash-woman. Billy soon built up a reputation as a gambler, stealing horses, killing Indians as well as a handful of white men. The Kid was now old enough to be dangerous, and his life had been one of irresponsibility and lawlessness. He had nearly reached his full physical growth at this time, around 5 feet 7½-inches in height, and weighing 135 pounds. A hard rider all his life, he was lean and sinewy. His hair was light brown, and his eyes a blue-gray, with curious red hazel spots in them. His face was long and his chin narrow and long. His front teeth were a trifle prominent, and he always displayed them with a wide beaming smile when talking. It was sheriff Pat Garrett who ended Billy's life on 14 July 1881, at Fort Sumner, New Mexico.

75. Bob Dalton was born in Cass County, Missouri, in 1868, during which he became a father, law officer, train and bank robber. As a law officer in his teens, Bob was awarded a deputy marshal's badge along with his brothers Grat and Emmett. Bob was soon fired for taking a bribe. Rumors also were spread around that Emmett and Grat were engaging in cattle rustling on

the side. Soon the latter two resigned and joined Bob in terrorizing the Kansas and Oklahoma terrain for over a year and a half in bank and train robberies. (Members of the gang included Grat, Emmett, Bob, Bill Doolin, Dick Broadwell, Black Faced Charley Bryant, William McElhanie, Bitter Creek Newcomb, Bill Powers, Charley Pierce.)

In the Coffeyville, Kansas, raid on 5 October 1892, while trying to rob two banks at the same time, Bob was killed and his gang was mowed down in what is now called 'Death Alley'.

76. The French prepared unique uniforms for their convicts, which in this case were black and white bars running horizontally. On many of their Islands, where prisons were built, the individual cells had overhead windows enclosed with iron bars. As guards patroled the cat walks during the day, they could look down and see the prisoners below projected with shadows of overhead bars, like a man in a striped suit. These black and white stripes were adopted into uniforms for all prisoners thereafter. It was also effective when convicts escaped as they could easily be identified with this clothing by anyone. Someone said, 'No man shall escape punishment if found guilty, be it a man who is 'black or white'!' Cole Younger is shown here serving a life imprisonment at Stillwater, Minnesota, in the (early) 1880s. He was paroled along with his brother in July of 1901. In 1903, he received a full pardon and was able to leave the state. Back in Missouri he looked up Frank James, and went into business with him managing a Wildwest Show. Born 15 January 1844, he died 21 March 1916.

PLATE 24

74   'Billy the Kid', 1879

76   Cole Younger, 1897

75   Bob Dalton, 1892

Strange as it may be, Calamity Jane mentioned Jesse James in her diary, dated November 30, 1889. 'I met up with Jesse James not long ago. He is quite a character – you know he was killed in '82. His mother swore that the body that was in the coffin was his but (I know) it was another man they called either Tracy or Lynch. He was a cousin of Wild Bill (Hickok). You won't likely care about this but if Janey[1] outlives you and me she might be interested. He is passing under the name of Dalton[2] but he couldn't fool me I know all the Daltons and he sure ain't one of them. He told me he promised his gang and his mother that if he lived to be a hundred he would confess. You and me won't be here then Jim.[3] To make it strange Jessie sang at his own funeral. Poor devil he can't cod me – not even with long hair and a billy goat's wad of hair on his chin. I expect he will start preachin'. He is smart maybe he can do it.' (From a diary belonging to Stella Foote, Billings, Montana.)

Alexander Franklin ('Buck') James was born at Kearney, Clay County, Missouri, on January 10, 1844. During the Civil War, Frank fought with the Confederate irregulars under General Sterling Price, and was captured at the Battle of Wilson's Creek, August 10, 1861. He was released on parole when he promised never to bear arms against the United States again. After telling many wild stories of the war, his bragging led to his arrest, but his mother effected his release by further promising that Frank would not step out of line again. This evidently angered Frank to the point where he couldn't face his friends any more. Hearing of Quantrill's band, he decided to join them. Frank remained with that guerrilla movement until Quantrill was shot in Kentucky, then he surrendered to the Federal authorities in that state. Had the authorities known that Frank had violated his parole, he would have been shot instantly. Historians still believe that Frank James not only participated in many train robberies and holdups but also planned the tactics and headed the gang as well.

With his brother Jesse dead, Frank decided to surrender to the Missouri authorities in October, 1882, stood trial and was acquitted of the Gallatin, Missouri, bank robbery. Governor Crittendon refused to surrender him to the Minnesota authorities, and he subsequently settled in Western Missouri, leading a straightforward life. Frank occupied the old James homestead near Kearney, Missouri, but made frequent trips to his ranch near Fletcher, Oklahoma. He also spent a little time working with Cole Younger who was just released from the Stillwater penitentiary. The two former outlaws appeared before the public in a traveling tent show, telling stories of their adventures. Frank James died on February 18, 1915, still bragging and boasting of his days as a bandit.

At the beginning of the Civil War in Jackson County, Missouri, lived Louis Dalton, a farmer and veteran of the Mexican War. In 1851, he married Adeline Younger, a half-sister of Colonel Henry Washington Younger, father of the outlaw Youngers. She therefore was an aunt of the Younger brothers and blood relation to Frank and Jesse James. A small army of 13 children (nine sons, four daughters, of which eight sons and three daughters reached adulthood) were ruled by their mother with a firm hand and an iron will, especially since her brother's boys had gone bad. When the Dalton family followed the homesteaders into Indian Country in Oklahoma, they finally settled down near the southern border of Kansas near the little town of Coffeyville.

Federal Judge Isaac C. Parker, 'the Hanging Judge', held the law of the territory in one hand, and a rope to all sinners in the other. Frank Dalton, a Marshal on the Parker staff at Fort Smith, Arkansas, died in a gun battle with a trio of whiskey runners. Brothers Grat, Bob and Emmett followed in Frank's footsteps as law officers, probably with vengeance in their hearts, but not too long after adopting their new badges they moved on to serve as Police in the Osage Indian nation. One of the reasons for leaving the Federal authorities, they stated, was because they couldn't collect their fees. However, Bob Dalton was fired for taking a bribe. While supposedly hunting cattle-thieves, they all were doing a little 'rustling' of their own. Grat left the force and went to California, where two other brothers, Littleton and Bill, had settled earlier. Bob and Emmett were wanted for sticking-up a Faro game in New Mexico, and when the trail got too hot, Bob followed Grat to California and Emmett went back into the territory he knew so well to find a hide-out for his brothers.

On February 6, 1891, near a fast growing town called Los Angeles, California, a Southern Pacific train loaded with passengers came to an abrupt stop. Four masked men waving a red lantern appeared in the dark before the engine, brandishing weapons and covering the train crew. They pounded the butts of

[1] Janey was Calamity Jane's daughter (Jean Hickok McCormick).
[2] J. Frank Dalton – claimed to be Jesse James in the mid-1940s.
[3] Jim was a close friend – an aristocrat, Captain James O'Neil, a Sea Captain living in England who raised little Janey.

their weapons on the Express car door and messenger Charlie C. Haswell peered out of the window into the darkness. 'Open up and be damned quick about it!!' A shot rang out and several pieces of buckshot creased his forehead. He jumped back and reaching for his shotgun slid the door back swiftly. His shotgun roared, hitting one of the bandits, possibly two, driving them back. Back in the tender, fireman George Radcliff, shot in the abdomen, lay dying while the masked men had their encounter with messenger Haswell. Grat and Bill Dalton were soon arrested and tried for a profitless holdup. Bill was acquitted, but Grat was convicted and sentenced to a 20-year term, from which he later escaped. (While being transferred to prison by train, Grat leaped out of the car window into a river below.) Bob Dalton was also on the wanted list but managed to escape. The railroad finally put up a $6,000 reward for Bob and Grat. Emmett, in his 1931 book *When the Daltons Rode*, blamed it all on false charges trumped up in the California train holdup. 'They put the runnin' irons on our hides', he said.

Once the gang was fully reorganized and ready to strike, its scope and objectives were somewhat changed. Instead of the group acting as mere horse thieves and petty holdup men, they began to operate on a much loftier scale, as bank and train robbers, modeled on the James-Younger methods. Bob Dalton, in his early twenties, was the leader of the group which operated for 18 months. Besides his own brothers, Bob had the services of seven other outlaws: Charly (Black-Faced) Bryant, George (Bitter Creek) Newcomb, Bill Powers, Charley Pierce, Dick Broadwell, Bill Doolin and William McElhanie. Doolin would later head a gang of his own with Bill Dalton, the fourth and last bad man in Mother Dalton's tribe.

Any man with a 'wanted dead or alive' poster on his head became fair game for every bounty or potshooting kid who was looking for a reputation. Wherever he went he was in constant fear of being shot in the back or ambushed at every turn of the trail. At the beginning he wasn't bothered too much by the thought, but, as time went on and his name became household gossip, in addition to newspaper accounts of his activities, he began to feel that he belonged to the 'living-dead'. The Daltons, in comparison to the James gang who rode unrestrained over the West for 16 years, were fly-by-night desperados. Their trail of depredation across Oklahoma in its homesteading days spanned only 18 months. But it was a busy 18 months of robbing trains and losing a few men in the process.

The notorious 'Wild Bunch' gang. Left to right, standing: Will Carver, Harvey Logan (Kid Curry). Left to right, seated, Harry Longabaugh (Sundance Kid), Ben Kilpatrick (The Tall Texan) and Robert Leroy Parker (Butch Cassidy). Over Cassidy's shoulder, on the backdrop, are seen what look like bullet holes. Legend has it that while the photographer was posing the boys, Butch stood up, flashed his six-shooter, turned to the wall and emptied his weapon (courtesy University of Oklahoma).

The reward money for any member of the Dalton gang reached $5,000. Several members of the outfit wanted to quit; even Grat and Bob thought of going to South America. But there was one more foray, the biggest and boldest venture, a twin holdup in daylight of the two banks in Coffeyville, Kansas. Cole and Jim Younger, their cousins, were still in the Minnesota State Prison at Stillwater, paying the price for the raid on the First National Bank of Northfield with the James boys in 1876, and Bob Younger had died in his cell.

Six outlaws huddled around a roaring campfire on Onion Creek in Indian Territory, discussing the Coffeyville daylight holdup. Bob Dalton and his brothers knew the streets, alleys and principal buildings well. Bob had visited the town on the quiet, taking the chance of being recognized. The boss bandit believed that both banks could be taken quickly and with a minimum of risk, knowing that each bank had so much cash on hand that that kind of 'stake' would allow them all to hideout for quite a spell, even leaving the country if necessary. In any event the 'take' would place them in the lap of luxury for a long time. Ironic as it may seem, the town had received a warning from law officers in the territory that they might be visited by the Dalton gang. However, no one paid any attention to the warnings and so the community was totally unprepared for the robberies.

Out of the six outlaws that planned the Coffeyville raid on October 5, 1892, only five rode into town. Bill Doolin's horse became lame on the trail coming in and he said he would be right along just as soon as he could steal a fresh mount. But he never did rejoin the band. Shortly after nine-thirty, as the town was just beginning to stir, the outlaws jogged down Eighth Street into the bright and sunny plaza. Somewhat surprised by a gang of workmen tearing up the street for repairs, Bob noticed that the hitching-rack near the banks had been torn down. He then directed his band into the alley which ran behind the city jail, one block below the Condon bank. Here the outlaws dismounted and tied their mounts to a fence. Whipping out their Winchesters from their saddle scabbards, they continued down the alley passing Alex McKenna's stable. Bob and Emmett were sporting false beards for disguises and Grat had grown chin whiskers. But McKenna thought he recognized the Daltons as they passed him and continued to watch the heavily-armed quintet as they passed out of the alley. Grat veered left into the Condon bank with

Broadwell and Powers as Bob and Emmett crossed swiftly over to the First National. Peering through the Condon's huge plate glass window, McKenna strained his eyes and much to his surprise he saw one of the outlaws raise a Winchester at the cashier's counter. At the top of his voice he shouted: 'The bank's being robbed! The bank's being robbed!!'

As his shouts rang throughout the plaza, others picked it up. Inside the bank, the holdup men heard the alarm also but continued their business. The town, electrified, began arming themselves and scattering in different directions. Boxes were kicked over, barrels placed in position, bales of hay and other protective items were piled high to use as barricades. In the meantime the Daltons were going about robbing both banks. 'Open the safe and be quick about it,' Grat Dalton snapped at Cashier Charley Ball of the Condon Bank. 'It's a time lock. Won't open till 9.45,' Charley answered nervously. 'Open it or I'll kill you,' demanded the outlaw. 'That's only three minutes yet,' the oldest of the Daltons said, 'and we'll wait.' At that moment gunfire sounded in the plaza; the next three minutes would be crucial. Things were going a little smoother across the street for the bandits. Teller W. H. Sheppard was stuffing $21,000 in bills into grain sacks that were flung at him by Bob Dalton. 'Keep the silver out,' Bob said sharply, 'It's too heavy.' When the safe was empty, Bob and Emmett started to herd their captives out ahead of them, but a bullet smashed into the door's glass pane as they opened it.

The citizens of Coffeyville were by now rallying

PLATE 25

77 Pearl Hart (Taylor), 1898
78 Annie McDougal, 'Cattle Annie', 1894
79 Jennie Stevens, 'Little Britches', 1894

77. *Pearl Hart (Pearl Taylor) was born in Lindsay, Province of Ontario, in 1871. Brought up in a boarding school until she was 17 years old, she met and married a man named Hart. In 1893, she separated from her husband, taking up residence in Colorado. Later she was reconciled with Hart and for three years they lived in Phoenix, Arizona, raising two children, a boy and a girl. Again, in 1898, she separated from her husband, working in Arizona's mining camps as a cook and 'hard-rock' miner. Pearl met a man named Joe Boot who persuaded her to assist him in holding up the Globe stage. Not long afterward, the pair were captured near Benson, Arizona; their 'take' was a little over $400. Boot received a sentence of thirty-five years, and Pearl received a five-year sentence, but she was released after serving half her sentence. Three years later she was implicated in a train hold-up near the*

border of Arizona and New Mexico. However, having not been convicted for that crime, she was soon released. With the law enforcement office keeping an eye on her, it was hard for her to do anything without being investigated. She soon dropped out of sight, no one knowing where to or when.

78 and 79. *Annie McDougal, alias 'Cattle Annie' (center), and Jennie Stevens, alias 'Little Britches' (right), were both consorts of the Doolin gang. They were daughters of respectable but poor families living near each other in the Osage Indian Nation. If the two weren't peddling whiskey to the Indians, they were stealing cattle and horses, until they were rounded up by law officers in 1894. Both girls were sentenced to a Federal reformatory at Farmington, Massachusetts. Their short-lived outlaw days promoted many newspaper stories of their daring robberies, which, of course, were untrue . . . but, papers sold. After their release, 'Cattle Annie' returned home to live a respectable life. It was reported that 'Little Britches' returned to the slums of New York City, where she died while engaged in religious work.*

PLATE 25

77 Pearl Hart (Taylor), 1898

78 Annie McDougal, 'Cattle Annie', 1894

79 Jennie Stevens, 'Little Britches', 1894

from every direction to repel the bandits, borrowing shotguns and rifles from the hardware stores. The roar of the guns rose to a pitch that sounded like a full-scale battle. Flying lead zipped and hummed, splintering wood and sending glass crashing into slivers everywhere. Grey smoke enveloped store fronts and second-storey windows, as citizens leaped about firing and taking cover at the same time. Bob and Emmett stepped back into the bank again slamming the heavy door. They decided to leave with teller W. H. Sheppard as hostage, by the back way, which meant traversing an extra block to get to the alley. As the bandits dashed out the rear exit, they were met with heavy fire by men posted by City Marshal Charley T. Connelly to cut off just such a retreat.

Lucius Baldwin, a youth who clerked in Isham's hardware store next door to the bank, ran out of the rear entrance the same time the bandits did. Excited, Baldwin tried to head them off with pistol in hand. Bob Dalton warned the boy to drop it, to no avail. He lowered his Winchester and pulled the trigger. Baldwin dropped like a sack of potatoes with a hole in his chest. He was the first casualty. Shots were coming at them from every direction but it seemed as though the citizens were concentrating their fire at the Condon Bank. This gave Bob and Emmett hope that they might run down the street unnoticed, and turn south through an alley to reach the horses. This was their only means of escape. Two more citizens were killed, G. W. Cubine, the boot maker, and Charley T. Brown, his partner. When Baldwin fell, the bandits abandoned Sheppard and started to run, Bob with his rifle in hand at the ready, while Emmett hung on to the grain bag filled with the loot.

Arriving at Union Street, Bob spotted Cubine standing in the doorway of Rammel's drug store cradling a Winchester facing the opposite way. Bob's shot tore through his back and into his heart. Cubine's partner, Brown, an old man, reached for the rifle on the ground but Bob's deadly fire plunged him backwards onto the ground, dead. It must be said, at this point, that all the bandits carried rifles. They also carried revolvers, but evidently considered them too unreliable at the distance and relied on their Winchesters all through the battle.

Meanwhile in the Condon Bank, the remaining three minutes ticked past slowly. Bullets began shattering the bank's huge windows, and the customers who were lined against the wall, arms raised, were now hugging the floor for protection. As Dick Broadwell surveyed the street with Winchester in hand, the weight of his boots smashed thousands of glass splinters making a sharp cracking noise as he walked across the floor. Suddenly, a slug hit Broadwell's arm. 'I'm hit,' he said, grinding his teeth. By now the three minutes had passed and the vault was thrown open. While the grain sacks were being filled with paper currency, searching bullets tore through windows. It wasn't long before both customers and bankers scrambled behind and under the counter, while the bandits prepared to make a dash to safety.

Cashier T. G. Ayres, of the First National Bank, ran across the street to Isham's Hardware Store, armed himself with a Winchester and took up a position in the doorway. Not knowing that the outlaws had taken the long way around, coming up behind him, he was surprised to see Bob Dalton lower his Winchester at him and fire, the bullet striking into his cheek bone below the left eye. Bob and Emmett reached the alley almost at the same time that Grat, Broadwell and Charley Powers did. Grat ordered a fast retreat from what is now called 'Death Alley'. Bullets continued to smash and splinter anything in the way. Bill Powers was wounded in the arm, Broadwell and Bob Dalton fell almost at the same time. The heaviest fire came from Isham's hardware store and from behind wagons in front of Boswell Company Hardware.

Emmett was hit twice, in his right arm and hip, but as he fell he still clutched the sack containing the $21,000 haul. Bill Powers rose and tried to mount his horse, but a second slug brought him down. Broadwell, mortally wounded, managed to break away on horseback, but finally slipped from his saddle dead, before he had gone half a block. Emmett, seeing his brother Bob lying wounded against a pile of rocks, grabbed his horse's reins and moved toward the brother he worshipped. The 20-year-old outlaw tried to lift his bandit chieftain with the one good arm, but failed. 'I'm done for ... don't surrender ..,' Bob gasped, 'Die game!!' Just then the town liveryman and the barber stepped into the alley from behind an outhouse, and both of their double barreled shotguns roared. Emmett plunged forward with 18 buckshot in his back and shoulders. Someone shouted 'Hold your fire, boys – they're all down.'

A little more than ten minutes had passed since the Dalton gang had entered Coffeyville and wrote their bloody chapter in the annals of outlaw history. The *Journal* newspaper describing the battle counted four citizens dead, and three wounded. Out of the five outlaws, four were dead, and Emmett Dalton was badly wounded.

Five months passed before Emmett was able to face the court for the killing of two citizens of Coffeyville, Kansas, George Cubine and Lucius Baldwin, during the double bank hold-up. He was finally sentenced to a life term in the Kansas State Penitentiary at Lansing. In 1907, some 15 years later, Emmett Dalton was pardoned by Governor E. W. Hoch, after the citizens of Coffeyville presented a petition to the governor for his pardon. After his release from the 'Iron Corral', he turned churchman, and a crusader for prison reform. His sweetheart, Julia Johnson, who had waited for him all this time, now became his wife.

Thirty years after Coffeyville, they were still picking pellets out of his huge 200-pound frame. In 1931, Emmett and Julia, on what they called their second honeymoon, visited Coffeyville and the graves of his brothers, Grat and Bob Dalton. A newspaper reporter was with the pair and recorded Emmett's comments. 'I challenge the world to produce the history of an outlaw who ever got anything out of it but that – ,' Emmett remarked, as he pointed an unsteady finger at the graves of his brothers, 'or else to be huddled in a prison cell.' He died peacefully at his home in California, on July 13, 1937, the only survivor of the carnage at Coffeyville, Kansas.

Johnny (John Ringgold) Ringo was born in Texas, around 1844, was well educated and loved to read good books. Frequently moody and easily irritated, he often threatened to commit suicide. He came into prominence in Tombstone, Arizona, as a lieutenant in Curly Bill's gang of cut-throats, rustlers and holdup men. He was like a Hamlet among outlaws – introspective, darkly handsome, six foot two, lean, with somber blue eyes, and absolutely fearless. A romantic but tragic figure, Ringo had a great respect for women, good or bad; he treated them as a gentleman would. He shortened his name from Ringgold to Ringo so his three sisters, living with his grandfather Colonel Coleman Younger in San José, California, would not know of his outlawry. Ringo gambled and drank with the best of them, robbed, plundered and killed without a second thought. When Billy Breakenridge, deputy Sheriff and gunfighter in his own right, was asked who was the most outstanding gunfighter he had ever run up against, 'Johnny Ringo would have made me look like an amateur . . . ,' he said.

When drinking heavily, he once challenged Wyatt Earp to fight a handkerchief duel, but Earp, at the height of his political career, declined. When Wyatt, Virgil Earp and 'Doc' Holiday rode out to Curly Bill's

Harvey 'Kid Curry' Logan, 1865–1904, with his wife, Annie Rogers. By 1901 this noted train robber and desperado was one of the most wanted men in the country. He was the 'tiger' of the wild bunch. After Butch Cassidy fled to South America, Logan tried to organize another gang, but, after an unsuccessful train robbery, he was pursued and killed (Union Pacific Railroad Museum).

ranch to arrest him, Ringo, under the influence of alcohol, confronted them at the San Pedro River with a sawed-off shotgun. It was either turn back or face an agonizing death. The trio didn't make any fuss, and returned to town without Curly Bill.

The untimely death of Ringo is shrouded in mystery. A teamster stopping off for his noon-day lunch happened across Ringo's body, a single bullet hole in his head. He was seated on a flat rock, his head fallen onto his chest. In his right hand was his six-shooter, the hammer resting on an empty cartridge. The other five chambers were loaded and unfired. His coat, boots and horse were gone, and a portion of his underwear bound his bare feet. He had not been robbed, as his personal possessions were on him. A coroner's jury was convinced that he had committed suicide. Deputy Billy Breakenridge had run across Ringo earlier that day and stated that he was drunk and disorderly. Breakenridge was the last person to see him alive.

Ringo was buried under a giant live oak tree, and his grave can still be seen there today.

William H. Bonney (alias Billy 'the Kid'), was born in a tenement in New York on November 23, 1859. At the age of three, his parents left the slums and moved to Coffeyville, Kansas. When his father died, his mother moved to Colorado taking Billy with her. There the pretty Irish widow married William Antrim, a miner, who finally settled in Silver City, New Mexico. In a raw boom town in the early 1870s,

there were no schools. While his mother was busy running a boarding house and his stepfather off prospecting, Billy got his education in the mud-caked streets.

Stories of bandits were coming out of war-torn Missouri, of daring bank raids by a border bandit by the name of Jesse James. Young Bonney listened to these stories told by drifters who glorified them a little more each time they told them. It was probably here that the boy cultivated an interest in outlawry, and, as he took the plunge, he would have no idea that his name would rank next to the James gang in American outlaw folklore.

Billy's first disregard for the law was when he stabbed to death a bully who earlier had insulted his mother. It happened in a saloon, and the weapon he used was a penknife. The young lad fled the scene; marking the beginning of a long flight that didn't end until he walked into Pat Garrett's ambush in Pete Maxwell's bedroom in Fort Sumner, nine years later.

Ash Upson, the itinerant newspaperman who wrote a 25 cent pamphlet of *Saga of Billy the Kid* for

---

PLATE 26
80 'Butch' Cassidy, 1897
81 Mexican bandido, 1915
82 Torn Horn, 1903

80. *Robert LeRoy Parker ('Butch Cassidy') lived from April 13, 1866, to July 20, 1937. As a young man, 'Butch' worked as a cowboy on numerous ranches around Wyoming. In between jobs, he began rustling cattle but was caught and sentenced to two years in the Wyoming State Penitentiary. After being released in 1896, he returned to crime, forming the notorious 'Wild Bunch'. Cassidy engineered a number of bank and train robberies. After each hold-up, they would retire to their hideout in the 'Hole-in-the-Wall' country of Wyoming, and after the excitement had blown over would return to their headquarters in small cities of Texas. The gang slowly was apprehended or killed, besides, the long arm of the Pinkertons was always close at hand. Cassidy and Harry Longbaugh, along with Etta Place, a clever master of horsemanship and expert rifle shot, fled to the Argentine Republic in South America, where they, it was said, had joined Harvey Logan. Retiring there as cattle ranchers for two years, they began holding-up banks and mule trains from rich mines. They were last heard of shooting it out with soldiers in the Spring of 1908 in San Vicente, Bolivia, where Longbaugh was reported killed and Cassidy slipped through the soldiers in a stolen uniform, and managed to escape to the coast. Illustrated here is Cassidy dressed as a rancher.*

81. *A typical Mexican bandido (or bandit) of the early turn of the century. Banditry in Mexico had its deep roots not in Mexican depravity but in the social-economic situation, and derived*

historically directly from a hundred years of civil strife. Guerrilla warfare is the characteristic fighting technique of the peon. After every great wave of invasion or rebellion, there always were certain guerrilla bands who refused to go back to the clutches of the hacienda—store and the mercy of the 'jefe politics'. Armed and trained for instantaneous action, these hardened men, accustomed to living off the country, turned to banditry as readily as a masterless mustang returns to the mesa.

On March 16, 1916, the revolutionary bandit leader, Pancho Villa, with a force of 400 bandidos crossed over the Mexican border into the United States and ruthlessly raided Columbus, New Mexico, which almost brought the USA to the brink of war with Mexico.

82. *Tom Horn, (Nov 21, 1860, to Nov 20, 1903) held many jobs. The way he dressed, he looked more like a well-to-do businessman than a hired killer. He hired out as a cowboy, railroad worker, stagecoach driver, army scout, teamster, part-time law officer, Pinkerton detective and a hired range detective, his last function. While working for a cattle company, in 1894, technically as a bronc buster, his real job was eliminating both rustlers and troublesome homesteaders. After his victim had fallen with a .30-.30 rifle shell through him, Horn would leave his trademark — a set of two stones under the head of the dead man. Each job gained him $600, and he would travel to Denver or Cheyenne to spend his bloody earnings on women and drown his brain in a drunken spree. Tom Horn was finally pushed into a drunken confession, and his statement led to a conviction for murdering a 14-year-old boy. Up until his hanging, Tom insisted on his innocence.*

PLATE 26

80   'Butch' Cassidy, 1897

81   Mexican bandido, 1915

82   Tom Horn, 1903

E. D. Nix, former US Marshal of Oklahoma; Al Jennings, former train robber and bandit who led the Jennings Gang; and Chris Madsen, former deputy US Marshal, who delivered the outlaw Jennings to the Penitentiary after he was convicted. Photographed in Houston, Texas, in 1937 (author's collection).

Colt Frontier sixshooter. Other weapons varied from a concealed sawn-off shotgun to a big caliber Winchester rifle. Gunfights were generally narrowed down to pistols, which were much more easily carried around on the person in a concealed fashion. Many styles of carrying a pistol were devised by the shootist. Two or more pistols were tucked into a man's waist band, which was a wide scarf doubled over and wrapped around his middle. Hidden pockets were preferred by gamblers and were sewn in a number of places throughout their clothing ... where a weapon could be easily reached when necessary. Shoulder holsters were becoming fashionable. Hidden directly beneath the arm pit and strapped around the chest, they showed little evidence of a concealed weapon. Only a few books on today's market have bothered to mention the types of weapons used by the famous

Tom Horn (1860–1903) had many unusual talents. From being a cowboy, railroad employee and stage driver, he also worked as an Army scout, law officer, Pinkerton detective, range detective, soldier and hired gun. As a cattle detective in Wyoming he was accused of murdering a young boy, which resulted in his hanging in 1903 (courtesy Carl Briehan).

Pat Garrett, the man who shot the Kid one year earlier, tried to make a legend out of him. Years later, Upson ghosted another paperback for Pat Garrett, *The Authentic Life of Billy the Kid*, a hair-raising legend of a boy in his early teens roaming the Western plains as a fearless gunslinger, dead shot, superb horseman and a polished gambler – all boldly achieved in knee-pants.

Billy was 21 when he was planted beneath the sod at Fort Sumner, July 15, 1881, and, as legend has it, he had killed 21 men for his 21 years, not mentioning Mexicans and Indians.

The outlaws covered in this chapter are only a small segment of breeds that terrorized the West and kept lawmen uncomfortably on their toes tracking them down. There are far too many to mention; however, listed here are their weapons and calibers that they felt comfortable with while they committed their cruel acts against the public. The era of the Western Gunfighter lasted only 35 years on the American frontier, from the end of the Civil War until a little after 1900 when frontier justice put an end to this lawlessness.

The gunfighters' and outlaws' 'tools of trade' covered a wide selection, from a pin fire pistol, which put a somewhat large hole in a man, to the popular gunfighters, who drew their weapons on impulse – and asked questions later. This list is an attempt to identify the individual gunfighters' weapon, as well as its manufacturer and caliber.

The names of criminals below were picked at random and are not in alphabetical order.

Jesse James: Smith & Wesson Schofield, Single Action, 6 shot, .45 caliber (1875). Colt Single Action, 6 shot, .45 caliber, (1873).

Frank James: Remington Army model, .44 caliber (cartridge).

John Wesley Hardin: Colt, double action Lightning, .38 caliber.

Sam Bass: Colt, Single Action Army, .45 caliber.

Billy the Kid: .38 caliber double action Colt Lightning, and .44 caliber Colt, sheriff's model.

Butch Cassidy: .44 caliber, Colt Frontier model (cartridge).

Cole Younger: Colt Navy, .36 caliber percussion, model 1851, also Colt Single Action Army .45 caliber (7½ in barrel).

Jim Younger: Same as his brother Cole.

Dalton brothers:

  Grat: Colt, Single Action Army, .44–40 caliber.

  Emmett: Colt, .44–40 caliber.

  Bob: Colt, .44–40 caliber.

  Bill: A variety of calibers, Colts, .44–40 and .45 calibers (cartridge).

  Frank: A variety of calibers, Colts .44–40 and .45 calibers (cartridge).

Poncho Villa: .44 caliber, Mervin & Hubert.

Clay Allison: Colt Single Action, .45 caliber, Peacemaker (Model 1873) 5½ inch barrel.

Frank Leslie: Colt Single Action, .45 caliber, Peacemaker (Model 1875) 7½ inch barrel.

Henry Starr: Colt Single Action Army, .45 caliber. New service model of 1909.

Wild Bill Longley: Confederate Dance, .44 caliber, Model 1863, percussion.

Al Jennings: .45 caliber Army Colt.

Joaquin Murriette: .44 caliber Colt Dragoon, percussion.

Tom Horn: .30–30 caliber Winchester rifle.

Most of the Western characters presented here had numerous other weapons during their heyday as out-

Myra Maybelle Shirley (Belle Starr) 1848–89, shown here with her outlaw-lover, Blue Duck. Belle married Bruce Younger, Sam Starr and at various periods went around with Blue Duck, Jim French, Jack Spaniard, and finally settled down with Jim Starr. Both Belle and Sam Starr were wanted for robbery, murder and treason with a $10,000 reward over their heads. Next to Belle (sitting) is Blue Duck, an Indian outlaw leader who rustled cattle and horses and held up small banks and stages in Indian Territory. Belle was queen of his gang for a short period. At far right is Jim Reed, son of Belle Starr.

laws. Because of the many other weapons they possessed, it would be difficult to list them all.

When we talk about the Wild West, we do not mean the wild wilderness but the lawless wild living – with fighting, violence, disorder and killing. Not the grandeur of an untamed wilderness but a staged setting of undisciplined and violent men who defied the frontier laws. Journalists misapplied the acts of outlaws by portraying their exploits in newspapers and books as heroic deeds. The West was not 'romantic' to a Westerner, but to the Easterner, who could not shake hands with famous lawmen, sit in on Indian parleys, scout a vast wilderness, tote a six-shooter, ride a horse in a cattle drive or walk the wooden sidewalks with high heeled boots. It was the East that set the standards, and dubbed the cowboys, bandits and a few marshals as 'romantics'. The public chose to depict them as heroes who robbed the rich only to give to the poor. These so-called heroes will forever ride their gallant steeds across the Western Plains in memory and in novels.

9 Famous Lawmen and Agencies

A great proportion of superb lawmen in the early West did not use their badges as a shield for illegal acts. These men usually found their way to 'boot-hill' with but a few words said over them, and as for their epitaphs – few had any at all. Their deeds were not immortalized in song but their authority in office was praised by law-abiding citizens. Yet their stories were buried in the back pages of newspapers, simply because they were not colorful enough to become heroic figures. Of the more famous lawmen, here are a number of colorful characters the West produced.

'Wild Bill' Hickok bragged that he was an expert with a six-gun and boasted of killing over 35 men. He was more the professional gambler during his career as a lawman and probably fought most of his duels in a saloon rather than in the streets of a frontier town. Bill was born in Troy Grove, Illinois (LaSalle County) in 1837, and was an Army scout during the Civil War as well as in the Indian Wars in 1868. In 1871, he was the two-gun Marshal of Abiline who gunned down a boisterous cowboy and accidentally killed one of his own policemen. His career ended shortly after that incident, and he roamed the West, boozing, gambling and was even thrown in jail for vagrancy. He finally landed in a Deadwood city saloon, in 1876, and, while playing poker, was shot in the back of the head by 'Crooked Nose' Jack McCall. In his hand he held a pair of Aces and Eights – 'dead man's hand'.

When he worked at it, Wyatt Earp was an efficient lawman, but whatever history writes of the man he was not the town tamer. In Wichita, 1875–76, he served as a policeman without much success, and later on two occasions he acted as assistant Marshal in Dodge City in 1876–77, and again in 1878–79. Tombstone was just emerging as a new mining town, and with his brothers, Virgil, Morgan and James, Wyatt Earp took up residence there, followed later by Doc Holiday. Virgil became assistant Marshal, subsequently serving as acting Marshal. Morgan rode shotgun on a Tucson stage, and James served as bartender in the local saloon. Wyatt was fortunate enough to find a Faro table where his brother James served the local townspeople. Trouble soon erupted between the Earps and the Clanton and McLowery brothers, supposed cattlemen who were suspected of rustling cattle in addition to raising hell in Tombstone. The feud reached a climax at the famous OK Corral, where the Earps and Doc Holiday killed Billy Clanton, Tom and Frank McLowery on October 26, 1881. Virgil was wounded in the leg, and Morgan was wounded in the shoulder. Doc Holiday was also wounded but recovered. Three months after this battle at the OK Corral, Virgil Earp was shot from ambush and again wounded, and before he recovered, his brother, Morgan Earp, was killed in March, 1882, while playing a game of pool. His slayer was identified as Frank Stillwell, who was later killed by Wyatt Earp.

Virgil Earp died of pneumonia on October 19, 1906, at the age of 65, in Goldfield, Nebraska. James Earp expired in Los Angeles, California in 1926, at the age of 80 years. Wyatt went to the Klondike region and opened a saloon, where he spent several years, returning to spend his last days in peace and quiet in the California circles. He finally died at his Los Angeles home in California, January 13, 1929.

After working a few years at buffalo hunting and scouting for the US Army, Bat Masterson showed up in Dodge City in 1876, where his brother Jim ran a saloon and his older brother Ed was assistant Marshal. Ed was killed later by two drunken cowboys in 1878, and Jim served as Marshal from 1879 to 1881. Bat kept busy with his gambling, but was also elected sheriff of Ford County. In 1879, he was defeated, and after several years he pulled up stakes and headed for Trinidad, Colorado, where he established himself as town Marshal. But he insisted on gambling, losing both money and friends, and finally, heavily in debt, he was asked to leave. Bat dealt Faro in Denver in 1900 and again he was invited to leave. In 1902, he found his way to New York, and was arrested for cheating at cards. His influence with local politicians helped him beat the rap. Bat became a well known sports writer in New York and Denver, where he also operated Faro games and other forms of gambling.

President 'Teddy' Roosevelt was enchanted by the romance of the adventures Bat had experienced in his

Right to left: James, Virgil, Morgan Earp (Arizona Historical Society).

early life and appointed him deputy US Marshal, which he served in good capacity for two years. When a change of political parties deprived him of his office, he became a sports editor for a New York newspaper, where he died at his desk in 1921 while writing this last entry, 'Pretty good world after all . . .' etc.

Chris Madsen was born in Denmark in 1857, and later served in the Franco-Prussian War while still a young man. When he heard of the American Indian Wars, he left Europe in 1870 for America and headed West for adventure. Before he entered the US Army, Chris served as a government scout for some time, where he had full charge of the Indian Scouts in Wyoming and in the Indian Territory. Later he became a Quartermaster Sergeant with the 5th Cavalry.

Madsen participated in a number of Indian engagements where he served in Arizona against the Apaches, campaigned in Wyoming against the Sioux and Cheyennes, and managed to keep his scalp in the Nez Perce engagements in Idaho and Utah.

Because he fell in with the right groups at the right time, he was selected as escort for President Arthur's Yellowstone Expedition as Deputy US Marshal in 1889 and then under US Marshal Evett Nix in the 1890s. His service as a law officer compelled him to take part in many gun battles with outlaws. He delivered the notorious train robber Al Jennings to the penitentiary, and after Jennings' release they became great friends.

The 7th Cavalry, under the command of Lt Col George A. Custer, enlisted Madsen's service as scout in 1876, but Madsen was away on scout duty when

Custer fell under the mighty Sioux on June 25, 1876, at the Little Big Horn.

This remarkable man's life ended peacefully in 1947, when he expired at the ripe old age of 90 years.

Heck Thomas was born in Atlanta, Georgia, on June 5, 1850, where he grew up and enlisted into the Confederate Army at the age of 12 years. He was a courier for Stonewall Jackson's Brigade, and after the war he was an express messenger on the Texas Central Railroad, when he saved $22,000 of the Express Company's money by hiding it in a stove. Sam Bass, one of the holdup men, shot through the door of the express car with his pistol, the bullet striking Thomas in one of his eyes, seriously injuring him. When Thomas was appointed a Deputy US Marshal, he worked under District Judge Parker, 'The Hanging Judge', out of Fort Smith, Ark. He helped break up the Sam Bass gang in Texas, and the Dalton and Bill Doolin gang besides several other gangs terrorizing the Oklahoma and Indian Territories.

Heck was elected the first Chief of Police of Lawton, Oklahoma, later to be accepted into the US Marshal's office again. He helped introduce the French 'Bertillon System', which was just being instituted in this country. It was a system of identification based on measuring the human body and its parts and photographing images and any scars or blemishes that were noticeable. Thomas carried two pistols, but his favorite weapon was a shotgun, the same one that cut down the notorious Bill Doolin. Chris Madsen, Bill Tilghman and Heck Thomas were known as 'the Three Guardsmen' in the wild outlaw days. Death came peacefully to Heck Thomas at Lawton, Oklahoma, August 15, 1912.

Bill Tilghman was born at Fort Dodge, Iowa, in 1854, during the time his parents were searching for a new route westward. Fort Dodge was already abandoned in 1849, because the removal of the Winnebago Indians made the post unnecessary. After realizing there wasn't any future in settling down there, the family moved to Kansas where young Bill grew up and found a lucrative trade as a buffalo hunter and an Indian scout. As he began to travel, he found a steady line of work, but a dangerous one, as city Marshal at Dodge City during the town's wild and hair-raising days. There he served a short term of three years experiencing everything imaginable in a flourishing frontier town of itinerant lawless men. It was here that Tilghman chalked up a distinguished gunfighting record.

Bill was offered the Sheriff's office in Ford County, Kansas, and he took it. For four years he hunted and captured some of the meanest outlaws of the Southwest.

When Oklahoma territory opened in 1889, Tilghman agreed to serve as the first City Marshal of Perry, another town just as rough and tough as Dodge City. Later he became a deputy under US Marshal Evett Nix, where he apprehended such outlaws as Henry Starr, Bill Doolin, and two teenagers 'Cattle Annie' McDougal and Jennie 'Little Britches' Stevens, whose careers in crime were short-lived.

Tilghman later served as Chief of Police in Oklahoma City and subsequently as City Marshal of Cromwell. On November 1, 1924, while eating in a restaurant, he heard several shots outside. Hurrying outside he found a disorderly drunk trying to 'tree the town'. While disarming him and searching for some identification, the drunk produced another pistol hidden in his coat lining and shot Bill. Later it was found that the drunkard was Wylie Lynn, then a federal prohibition agent. Bill died in a few minutes on a dusty couch in a nearby used furniture store.

Probably the most outstanding early Western judge to ever hold a seat on the bench of the Frontier was Isaac Charles Parker. This former Congressman from Missouri was appointed to the Federal District Court in Fort Smith Arkansas in 1875, with jurisdiction over Indian Territory, so infested with outlaws and cut-throats that newspapers refered to that area as 'Robber's Roost'.

In his 21 years on the bench, Parker sent more than 74 men to the gallows that he had erected outside his courtroom. Sixty-five of his Deputy Marshals were gunned down in the line of duty during those years.

His swift justice and sternness came from his dealings with hardened criminals, and he would not tolerate anything that would weaken justice in his jurisdiction. He was 36 years old when he was appointed to the bench and he expired in 1896 at the age of 57. He was the only judge known in the early West as the 'Hanging Judge'.

Not every peace officer had a badge pinned to his coat to show official rank. Ribbons were used in place of badges with an imprint of the official office upon it. A hat band may have also served the same purpose, until a badge could be struck. Companies manufacturing badges were in business as early as 1868. Catalogs showed nickel-plated badges, and those made of German silver, all engraved meticulously in a variety of shapes and designs with gold inlaid, silver, steel, copper, brass and tin. Prices ranged from $1.50 and up. Stock items were cheaper and only the engraving was additional. Eastern salesmen from various companies brought with them a number of cases with various styles along with blank badges, a letter punch and number set, tools, and a chart of available letters to choose from. Many badges were made in a makeshift manner. Mexican silver pesos were fashioned into badges by jewelers with a five point star inside a circle carved from it. The term 'Tin Star' was a slang expression for a small town law man. More than one tin star was cut from the bottom of a tin can, until an official badge was presented.

THE TEXAS RANGERS

The Texas Rangers originated in 1823, when Stephen F. Austin, known as the 'Father of Texas', contracted to bring 300 families to settle in the Spanish Province of Texas. There were already more than 600 hardy colonists from all parts of the United States in Texas at that time. These people settled not far from the Gulf of Mexico. Their neighbors were comprised of Mexicans, who lived as far North as San Antonio, and the troublesome Indians, mainly Comanches. There was no army on that remote frontier to chase Indians and keep peace, and thus Austin became concerned for the settlers' safety. He organized ten dedicated men to 'range' over wide areas between designated rivers and scout the movements of Indians. From these 'ranging' activities, the Rangers derived their name. On the eve of the Texas War for Independence, the leaders of Texas were impressed by Austin's paid volunteers and their success. Realizing the need for a national law enforcement agency, they officially organized three companies of Texas Rangers in October, 1835. During the period of the Republic of Texas, 1836 to 1846, the Rangers became better established.

There were many efforts to disband the group, but because they were less expensive than an army and more effective and dependable, they were always called back into service. Rangers knew no military discipline. They were always independent. They did not accept a leader unless they knew he had courage, better judgement and physical strength to outlast his men on long hard marches. The leader, or Ranger Captain, never ordered his men to 'go', but to 'come', and it was part of their tradition for an officer to be the first to lead the way in any place of danger.

When the disastrous Texas-Santa Fe Expedition set out from near Austin to open trade with Santa Fe in June of 1841, it resulted in misfortune and was captured by the Mexicans. When the Mexican Government learned of this, General Rafael Vasquez was dispatched to the town of San Antonio in 1842, holding the town for two days before he withdrew toward the

Commodore Perry Owens (1852–1918) held many professions before becoming Sheriff of Apache County, in Arizona. He sported long hair and carried a brace of .45 caliber, 7½ inch barrel Colts and two rifles. Owens had a reputation as a dead shot against Apache Indians. In 1887 he was involved in a gunfight in which he shot down four opponents resisting arrest. Tom Horn served as deputy Sheriff under Owens.

Henry (Heck) Andrew Thomas, in later years (1850–1912). One of the famous 'Three Guardsmen' Thomas served as deputy US Marshal in 1877 and tracked many outlaws in the Indian Nation territory. In 1883 he was appointed Texas Ranger and was credited in helping break up the Dalton, Doolin and Casey Gang, along with many others (author's collection).

Rio Grande. The Texas Rangers followed him, but faced with such a large enemy force, were unable to attack. Battle after battle ensued between the Rangers and Mexican forces, with the Rangers winning some and losing some. Meanwhile the Texans who came from the United States grew tired of being a separate colony; help from the North was needed to carry on a continuous battle with the Mexicans and Indians. In 1846, the Lone Star flag was lowered and the Stars and Bars were raised. Mexico was furious about Texas joining the Union, and promptly sent an army in protest. General Taylor called upon the Rangers to act as scouts and spies. The US Army did not continue on until the Rangers had scouted the way and then led the charge when the battle began.

Sam Colt of Connecticut, famous for his revolver, was contracted to produce over 100 revolvers for the Rangers. When the weapons arrived in the hands of the Rangers they were eager to try them out on the

PLATE 27
83 'Wild Bill' Hickok, 1876
84 Ben Thompson, 1880
85 'Bat' Masterson, 1889

83. *James Butler Hickok ('Wild Bill') (May 27, 1837, to August 2, 1876) was born in Troy Grove, Illinois. As a young man in his teens, he proved to be a crack shot with firearms and seemed to be adept with his fists. At 18, Hickok wandered to St Louis, and from there to Kansas. Bill drove a stage coach on the Santa Fe Trail, and in 1860 Russell, Majors and Waddell employed him as wagon master. Hickok's first gunfight was with Dave McCanles, at the Rock Creek Station on the Oregon Trail in Nebraska. During the Civil War, Hickok was hired on as a Union wagon master in Sedalia, Missouri, and later posed as a spy and guide. After the war, he fell into gambling, and while in Springfield, Missouri, he killed Dave Tutt in a street fight. When Hickok fled to Fort Riley in the late fall of 1866, he was hired out by Lt. Col. Custer to scout for the 7th Cavalry. Later, he found employment in law enforcement as a deputy US marshal, chasing thieves that stole government livestock and army deserters.*

In August, 1869, he was elected sheriff in Hays City, a wild and most dangerous town on the frontier. In less than three months, he killed two men. From a Wild West show he went to Abilene in 1871, where he accepted to be city marshal for $150 a month. Here he became involved in a tragic shooting incident. Hickok killed Phil Coe and accidently shot and killed his own deputy. In 1872, 'Wild Bill' teamed up with Buffalo Bill Cody's troupe and was billed as 'Scouts of the Prairie'; 1874 found Bill back in the West, but two years later he was arrested in Cheyenne for vagrancy. The same year he married circus owner Agnes Lake, but after two weeks the lure of gold in Deadwood City broke up the honeymoon. Arriving in Deadwood City, Dakota Territory, he picked up at the gambling tables. On August 2, 1876, in Deadwood's saloon number 10, while playing cards with three other friends, his back to a partially open door, Bill was shot in the back of the head by 'Crooked Nose' Jack McCall. In his hand he held 'Aces and Eights', later termed as Dead Man's Hand. In this illustration, Bill wears 2 pistols tucked in a red sash, butts forward beneath his coat.

84. *Ben Thompson, (November 11, 1842, to March 11, 1884), had many occupations. As an ex-confederate soldier, Ben worked as a printer, gambler, Texas Ranger, saloonist and as a law officer. He participated in fourteen gunfights during his lifetime. Fond of gambling, Thompson traveled to Kansas in 1871, and opened the Bull's Head Saloon in the roaring cattle town of Abilene, Texas. His partner was an old friend, Phil Coe, whom 'Wild Bill' Hickok later shot and killed. A series of problems followed Ben. He and his family had a serious accident, injuring*

his wife, son and himself. He soon sold the business and returned to Texas. After 2 years, he returned to Kansas after having sampled the prosperity of the cattle towns. Again, he became involved with a number of shoot-outs and was arrested many times and thrown into jail. In 1879, Ben was defeated for the office of Austin City Marshal, but ran again in 1881 and won. He proved to be a fair and excellent officer; however, after killing Jack Harris in Harris' Variety Theatre in San Antonio, he resigned his office and turned to drinking. In March, 1884, Ben and a friend Kingfisher were killed in a shoot-out at Harris' Variety Theatre in San Antonio.

85. *William Barclay ('Bat') Masterson (November 26, 1853, to October 25, 1921). From farming, buffalo hunter, army scout, gambler, saloonist, law officer, gunfighter, to sports writer and prizefight promoter, Bat had led an exciting life. In 1872, he and brother Ed journeyed to Dodge City, where Bat accepted a grading contract for the Atchison, Topeka and Santa Fe Railroad. However, buffalo hunting was reaching its peak by this time and Bat wanted to get in on some of the kill. Following the Adobe Walls battle in the Texas panhandle, Bat joined up with General Nelson A. Miles as a scout, where he served for three months and was discharged on October 12, 1874. Dodge City saw Masterson again in 1877. He somehow received an appointment as deputy sheriff of Ford County, and his brother Ed became policeman in Dodge City. In November of the same year, Bat was elected sheriff of Ford County, where he apprehended numerous thieves and killers. In April, 1878, Ed was killed in a shoot-out, but Bat continued his duties as sheriff until he was awarded an appointment as deputy US Marshal in January, 1879. Bat, unconcerned by his present duties, was hired out to lead a posse of gunmen to back up the Santa Fe Railroad in a dispute with the Denver & Rio Grande line over right-of-way territory. In 1879, Masterson was defeated after a close election for sheriff. Footloose and fancy free, he drifted into Colorado, New Mexico, and then to Nebraska. He lived in Kansas City for a while until 1881, where he and a few friends visited the new boomtown of Tombstone. Bat stayed for a few months before returning to Dodge City for the serious business of helping brother Jim in another shoot-out. Around 1883, Bat began writing short columns for newspapers besides being interested in the line of sports, especially as promoter of horse races and prizefights.*

After he married Emma Walters in 1891, Bat continued writing, making his home in Denver. Eleven years later he moved to New York, where, for two decades, he continued as a sports writer. In 1905, President 'Teddy' Roosevelt appointed Bat as deputy federal marshal, but after two years he resigned. After establishing himself with noted figures and various night spots of New York, a tired Bat Masterson slumped finally over his work desk, dead from a heart attack. He was 68 years old.

PLATE 27

83 'Wild Bill' Hickok, 1876

84 Ben Thompson, 1880

85 'Bat' Masterson, 1889

Tracking outlaws. A man had to be an outdoorsman, knowledgeable in scouting and tracking, as well as being 'half-Indian'. He chose the best in firearms, equipment and horses. It did not make any difference if they were Rangers or half-baked deputy Sheriffs, bringing them in dead or alive was their job (Red River Gun Leather and Clothing, posing is Bill Evans).

Indians. While in pursuit of a band of Indians, guns blazing, the Indians escaped, wanting no part of the men who had a shot for every finger on one hand. It seemed that, finally, an ideal weapon had been introduced to the Rangers, who found it very effective. Some changes were later made at the suggestion of Sam Walker, and a second Colt Model revolver was developed known as the famous 'Walker Colt'.

Between 1848 and 1858, the Rangers saw active duty off and on. Fugitives, Indian bands, and small groups of Mexican raiders were chased. In 1858 they were officially called back into service and paid with Texas funds. Finding their enemy and hitting him hard became tradition. As more white settlers moved into Texas to settle, the Rangers found that it was now the white man who became a problem. The difference did not stop there. White fugitives were

apprehended and dealt with the same as a Mexican or Indian.

From 1860 through the Civil War, and continuing for ten years after, the Rangers were heard little of. But, in 1874, they were reorganized by the new Governor when the Indians began battling the white migration. And since the army had been withdrawn from service to carry on the Civil War, 'Lawless Men', either alone or in groups, were terrorizing the settlers. Also, in 1874, Major John B. Jones organized a Frontier Battalion of Rangers, totalling five companies. They patrolled the territory from the Red River to the Rio Grande along the Western front. It was common practice for an officer to visit each company periodically. The Rangers wore no uniforms. Each man slept on the ground on a blanket from his bedroll and had a good horse, a good pair of boots, a wide-brimmed hat, and chose whatever garment to wear in between. His rifle and pistol was of a large caliber and always kept close to him night and day. Food was very simple and he cooked it himself. All in all, he traveled very light and was often gone for long periods of time.

The border counties were besieged by desperados who were more cunning and dangerous than the Indians. In order to track down each of these 'Lawless Men', a list containing 3,000 names of thieves, robbers and highwaymen was prepared and issued to each Ranger Captain. Since the only problem now was that these men were white, dressed the same and were nearly as intelligent as the Rangers, they were hard to identify. The Ranger became more of a 'peace officer' than an Indian fighter. Rangers were organized into companies, not regiments or brigades. A company would be in the charge of a captain or lieutenant and might even have a sergeant. Headquarters were in Austin, Texas, where Captains reported to the Headquarters officer. Requirements were similar to those for a cowboy. 'Can you ride?' 'Can you cook?' 'Can you shoot a gun?' Rangers were often labeled a 'Cowboy with a commission'. By the late nineteenth century, Rangers were becoming involved in detective work, following violators known as fence cutters and isolated cases of horse and cattle theft. By 1901, the Frontier Battalion was abolished and a new Ranger force was created. Under this new regulation, each Ranger was considered an officer, and could perform all duties exercised by any other peace officer.

Through the Mexican revolution, around 1910, and the 1917 great West Texas oil boom, the Rangers were kept busy keeping peace. Revolution, Prohibition and oil booms all came at once, making demands on the Texas Rangers which they couldn't meet. The First World War even involved the Rangers when it was discovered that Germany and Japan were planning to assist the Mexicans to recapture Texas. Many innocent persons were killed and murdered by degenerated Rangers, causing an investigation of the Texas Rangers by the state of Texas Legislature. The investigation began in January, 1919, and caused a series of cutbacks in the force to four companies of not more than 15 men. Captain Frank Hamer, the last Ranger of the old school, was best remembered for his clean-up campaigns in the oil boom towns, 'Hamer's War' in 1927 and '28 on the Texas Bankers Association, and the pursuit and death of Clyde Barrow and Bonnie Parker in 1934. Today, as a law enforcement branch of the Texas Department of Public Safety, the Rangers, now a sophisticated force of 94 men that includes a Senior Ranger Captain, an assistant to the Senior Ranger Captain, six Captains, six Sergeants, and 80 Privates, have developed and kept peace over a century and a half with a proud tradition.

PINKERTON AGENTS

Allan Pinkerton left Scotland a fugitive, with a royal warrant for his arrest after being involved in workers' agitation for political reform in Britain. Dodging the authorities who were hot on his heels, he had enough time to pack his things, wed his sweetheart and head for the high seas, and sanctuary in North America. Landing first in Canada and later moving on to Michigan, Pinkerton and his bride finally settled in Illinois.

By 1843, this penniless fugitive from British justice set about manufacturing barrels in Dundee, Illinois, a trade he had learned in his homeland. After several years, his business acumen had won him a thriving trade; then, one day in 1847, a chain of events altered his life. Quite by accident, Pinkerton's alertness uncovered a band of coin counterfeiters which he led the county sheriff to arrest. Later, the town discovered that bogus bank notes were being passed around and naturally turned to neighbor Pinkerton for assistance. The runaway barrel maker soon found himself called upon from every quarter to undertake matters that required his detective skill. In 1848 he accepted an offer to serve as a deputy in the Cook County Sheriff's office. Now completely involved with crime solving, his good reputation earned him an appointment as Chicago's first full time police detective.

Charles A. Siringo (1855–1928). Well known as a cowboy detective all over the West, chasing rustlers, bandits and murderers. In the 1890s, Siringo worked for the famous Pinkerton Agency for 22 years (Union Pacific Railroad Museum Collection).

In 1850, Pinkerton and Edward A. Rucker, a young attorney, opened their own private detective agency, the Northwestern Police Agency. Business grew rapidly as it was the first of its kind in the country. By 1856, the agency signed contracts to protect the property of several Midwest railroads, and his clientele had become national in scope. Pinkerton's rapid success grew out of the circumstances of the times, where there was no local police force capable of handling a delicate situation in crime detecting, because most were undermanned, and there was no centralized federal police agency at all. Where the local police was unable to pursue a fleeing criminal into a jurisdiction other than their own, the Pinkerton agency could. By 1860, Alan Pinkerton's offices rapidly expanded geographically and its activities broadened as criminals multiplied and crime increased. A staring, unblinking eye and the phrase 'We Never Sleep' was the agency's advertising identity.

Just before the Civil War exploded, Pinkerton was on the trail of rebel conspirators. In 1861, he learned of an alleged plot in Baltimore to assassinate President-elect Abraham Lincoln. The cunning Pinkerton helped pursuade Lincoln to travel at night in disguise. Lincoln arrived safely in Washington aboard a special train early the next morning. In August, just

after the Union defeat at the first Battle of Bull Run, Pinkerton went to Washington to officially organize and head the Secret Service for General George B. McClellan's new Army of the Potomac. However, in November 1862, he resigned as Chief of the Secret Service, and following the surrender of the Confederates he returned to Chicago to resume his office as private investigator. During the Civil War, both sons of Allan Pinkerton, William and Robert, had worked with their father, and now joined the Chicago firm. At the death of their father in 1884, both sons proved themselves able administrators.

By the turn of the century, the Pinkerton Agency's

PLATE 28
86 Wyatt Earp, 1881
87 'Doc' Holliday, 1881
88 'Heck' Thomas, 1894

86. *Wyatt Berry Stapp Earp (March 19, 1848, to January 13, 1929) came from a farm family in Monmouth, Illinois. He also worked as a section hand on a railroad, was hired as a buffalo hunter, keeper of a saloon, gambler, law officer and prospector. By 1875, Wyatt served as city policeman in Wichita, where he made routine arrests. Shortly thereafter, he was relieved of his duties and told to 'get out of town!' From there he wrangled another job as policeman in Dodge City, in 1876. After two years of wandering around Texas, he assumed a position as assistant marshal of Dodge. In the late fall of 1879, Earp left Dodge City with his tail between his legs. He was publicly beaten up by a huge cowboy named Red Sweeney, over the affections of a 'soiled dove'. Upon an invitation from his brothers, Earp headed to Las Vegas, New Mexico, where he met up again with 'Doc' Holliday. Within a few months, brothers James and Virgil Earp settled in Tombstone, Arizona, along with their families, and Wyatt followed. Tombstone was an open town. Here Wyatt became a shotgun guard for Wells Fargo, and was frequently fond of collecting 'easy money' across the poker tables. Soon Morgan and Warren Earp appeared in Tombstone, followed by John Henry ('Doc') Holliday.*

By July, 1880, Wyatt, after unsuccessfully trying to obtain a sheriff's appointment, settled for deputy sheriff of Tombstone. Within a year, a feud developed between the Clanton and McLowery brothers and the Earps. The feud spilled over in gunplay at the 'OK Corral', October 1881, with Wyatt, Morgan, Virgil Earp and 'Doc' Holliday on one side, and Ike and Billy Clanton, Tom and Frank McLowery and Billy Claiborne on the other. Tom, Frank McLowery and Billy Clanton were killed, Virgil Earp was wounded in the leg and Morgan Earp was wounded in the shoulder. Both recovered. After that, Wyatt traveled considerably, and finally settled down for several years in the Klondike region, prospecting and running a saloon. California was his last home. At his Los Angeles home, Wyatt Earp died peacefully on January 13, 1929. For six years, he had

an exceptionally good record for a man who upheld law and order in a country where killing a man was of frequent occurrence.

87. *John Henry ('Doc') Holliday (1852–1887) had all the qualities of being a great dentist, if . . . tuberculosis had not cut his career short. By 1873, 'Doc' traveled west, seeking a climate which might postpone his imminent death. However, after 15 years of dodging the 'grim reaper', he acquired a staggering reputation as a beady-eyed executioner while still practising his occupation as a part-time dentist. At times, it looked like his occupation was nothing more than drinking and gambling. 'Doc' appeared in many Western boom towns during their heydays. In Dodge City he killed a man who had drawn a gun on Wyatt Earp, saving Earp's life by a split second. The two became close friends from then on. When Wyatt left Kansas for Tombstone, Arizona, 'Doc' followed later.*

At the OK Corral battle, 'Doc' stood shoulder to shoulder with the Earps, where he was slightly wounded. His sawed-off double-barrel shotgun, with its stock cut considerably back, was a great help to his friends in holding off Earp's arch enemies. Holliday figured prominently in Tombstone's affairs, along with his mistress, 'Big Nose Kate Elder'.

As his health continued to wither he was advised by friends to travel to Colorado, a sanitarium at Glenwood Springs. It was here, in 1887, that he died as a young man of 35 years old.

88. *Henry Andrew ('Heck') Thomas (January 6, 1850, to August 11, 1912) served in the Confederate army in Stonewall Jackson's brigade as a courier, then afterwards as a railroad guard, detective, and law officer. Heck appears here as he usually looked while serving as a Deputy US Marshal in Oklahoma. He served with Bill Tilghman and Chris Madsen under US Marshal E. D. Nix. During a three-year period, 1893–96, Heck was responsible for arresting more than 300 wanted criminals. He became noted as one of the 'Three Guardsmen' (Heck Thomas, Tilghman, and Madsen). Thomas also spent seven years as chief of police in Lawton, but in 1909 he lost the job due to ill health. He died within three years at age 62. He is also credited for incorporating a number of systems in criminal identification, including experimenting with 'Match-up' finger prints found at various crimes.*

PLATE 28

86   Wyatt Earp, 1881   87   'Doc' Holliday, 1881   88   'Heck' Thomas, 1894

Burt (Cap) Mossman (1867–1936), farmer, cowboy, rancher and lawman (Deputy Sheriff of Navaho County, Arizona). 'Cap' Mossman was appointed first captain of the newly created Arizona Rangers in 1901. With a staff of only fourteen Rangers 'Cap' was able to run down and jail most of Arizona's outlaws (Arizona Historical Society).

reputation was global. Under four generations of Pinkertons, it is still a steadily growing enterprise. Famous criminals and outlaws, like Jesse James; Butch Cassidy and the Wild Bunch; the Molly Maguires; 'Scratch' Becker, a forger; Adam Worth, 'Napoleon' of International Crime; 'Piano Charley' a skilled pianist and just as skilled in robbing banks, plus many others, all tried to keep out of reach of Pinkerton's long arm of the law to no avail.

ARIZONA RANGERS

As far back as the Civil War, there were a number of attempts to organize an effective law enforcement organization to protect the lives and interests of Arizona's fast growing population. However, because of political red tape and poor communications, this effort failed to make any significant improvement or advancement. The territory of Arizona remained a lawless land, plundered at will by the many roving hostile Apaches and an ever increasing number of outlaws.

In 1901, Governor Oakes Murphy pushed through the Arizona legislature a bill organizing a militia of

men called the 'Arizona Rangers'. These paid professionals were to be well organized and well trained, and to deal with almost any type of situation ... enforcing the law and apprehending criminals in a just way. It did not take long to compile a crime-fighting record, unique in Western history, paving the way to statehood for Arizona. The 1901 force of Arizona Rangers included 14 men: one Captain, a sergeant and 12 privates. Many of the men were ex-cowboys with some previous experience as lawmen. Captain Burton 'Cap' Mossman was paid a monthly salary of $120, the next rank down was the sergeant who received $75, and each of the privates earned $55 a month. When in the field, each man was allowed $1 per day for subsistence and 50 cents per day to feed his horse. Under their military code, each Ranger outfitted himself with a suitable horse, camp equipment and large caliber army six-shooter. Provisions such as ammunition, food and breech-loading cavalry arms were supplied by the Territorial Government. The enrolment was for the full year, unless a man was discharged earlier.

Each man had to pass a rigid physical examination to prove to his superiors that he could ride a horse well, shoot both pistol and rifle with some expertise and have a general knowledge of the Territory's geography. After each was indoctrinated they became known as the 'Fearless Thirteen'. Their operational and base headquarters was located at Bisbee, Arizona. From here they could operate and enforce the law throughout the vast Territory of Arizona. Rangers had full authority to pursue and arrest criminals in any portion of the Territory. Their responsibilities were to deliver the outlaws to the nearest law office in the county in which the crimes had been committed. The arraignments often took weeks of travel over rugged country, and the threat of ambush was ever constant. Similar to the Texas Rangers, it was said that the Arizona Rangers had a bad habit of 'shooting first and serving the warrant afterwards'. However, they actually returned with live prisoners in more than 90 per cent of their cases.

On March 19, 1903, the Governor increased the number of Arizona Rangers to 26 men with a pay raise. Medical treatment was provided for injuries sustained while on duty and repayment for horses killed in action. During the first few years, Rangers were working in secrecy, wearing no badges at all. In 1903, they were authorized to wear badges in plain sight. Twenty-five badges were struck: one for the captain, one for the lieutenant and one for each of the four sergeants and 19 privates. Each badge had numerals to identify the officer wearing them. A five-point, ball-tipped star with the name 'Arizona' on top and 'Rangers' on the bottom was engraved across the front and the identifying number above. After only eight short years (1901 – 1909) because of political controversy, the Rangers were abolished and the force disbanded. This group of men, small in numbers, compiled a record equal to that of the Texas Rangers.

THE BOUNTY HUNTER

It wasn't until after the Civil War that the words 'Bounty Hunter' became an almost common phrase on the lips of both policemen and the men who committed crimes in an era when our frontier towns could only afford one or two constables. Often working alone and sometimes politically corrupt, an officer was frequently disinclined or unable to pursue the fleeing criminal into jurisdictions other than his own and soon, after a short chase, would call off the hunt. When the townspeople found their local police agency of no use in capturing the wanted criminal, they enlisted the aid of the Bounty Hunter.

The Bounty Hunter was often hard to contact because he was always on the move. However, insurance companies, local post offices and a few select attorneys knew where and when to make contact with him. Newspaper personal columns were another way of reaching him, as well as a post office box number or general delivery. By these means of communication, meetings could be set up and enough information could be passed on to him describing the wanted individual and his last known location. The Bounty Hunter was not a sworn lawman but a middle-man who tracked down horse thieves, bank robbers, rustlers and murderers and returned them to a place where justice could duly and properly be served. When the desperado was returned, the Bounty Hunter remained long enough to pick up his reward and silently disappeared, having nothing more to do with the whole affair. This sometimes lucrative but lonely life was not generally a full time job to him. He might take work as it came to him,

sometimes not being too particular about what kind of job it was. Gambling might suit him more or ranch work might give him plenty of cover to preserve his identity. Some Bounty Hunters left families back East to fare for themselves, while they worked the Western Frontier towns looking for wanted individuals. Researching a criminal's activities must come from reliable sources, people who would protect his identity and constantly keep him informed, for a slight fee.

His 'tools of the trade' which he depended on daily were by far the most updated, precisioned, and highest in caliber that could be obtained. A good horse and saddle at top dollar insured the best in traveling. He carried nothing over 75 pounds in addition to his own weight, as his horse might become over-exhausted on long trips. Several hide-a-way weapons might be found in his boots and another in the saddle bag, tucked snugly into a sewn holster on the inner flap. An advantage in the favor of the Bounty Hunter was that he was usually unknown by the hunted. One thing that made it harder to return a fugitive alive to his own grounds was if the wanted poster demanded him in his whole-skin (alive). The easiest part was when the poster suggested a man be brought back 'dead or alive'.

It seems almost far fetched to believe that even today in these modern times we still have at least six Bounty Hunters in the United States who practise their trade with tradition and dedication. Instead of horses they travel in automobiles. Their weapons are highly devised semi-automatics with silencers attached. Communications sent and received take only a few minutes and confirmation is easily established. They work alone, selecting a stakeout in order to observe the wanted man or woman, staying up all hours of the day and night and chancing that they themselves might end up on a slab in the morgue. There is no use in asking for help from the local police departments. It was the same during the days of our hectic and lawless Western Frontier. The contemporary Bounty Hunter faces many hardships and ordeals as did the old-timers who fashioned this part time business in crime. And only in the eyes of the hunted will the reputation of the Bounty Hunter earn him an appointment down the barrel of a fugitive's pistol.

THE FAST DRAW

With all of my research for books, magazine articles and illustrations, I am still not convinced that the early gunfighter practised the art of 'fast draw.' By that I mean the art of fast draw as it is exercised today by gun enthusiasts in various clubs all over the country. Competitions are staged between opponents to see who can draw the fastest and fire a handgun from a holstered position on a man's side. This is timed right down to the split-second. Most used is the famous Colt single action six-shooter, with the accompaniment of the low slung fast draw belt and holster rig. In 1959, there were at least 186,000 fast draw enthusiasts enrolled in clubs across the United States and thousands more in Europe. And who would deny the havoc of at least another 20,000 Americans practiving fast draw in their own back yards or basements, without any supervision, instruction or advanced practice. It was these unskilled users of fixed ammunition who were responsible for a host of accidents that made up what the newspapers labeled 'the wounded knee syndrome'.

During the heyday of the Wild and Wooly West, when gunmen lived from day to day by their wits and their weapons, the term 'fast draw rig' was never heard of. By making a study of the many factory made belts and holsters of that day, it is found that the belts were worn high on the hip and the holster snug to the body. Examining many old photographs reveals this to be true. This writer, after much research through pictorial books of the Old West, had found a few men wearing gun belts low and over their hips, but in most cases it was out of necessity as the belt could very well have been taken from another person with a larger waist. The holsters were not tied to the leg and no indication of a fast draw rig was present.

Going back a little further in the history of the holster, we find the Russian Army wearing holsters attached to belts strapped around their waist. It was Captain George B. McClellan who in 1854 was one of the few chosen by the War Department to observe and study foreign military systems during the Crimean War, and incorporate their best features into a revision of our Army's tactical manuals. In his later report, McClellan introduced the Russian system of

---

PLATE 29
89 Arizona Ranger, 1901
90 Texas Ranger, 1886
91 North West Mounted Policeman, 1897

89. *In 1901, the original Arizona Ranger force was fourteen men; one captain, one sergeant and twelve privates. These men were carefully selected from experienced law officers to ex-cowboys. Each Ranger was required to outfit himself with a mount, six-shooter and camp equipment. It was up to the Territorial Government to supply the men with provisions, ammunition and the best available breech-loading rifles. From their base camp at Bisbee, Arizona, they became the relentless enforcers of the law, reaching out with long tentacles to pursue and arrest criminals in any part of the Territory. In 1903, the Governor was empowered to increase the Rangers to 26 men with a raise in pay. For several years, Rangers worked in secrecy and wore no badges, but this proved a problem. Later, their captain was authorized to provide badges to the men to redeem their authority to the citizens who sometimes questioned it. Twenty-five badges were struck, a five-point ball-tipped star, handmade in silver with 'Arizona Rangers' engraved across the front with an identifying number on top. The Rangers soon became the subject of political controversy, and in 1909 they were disbanded. In eight short years, these daring and dedicated men tamed a 'lawless frontier' that is still unequalled in the Southwest.*

90. *The Texas Rangers was first formed loosely as an organized semi-military police force in 1823, while Texas was still a part of Mexico. Even though they were outnumbered, their object was to provide settlers a minimal amount of protection against Indians.*

After much of Texas and surrounding territories had settled, the white man or outlaws became a nuisance. In 1844, Sam Houston re-organized them to the strength of over 1,500 men. Each man provided his own mount and wore no uniform. Their major weapons were Colt pistols and Winchester rifles in large calibers. Through the 1870s, the Rangers brought law and order to a lawless frontier from the Colorado line down through the Staked Plains and West Texas and along the Mexican border, against raiders of all races and colors. Later, they formed into military units and served as part of the national army of the United States.

91. *Canada's new 'Western Empire' was a troubled land in 1873. The Indians and Métes of the West resented the white man's takeover, seeing in it a threat to their traditional way of life. Storm clouds were gathering and bloody insurrection against Canadian authority was already in the wind. On the recommendation of various Government officers and Commissions, the newly-formed Canadian Parliament decided that a permanent force should be organized and stationed in what was then known as the North-West Territories. On May 23, 1873, the Prime Minister signed the new Act which became effective on November 1, 1873. This new force became known as the North West Mounted Police (NWMP). In 1904, the Force became known as the Royal North West Mounted Police, or RNWMP, and in 1920 as the Royal Canadian Mounted Police; it is now generally referred to as the RCMP. Every man was armed with a carbine in a bucket on the saddle, and a revolver carried over the left hip. In addition, one troop was armed with lances to be used for pomp and ceremonies and also to impress the Indians.*

PLATE 29

91   North West Mounted Policeman, 1897

90   Texas Ranger, 1886

89   Arizona Ranger, 1901

E. L. REEDSTROM

carrying a pistol on the waist belt for the military. During the Civil War, the heavy Colt percussion Army Model found its way into a large flapped holster, butt forward, and slipped onto the belt for both Army officers and Cavalry troopers. Before this, horse-pistols were carried in dual holsters slung over the pommel of the saddle called 'pommel holsters'.

As the war continued, these large holster flaps were usually cut off and discarded or used for inner soles for worn shoes or boots. As newer innovations came about and weapons, especially the hand gun, became easier to load with self-contained cartridges that replaced the percussion system, a change in holster design was necessary. Almost every holster was form fitted to the pistol, holding the weapon snug when new until the leather was well worn and the pistol easier to withdraw. Later a mule ear was usually placed on top of the holster and off to the side somewhat so the leather loop could slip over the hammer of the pistol. This secured it so that it wouldn't work itself out and fall to the ground with any quick motion. Leather straps later were attached and were designed to the owner's taste by a saddle maker. These straps had no fasteners and were tucked in between a leather loop. As the advancement of the holster continued, straps about half an inch wide with snaps fastened at the ends insured a secure hold. Not too many types of handguns could be fitted into one holster. Because of some pistols' similarity in design and form, the Colt, Remington and Smith and Wesson were about the only ones that would fit a single holster. Barrel lengths would be the only problem in a proper fit, and this was usually easy for the owner to rectify. This type of belt and holster could not be used too readily for quick draw by the old time gunslingers. Holster ties (two long leather thongs at the bottom of the holster) did not come about until the early or mid-1890s, and this was adopted by the US Army and Cavalry during the Spanish American War. The thongs were tied around the lower thigh above the knee so that the holstered pistol would not flop around during heavy activity. These thongs are still used with our modern type fast draw rigs to keep the holster in a stationary position.

Actually, most Western gunfighters had devised special and unique methods of getting out their weapon quickly without hanging it up in a holster. Wild Bill Hickok wore a cloth sash around his middle with two Smith and Wesson revolvers protruding butt first. He was comfortable with this system for a quick draw. By speedily withdrawing the weapon, all he had to do was point the barrel in a man's direction, and fire at close range. There certainly was no trick to that with the exception of a little speed and surprise. Even if Bill missed completely, the muzzle blast from his large caliber pistols would probably knock the other man over or throw him off balance. If that wasn't enough, the exploded charge could set his clothes on fire.

Wes Hardin's skill with pistols was not hearsay. While captured by the Texas Rangers in 1877, the bandit was asked to perform some of his tricks with empty weapons. Captain Jim Gillett said that nothing could compare with Hardin's stunts as he manipulated the pinwheel, boarder shift, rolls and quick draw from a gun harness he perfected himself. This holster vest or 'Hardin Vest' as it was called, was made out of soft calfskin and sewn upon its front were two holster pockets slanting outward from center to hip bones. Within these holsters he carried his six-shooters, butts inward so that, while drawing, the arms were crossed and the weapons were pulled out quickly. It would seem to anyone confronting Wes that with his arms crossed against his chest, his hands out of sight (but probably gripping both pistol grips), he was incapable of reaching for hip pistols. Any effort in drawing a weapon on Wes in this position proved fatal.

The Barns .50 caliber boot pistol, with its single heavy ball, was convenient only if a man was sitting down at cards or eating. Its accuracy was good for pointing at the man in front of you . . . at close range. As men's clothing was styled to show off the masculine chest by being rather roomy, it was not too hard to conceal two percussion pistols holstered and attached to a pair of suspenders, butts pointing at each other. As he reached under his coat in a slow manner, as if to hoist out a cigar or his watch, the man opposite the gunfighter was soon surprised. The old 'hat trick' was another diversion a gunfighter had working for him many times over. When confronted by a pistol-toting whiskey soak bent on carving another notch on the handle of his gun, the gunfighter watched the eyes of the man before him and when he thought the drunk was ready to draw, he quickly pitched his bowler hat in the man's face and, as he jumped to one side, drew his pistols and fired.

The cutaway trigger guard on a single action Colt was another way in saving the shooter a split second. Swivel holsters were later manufactured so that the pistol could be fired without withdrawing the piece. And similar to this was the 'quick-fire' rig of L. S.

Flatau's pistol and carbine holder, patented January, 1882. The construction of this device was a steel plate riveted to a belt and to the metal plate was riveted a metal spring similar to that of a tuning fork. The pistol is provided with a button, which in this instance forms a part of the pin upon which the hammer of the arm is pivoted, and which is adapted to pass between and under the parts or prongs of the spring. What secures the arm in a hanging position is when the arm's button settles down into a half oval. To release the arm one has only to pull up slightly and quickly move the arm forward horizontally until it has cleared the plate. This device was designed originally for the US Army Mounted Troops, and after failing the Army acceptance trials was offered to the civilian trade. Obviously, it was snapped up by lawmen and outlaws and used in their profession.

Motion pictures have recreated the old Western gunfighters and their notorious exploits against banks, railroads and stagecoach lines, and viewers marvel at their deeds. A fast horse, and a fast weapon showing the Prince of Pistoleers in action, make the fans go wild and clamour for more. If the bandits are fast, then the good guys have to be faster. Around the late 1920s and early '30s, the Western holster and belt changed considerably. It is now designed for faster action; its prototype was probably born on a movie set.

NORTHWEST MOUNTED POLICE

On May 23, 1873, the Dominion Parliament passed an act to provide for establishment of a 'Mounted Police Force for the Northwest Territories'. The Force recruited men between the ages of 18 to 40, being of sound mind, able to ride a horse, able-bodied and of good character. Payment was established at 75 cents per day for subconstables and $1 for constables. The men were also required to be able to read and write either in English or the French language. The Command was divided into troops and the commanding officer was termed 'Commissioner'. The full term of service was for three years and the men were trained as a paramilitary body. Their immediate objectives were to curb the liquor traffic among the Indians and once again gain their respect and confidence.

The Northwest Mounted Police officially came into existence on August 30, 1873, when the provisions of the Act were brought into force by Order-in-Council, and recruiting began. A force of 300 men was authorized, but only three troops of 50 men each were formed. This force was quickly activated after the government received reports from Cypress Hills that white wolf hunters had massacred a band of Assiniboine Indians. The Northwest Mounted Police's main task was to establish and maintain amicable relations with the Indians of the Northwest Territories between 1874 and 1885; a secondary concern was to avoid any American frontier wars, and settle differences between miners and settlers flooding the area challenging warlike tribes for their hunting lands. After the buffalo's rapid destruction, the Indians were forced onto Canadian reserves. By the time the white settlements got under way on the prairies, the Indian put away all warlike weapons and slowly adopted a quiet life on the reservations. As one prominent Chief of the Blackfoot tribe said after accepting and signing of Treaty Number Seven, 'The advice given me and my people has proven to be very good. If the police had not come to this country where would we all be now? Bad men and whiskey were killing us so fast that very few of us would have been left today. The Mounted Police have protected us, as the feathers of the bird protect it from the frosts of winter.'

Another problem arose, after the Custer battle in June, 1876, the hostile Sioux escaped into Canada for fear of the larger American military forces then closing in on them from all sides. The Sioux's arrival disturbed the peaceful relations which Canada was in the process of restoring with its own tribes. Now the Sioux, traditional enemies of many Canadian Indian tribes, had to be watched. Various outposts were built and reinforced and small scouting parties were sent out to keep a watchful eye on them. By 1879, many Sioux began slowly returning to the United States. After Sitting Bull had been informed that the 'Great White Mother' would no longer supply them with food, he and his small band of Sioux finally returned to the American authorities at Fort Buford, North Dakota.

Settlements did not begin to increase on the frontier until the railway construction crossed the prairies during 1881 and 1883. In its wake, there came a steady stream of white settlers. Construction camps, or 'end of track towns', sprang up along the railroad, with gambling, drinking, vice, and houses of ill repute going full blast to entertain the construction crews. Along with this, something new arose: labor unrest resulting in the first serious strike. Reinforcements were rushed to Moose Jaw to guard railroad property and settle the unruly strikers, and to provide the protection for those who refused to leave their jobs. For many years, force members fulfilled every duty concerned with civil authority in the Northwest. Services were extended for public order and welfare and assuming responsibility for the mail service in the early West resulted in awarding contracts for mail carriers between settlements. Criminals sentenced to short jail terms often served their time in Mounted Police guardhouses; those sentenced to hard labor swung axes on the post wood pile.

Early 1885, brought more and more settlers into the country and the Métes Indians, along the North Saskatchewan River, became concerned about the loss of their land and way of life. A report to the Force was a serious one, and a Northwest rebellion was likely to ensue. Hostilities did break out and a severe clash took place near Duck Lake between 56 Mounted Policemen, with 43 Prince Albert Volunteers, and a large party of Métes Indians, or half-breeds. Although Duck Lake was an important victory for the rebels, they were soon overwhelmed and crushed by a larger military force.

In 1896, the Canadian Government began a vigorous campaign to attract settlers to the prairies. Grants of 160 acres were given to anyone who wished to settle the land. By 1914 over a million settlers had arrived and established families, homes and businesses. The police became land agents, agricultural experts and welfare officials. Assisting the oncoming new set-

tlers became a burden on the Force. While this was happening, a new frontier was opening up to the north. Little was known of the 'Yukon' prior to 1886. In 1894, a gold strike on a small Yukon tributary, just inside the Canadian border, set off a stream of prospectors, attracted to the sudden gold discovery.

Over the next two years, tens of thousands of gold seekers converged via various routes to the Klondike. The 19 officers and men of the Northwest Mounted Police could not handle the 'rush', and they were quickly reinforced. Between 1898 and 1900, a 200-man force was sent by the Canadian Government to assist the Northwest Mounted Police to guard prisoners, banks and gold shipments. The Northwest Mounted Police and Union Jack became symbols of personal security and justice at the summits of the passes. Not many found their 'Eldorado', and most left broke and disheartened as quickly as they had come.

The end of World War I saw the entire northern mainland effectively brought under Canadian Government jurisdiction. In 1904, by command of King Edward VII, the prefix 'Royal' was added to the Force's title, and in 1920 its future and enduring fame was assured when it was renamed the 'Royal Canadian Mounted Police', with a new strength of 1,200 men. For over 100 years of a proud tradition, their motto still stands: 'Maintain the Right'.

10 The Cowboy

The American Cowboy is a curious blend of the Mexican 'vaquero' and the Californian 'caballero'. Our first true American cowboys were Texans, working and handling stock in open country with the aid of a well trained cow pony and a lariat. There are several accounts that lay claim to having originated the name cowboy, which is an American term given to a man who tends cattle. One story states that it was coined during the Revolutionary War, when groups of Tory loyalists roamed the region between the lines in Westchester County, New York, calling themselves 'Cowboys'. For some unexplained reason they had no association with cattle. The second anecdote seems more apropos and closer to the true source. A group of wild-riding, reckless Texans under the leadership of Ewen Cameron spent much of their time chasing longhorns and Mexicans soon after Texas became a republic in 1836, calling themselves cowboys.

When the longhorn breed of cattle were brought into Mexico by the Spanish Conquistadors as early as 1519, they were left to graze on the open range by Mexican settlers who moved northward over the Rio Grande River into Texas. At that time there was no market for beef, and as the herds increased, many wandered off and became wild. In 1821, when a small migration of Easterners settled in Texas, they found great herds of these wild cattle. After capturing many, they learned from the Mexicans how to brand and mark them. This was the beginning of the great Southwestern herds.

The increase of English speaking people soon alarmed the Mexican Republic who tried for many years thereafter to compel the Texans to acknowledge themselves as Mexican subjects, only to meet with defeat each time they approached the subject. The Texans claimed independence, but no nation would acknowledge their claim. Davy Crockett journeyed to Washington several times to intercede on their behalf but was scoffed at by the politicians of the East who made fun of him while he pleaded his case. In 1836, Santa Anna marched his large army across the Rio Grande into San Antonio and annihilated all the Texans there, including Davy Crockett, at the old Fort Alamo stronghold. In counteraction Sam Hous-

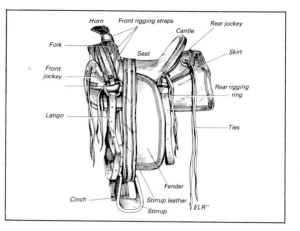

Among the many problems with early day saddles were the stirrups. They rotted under rain and heat, and when a cowboy started to saddle up his foot would crash through the stirrup under his own weight. In the late 1840s the steam-bent stirrup was stronger than the hollowed-out wood stirrup.

ton, Ben McCullah, Kit Carson, Pat Cannon and other distinguished fighters declared all of the people of Texas as members of a new Texas Army; men, women and even children had to shoulder arms and fight. They did not ask for any help from Washington, but alone fought bravely and were victorious. The rest of the nation was compelled to acknowledge independence of Texas as one of the States of the Union on December 29, 1845.

Now, the Texans turned their attention to the horse and the cattle industry, which was very profitable for hides, horns, hoofs, tallow and corned beef. People from the East and Northern states began to invest their money and a great emigration from the States took place. The Spanish language soon gave way almost entirely to English, and the name 'Vaquero' lost its significance but the title 'Cowboy' now took its place.

The vast stretch of country lying between the Missouri River and the Rocky Mountains was at one time a wasteland, useless for most purposes of man-

Black Powder Editor for Guns & Ammo *magazine, Phil Spangenburger, poses in some of Red River's gun leather and horse tack equipment. Phil is very authentic in early Western costumes & horse furniture. Here he poses for us in buckskins and chaps of a cowboy circa 1880 (Red River).*

kind. But to the stock growers it was open range territory for hundreds of thousands of cattle, one of the most important sources of the world's food supply. The treeless plains, though uninviting to farmers, were a paradise to the ranchman. To a freeman, life on the range, with all its outdoor activity, meant hard work.

The American cowboy, with his large sombrero, leather chaps and western saddle, rode his sturdy bronco like the centaur of Greek mythology. In the earlier days the Texas steer with his six-foot-wide spreading horns was the prevailing type of cattle. The breeds have since been crossed with others, the result being a type with a large frame which fattens readily and produces good beef, yet still retains the hardiness necessary to survive the hardships of winter and the droughts of summer.

The cowboy's outfit struck the people of the East with the general impression that the long hair, wide-brimmed hats, huge spurs, fringed buckskin leggings, including a holstered weapon on his hip, was worn for show and bluster. It was not a desire for picturesqueness that led to the cowboy's attire. Questions of usefulness and necessity were the only considerations that prompted the adoption of this peculiar dress. As an example, the cowboy's wide-brimmed hat has

been worn without changes in fashion for generations; this is enough to indicate that use, not vanity, dictated its origin. When wide-brimmed hats could not be obtained because of the great distance between sources of supply, the cowboy made his own. When the sun is hottest during midday, the hat is much cooler than a straw hat. During a heavy wind and sand storm, the wide brim protects the eyes. When mud was flying from a stampeding herd or hail stones were pelting down upon his head, these hats protected a man's face. When the Eastern manufacturers saw the potential in hat-making for the West, 'Stetson' won over all others as the hat made of the best fur. They could be washed, soaked in water, and, after being exposed to all kinds of weather, still held their shape. In addition, they would withstand rough wear for many years. Stetsons usually cost from $8 to $20, and if made to order would cost a great deal more. Some cowboys claimed that they could tell where another cowman hailed from by the look and shape of his hat. As an example, a huge plain crown, having no center crease or dent, came from Texas. A peaked hat, or a four-dented crown, came from Montana – hence the Montana peaked hat.

There were good reasons why some cowboys, not all, might sport long hair hanging down to their shoulders. Through rain or shine and in many changes of climate, they found from experience that the greatest protection to their eyes and ears in addition to their hats was long hair. Old-time hunters and mountain men knew this very well. As a rule most scouts, trailers and guides grew hair in ringlets about their shoulders. Those who were prejudiced against it have suffered the consequences of pain in the head, followed by sore eyes and loud ringing in the ears. A result of exposure without the protection of long hair was sometimes a loss of hearing in one ear, caused by one or the other of the ears being exposed more when the cowboy was lying on the ground. Healthy eyesight and hearing were of the greatest importance to a scout, hunter or cowboy. Some white men not related to, but living among the American Indians, found that letting their hair grow long gained favor with the noble red man of the plains.

There were many varieties of 'Chaps', a Spanish word for 'Chaparejos', which were buckskin leggings worn by cowboys to protect their clothing and limbs from the wear and tear of heavy brush and 'cat-claws', a bush with claws similar to a cat, thorns, cactus and many other varieties of desert undergrowth. 'Armitas' were worn by the Mexican 'Vaqueros', which was a leather apron tied to the waist and knees, but falling a little below the knees. This style was used before the 1860s. The late 1860s and early 1870s saw the evolution of the 'shotgun' pattern. The 'Batwings' appeared around 1900, and the 'Angora', 'Woolies' or 'Grizzlies' were worn in the Northern states but seldom seen in the Southwest, appearing after World War I.

The famous Levi Strauss breeches were first manufactured in 1850, mainly for the California miners who wore out a pair of pants in a week's time. The trousers were of a durable canvas ducking, and came in one color, tan, with rivets reinforcing pockets and seams. By 1877, Levi's could be purchased in two colors, and two fabrics; the off-white (frequently tan or duck) and the indigo-dyed denim. The pants had two suspender buttons in the rear and four in the front. Belt loops on trousers were introduced in 1922.

Cowboy boots were generally the most expensive part of his wardrobe. In 1880, store-bought boots sold for $7 and tailor-made boots went as high as $15. The high 'Cuban-heel' kept his boot from slipping through the stirrup and, while roping on foot, the heels 'dug in' the ground, giving him a sure footing. Pointed-toe boots (later introduced) allowed the cowboy to pick up a stirrup on a wheeling horse.

The 'Yellow Slicker, Saddle Coat, Fishskin or Tower' saddle coat was a perfect raincoat for the mounted man. It was designed especially for horseback riders and was made of heavy canvas or duck, and waterproofed with linseed oil. The coat covered the entire saddle when worn, as well as the rider, insuring a dry seat, while the lower extremities of the rider were also covered. The coat could be regulated for riding or walking, simply by adjusting one of the rear buttons. Standing, the coat fell to the cowboy's ankle. The coat was introduced in the early 1880s, primarily for the cowboy/cattlemen trade. Sizes ranged from 36 to 44, and sold for around $3 apiece.

Heavy, strong and enlarged spurs, or 'gut hooks', were usually chosen by the cowboys to work with and were called cruel by many, but, singular as it may seem, the light spurs used by Easterners were more cruel, as the heavier pair served a greater purpose. Generally, a cowboy's life depended upon how he used them, and many times his horse would not get up and out of the way of a wild steer's charge, during a stampede, unless he was severely spurred. If the spurs had small rowels, they could not reach the skin through the long hair and scurf that nature provides the horses with to protect them from the severe winters of the plains. The spurs must be strong enough

The mounted Frontiersman sports a lever-action rifle which typifies the Westerners' fondness for this type of action. Larry Demitter with Navy Arms 'Henry Carbine' .44–40 caliber (Guns & Ammo Magazine).

that they will not break down in times of danger, and will not wear out before they reach their destination.

The 'All Around Duster' can be traced back to the Civil War. Made of white canvas or a heavy ducking, it reached to the wearer's ankles, and was designed primarily for a horseman. (A split in the coat at the rear was designed for riding flexibility.) An adjustable back belt was sewn in the rear, permitting either a tight or loose fit. Field surgeons, army scouts, contracted civilian haulers and stage coach drivers all wore these long coats principally to keep the dust off their clothing beneath. A later model came out, similar to the earlier one, but the rear split was discarded and a side split was employed on both sides for the motor-touring car enthusiasts (1917–20).

The big kerchief, which was usually found around a cowboy's neck, was for a reason, instead of being stuffed into a rear pocket. It would have been an inconvenience, possibly causing suffering, had he not arranged it loosely about his neck. While trailing behind cattle, the dust was so thick and heavy it seemed to choke the air out. Handkerchiefs immediately went over the nose and mouths of cowboys who trailed the herds for stragglers. It was often used as a veil during heavy dust storms. During winters, when snow blindness was frequent, green or blue silk see-through veils or handkerchiefs were worn to cover a man's face. Loosely tied around his neck, it was handy and secure when needed in any emergency. On the other hand it was also used in stage holdups, train robberies and bank stick-ups – but not often. By pulling the bandanna over the face just up under the eyes, the holdup man could escape without showing his countenance; however, once in a while, a man or woman victim could identify the bandit by the color or oddity of the bandanna's pattern. However, large gunney sacks were the best protection against any identification. They were dropped over the head – protecting the whole face – with only two eye holes cut-out to see through, and possibly an opening for the mouth to breathe air.

Most work shirts were pull-overs, plain, striped, or patterned. Collars were the simple fold over, square ends, short round tips, or mule eared (long fold over) with either a three or four button front or the seven button bib front. It was not uncommon for a clothing manufacturer to make one particular type of shirt in a

---

PLATE 30
92 Californian 'vaquero', 1840s–60s
93 Texas cowboy, 1870s
94 Cowboy, 1880s

92. *A California 'vaquero' of the 1840s is dressed in his everyday working attire: a short jacket, a wide sombrero, heavy leather trousers buttoned on each side called 'chaparreras' (later abbreviated to 'chaps'), and half-breed leather leggings or 'botas' wrapped around the lower part of his legs to protect against snake bite and thorny brush. (He has also partially hidden his silent weapon – the knife.) His spurs have enormous rowels, and for a reason. The bigger the rowel and the more points in it the less damage it does. It is the smaller spur with few points that sinks in. However, when acquiring a new pair of spurs, each point is filed down until it is blunt. When used, a mere touching of the horse was all that was needed. In the 1870s, names such as 'gut-hooks', 'cartwheels', 'canopeners', 'tin bellies', and 'goosenecks' referred to the spur.*

He wore no boot, only soft, home-made leather shoes with low heels. A fancy, heavy, close-woven red sash was worn around his middle and tied to one side. He might carry papers, weapons or anything else of importance within. In Indian country, the sash was wrapped many times around his middle to protect his lower extremities as well as his upper chest from enemy arrows. Many vaqueros were saved by this means. From his wrist hangs a quirt, 'cuarta' (kwar-tah), or 'quisto', braided from rawhide: the stock was usually filled with lead shot and the over-all length might range from 12 to 18 inches in length. He used this in breaking a horse or to strike down on a rearing horse that threatened to fall backward.

93. *A young Texas cowboy, astride his mount, preparing to embark on probably his first trail drive, is fully equipped with his tied-down working rope beside him. After 1850, sailing ships brought an abundance of fiber rope into the country. It won a great and lasting preference over the native rawhide lariats (reatas). Ropes were responsible for much of the change and development in American western saddles. By the 1860s the bulky Mexican saddle horn was trimmed down from its saucer-sized top. Accompanying some changes, forks were heightened to bring the horns up into a handier position, and this called for stronger trees and better rigging. For added security and comfort the Mex-*

ican cantle grew from 2½ inches up to 5–7 inches in height. Breast collars and cruppers disappeared, while Martingales saw little service, and only for special purposes on certain horses. By 1880 newer saddles appeared showing full-covered seats, cantles and pommels, regular jockeys, full skirts with built-in sheepskin linings, and with all rigging concealed under leather covering. Narrower and stronger, one-piece bent-wood stirrups were added instead of the weak, carved stirrups, and the huge Mexican skirts were reduced in size and rounded off at the corners.

94. *The wide-brimmed cowboy hat was becoming a tradition; however, not all the beef-chasing boys wore them. Shown here, a cowboy of the mid-1880s preferred a 'Stetson', but one with a shorter brim. The large neckerchief would cover the nose and mouth from dust, covering the back of the neck from sunburn, a muffler in cold weather, to hold down his hat during windy days, keeping ears covered from the freezing cold, a sling for a broken arm, and as a towel to clean dust or dirt off. The bib pullover shirt was not often worn by the early cowboys, because they were expensive and were ordered from the East. Although they were warm pullovers with the added chest protector, only a few found their way into the cowboy's war bag. When Levis were first introduced in the West (1850), they were marketed for the hardrock miner, who went through a normal pair of pants in three weeks. At first the cowboy would not be caught dead in a pair because they were worn by poor miners. Not until late in the 1870s did cowboys begin to wear these copper-riveted, reinforced denim pants because they withstood a great deal of punishment. (Belt loops were not introduced until around the 1920s.) On his belt he wears a holstered Remington 1874 Army, 44/40 caliber, cartridge revolver, along with a Civil War cap box that holds a number of loose cartridges.*

As boots began to change in design for the cowboy's profession, the Civil War period square toe gave way to the rounded toe and reinforced arch. Higher heels appeared, as well as the 'mule-ear' grips on top. Large rowel spurs were popular, with 'concho' studded spur straps, and jinglebobs sometimes appeared hanging from the spur's shank to create a certain sweet music to any cowhand. The long pole he holds is to prod the cattle into chutes, then into box cars for shipment back East. Because of this he was nicknamed a 'Cow Poke'.

PLATE 30

92   Californian 'vaquero', 1840–60s

93   Texas cowboy, 1870s

94   Cowboy, 1880s

E.L. "REEDSTROM"

Probably in his teens and working his first cattle drive, this young cowpuncher poses for the photographer in his newly purchased 'Shotgun Chaps'. The side arm hardly posed a threat to anyone, as it was often called a snake gun. It was, however, very essential in his line of work: shooting a wild steer, putting a horse away because of a broken leg or stopping a stampede. With many rustlers waiting their chance to run off a few head, they soon changed their minds when seeing the cowboys well 'heeled' (Joe M. Gish Collection).

white color and a front pattern long enough to hang down to a man's knees. This particular shirt was made to use as a day shirt and a nightshirt, one that a man could sleep and work in.

The cowboy's belt revolver, cartridge and open holsters were not worn to express bravado. They wore them when crossing hostile country because it was necessary. Horse thieves, Indians, and other marauders kept on the run attacking the trail drivers whenever practical. Cowboys kept as well trained as possible with their side arms and saddle guns, practising whenever they could, but away from the herd. There were times when they might have to cripple or kill cattle to save their horses in a stampede, or save a man's life, and their pistols must be ready at their

sides. The caliber most cowboys used during the early days was the .44–40 caliber. The Colt pistol was manufactured in a .44–40 caliber which was interchangeable with the Winchester Model '1873', lever action rifle. The same shell could be fired in both revolver and rifle, making it easier to carry the same caliber cartridge round in pistol belts.

Many Easterners remarked that they could not understand why cowboys used such large heavy saddles. Their saddles were not made for pleasure riding, for they had to do heavy work with them. When roping cattle, the saddle must be secure, strong and made of the best leather. When a double cinch saddle was used, one cinch kept the saddle from pitching forward when a steer was on the end of a rope, the other secured the saddle in the usual manner and particular care was taken to insure settling the saddle on the horse's back. They always had a heavy load to carry in addition to their own weight. The burden had to be evenly distributed so that it was easier on the horse than if one of the smaller short horn saddles was used. The end of the rope was held fast by turning the rope several times around the saddle horn which stood about six inches above the pommel. The rider often hung heavily over the further side of the pony to prevent the saddle from being turned around.

The chuck wagon, or a home away from home, is believed to have been designed by cattle baron Charles Goodnight in 1866. An old army wagon was chosen because it was heavy and the iron axles were most durable. At the rear, a large mess box was added with many drawers and compartments with a hinged lid that closed the chuck box but also served as a work table when opened. Beneath the chuck box was the boot. This was another large compartment where heavy iron kettles and huge frying pans were stored. On one side was the water barrel that would have to last the cook several days. On the opposite side was the tool box containing everything from an anvil to horseshoeing tools, a wagon jack, saw, pick, shovel and sledge hammer. The wagon bed contained all the cowboy's bed rolls and extra saddles; it also served to store wood when trees were scarce on the prairie.

Here are some delightful cowboy recipes, over 95 years old.

CHUCK WAGON RECIPES

COWBOY BEANS

1 pound dry pinto beans (2 cups)	1 6-ounce can tomato paste

7 cups cold water
2 pounds smoked ham
  hocks
½ cup chopped onion

1 4-ounce can green
  chili peppers, seeded
  and chopped
2 tablespoons sugar

Rinse pinto beans thoroughly. In cold water, combine beans in kettle or Dutch oven. Bring to boiling. Simmer 2 minutes; remove from heat. Cover; let stand 1 hour. (Or add beans to cold water; soak overnight.) Do not drain. Add ham hocks and onion. Cover; cook over low heat for 1 hour, stirring occasionally. Remove ham hocks. Remove meat from bones; dice. Discard bones. Return meat to beans. Add tomato paste, chopped chili peppers, and sugar. Cover and cook till beans are tender, about 30 minutes more, stirring occasionally. Add additional water, if needed. Makes 6 to 8 servings.

SOURDOUGH BREAD STARTER

Soak a cake of yeast in water until dissolved. Add two tablespoons of sugar and enough flour to make a soft batter. Let stand two days if warm weather, longer if cold. To use it, add a tablespoon of sugar and a teaspoon of soda, stir, and it's ready to use. Save some of the starter by just adding flour and water. As you use from the starter, just add a tablespoon of sugar and a teaspoon of soda for your biscuits. An egg will improve your biscuits if stirred into the dough. Keep your starter covered, and warm, so it will continue to 'work'.

SOURDOUGH BISCUITS
NOTE: TO USE WITH SOURDOUGH STARTER

1 cup sourdough starter
1 teaspoon each of salt,
  sugar and soda

1 tablespoon shortening
3 to 4 cups sifted flour

Place flour in a large bowl, make a well in the center and add sourdough starter (above). Stir in salt, soda and sugar, add shortening. Gradually mix in enough flour to make a stiff dough. Pinch off dough for one biscuit at a time; form a ball and roll it in melted shortening. Crowd the biscuits in a round 8-inch cake pan and allow to rise in a warm place for 20 to 30 minutes before baking. Bake at 425°F until done.

CHUCK WAGON CHOPS (Pork or Lamb)

Season chops with salt and pepper. Roll in flour. Fry in hot lard (or margarine) until brown on both sides. Reduce heat to low. Add 1 cup water. Cover and simmer 30 minutes. Remove cover, pour off liquid. Leave chops in hot pan a few minutes, to re-crisp.

RED BEAN PIE

1 cup cooked, mashed
  pinto beans
1 cup sugar
3 egg yolks, beaten

1 cup milk
1 teaspoon vanilla
1 teaspoon nutmeg

Combine ingredients and place in uncooked pie crust. Bake at 350°F for 30 minutes or until set. Make meringue with the leftover egg whites; spread on pie and brown in oven.

COWBOY STEW

1½ pounds beef stew
  meat, cut in 1-inch
  cubes
2 tablespoons all-purpose
  flour
1 teaspoon salt
2 tablespoons shortening
1½ cups strong coffee
2 tablespoons molasses
1 clove garlic, minced
1 teaspoon salt
1 teaspoon Worcester-
  shire sauce

½ teaspoon dried oregano,
  crushed
⅛ teaspoon cayenne
1½ cups water
4 carrots, cut in ½-inch
  slices
4 small onions, quartered
3 medium potatoes,
  peeled and cut up
¼ cup cold water
3 tablespoons all-purpose
  flour

With a mixture of 2 tablespoons flour and 1 teaspoon salt, coat beef cubes. In a Dutch oven brown meat on all sides in hot shortening. Stir in the coffee, molasses, garlic, 1 teaspoon salt, Worcestershire sauce, oregano and cayenne. Cover; simmer over low heat till meat is almost tender, about 1½ hours. Add the 1½ cups water, carrot slices, onion quarters, and potato pieces. Simmer, covered, till vegetables are tender, about 30 minutes. Blend ¼ cup cold water into the 3 tablespoons flour; add to stew mixture. Cook and stir till mixture is thickened and bubbly. Serve in bowls. Makes 6 to 8 servings.

LEATHER APRONS

1 cup all-purpose flour
¼ teaspoon salt
⅓ cup cold water

4 cups beef broth or
  chicken broth

Take the flour and salt, and stir together. Add enough of the cold water to form a stiff dough. Roll dough paper thin. Cut into 2-inch squares. Drop into boiling broth; cook 15 minutes, stirring often. Makes about 30.

SONOFABITCH STEW

2 pounds lean beef
Half a calf heart

1 set brains
1 set marrow gut

$1\frac{1}{2}$ pounds calf liver
1 set sweetbreads

Salt, pepper
Louisiana hot sauce

Kill off a young steer. Cut up beef, liver and heart into 1-inch cubes; slice the marrow gut into small rings. Place in a Dutch oven or deep casserole. Cover meat with water and simmer for 2 to 3 hours. Add salt, pepper and hot sauce to taste. Take sweetbreads and brains and cut in small pieces. Add to stew. Simmer another hour, never boiling.

WILD CARD CHILI

1 pound chopped beef
$\frac{1}{2}$ cup chopped onion
1 16-ounce can red beans
1 16-ounce can refried beans

1 teaspoon chopped hot red peppers
$\frac{1}{2}$ teaspoon each salt and garlic salt
$\frac{1}{8}$ teaspoon each pepper

1 8-ounce can tomato sauce
1 cup water

and cayenne
3 tablespoons chili powder
1 tablespoon molasses

Brown beef with onions in a Dutch oven; pour off fat. Add remaining ingredients; cover and simmer for 1 hour, stirring occasionally. Makes 6 servings.

VINEGAR COBBLER

$1\frac{1}{2}$ cups sugar
$1\frac{1}{2}$ tablespoons flour
2 cups water

1 cup vinegar
Pinch of nutmeg
1 teaspoon vanilla

Mix sugar and flour dry, then add other ingredients. Place these in a baking dish and dot with butter. Cover all this with a pie crust. Bake at 375°F for 20 to 25 minutes.

PLATE 31
95 Cowboy, 1880
96 Texan cowboy, 1888
97 Cowboy, 1890s

95. *The 'Saddle Coat' or 'Pommel Yellow Slicker' was the most perfect raincoat ever to be manufactured for the use of the horseman. It was especially designed for horseback riders and was made of heavy cloth, canvas or duck, and waterproofed with linseed oil. This coat covered the entire saddle when worn, as well as the rider, ensuring a dry seat, while the lower part covered the length of the rider. It was a combination coat, which could be turned from a riding to a walking coat simply by adjusting one of the rear buttons. When standing, the coat would fall to a man's ankle. The slicker had many names; however, it was best known as the 'Fishskin' or 'Tower' saddle coat, names adopted from various manufacturers. This coat was first introduced a little before the 1880s, and primarily for the cowboy/cattleman trade. Sizes ranged from 36 to 44 chest sizes and sold for $2.65 to $3.00.*
96. *It was the Texans who adopted the idea of wearing leather leggings from their Mexican neighbors. These 'vaqueros' were using the old apron-like 'Armas' which were huge, tough leather flaps that fastened over the front of the saddle and hung down on each side. When a man saddled up, he laid these over his legs like a robe. This was for protection against thorny brush besides keeping the legs warm at night or in cold weather. Being too cumbersome, the Texan substituted the 'Armitas' which was a leather apron tied to the waist and the knees, but falling a little below the knees. This came about just before the 1860s. By the late 1860s and the early 1870s came the 'shotgun' pattern (center figure wearing 'shotguns'); these 'chaparreras', later called 'chaps', were like a man's trousers with the seat cut out. Large front pockets were added along with fringes running up and down the side seams. Conchos decorated the fronts as well as Mexican cartwheels, according to the cowboy's taste. Lower left shows three famous branding irons: the Lazy W, J.A. (Charley Goodnight's*

partner, John Adair), and the Bar None. The Colt Six Shooter is purposely placed incorrectly within the holster, as the Cowboy likes a 'cross draw'. He probably couldn't get a holster for that side, and any other one would do temporarily.
97. *Almost all cowboys wore pullover shirts in the 1880s, either lightweight or heavy wool, depending on seasons. Most shirts had the small, fold-over, soft collar with a row of three or four buttons from the collar to about four inches from the belt line. Sleeves were straight and loosely hung with close fitting cuffs. If a man's arm was shorter than the shirt sleeve, he would use an adjustable arm garter made from elastic. Favorite colors and patterns were stripes, checks, and solid patterns. Material varied from heavy knit Jersey to blue flannel, and from cashmere to percale, which is a closely-woven cotton fabric, usually with a print on one side. A few shirts were manufactured without breast pockets, but the majority had one pocket on the left side. Prices varied from $.75 to $.90 each. His chaps are the 'Angora', 'Woolies', or 'Grizzlies' and worn in wintery Northern states, but seldom worn in the Southwest, and never in brush country. They were introduced sometime during the late 1880s.*

Bucket-top gloves were worn in the early days of cowboying because they were easily obtained and reasonable in price; however, serious accidents occurred with this type of glove and everything seemed to get caught up in them as well. The tops were then hacked off and the shorter glove came into being for the working cowboy. His wearing of his gun belt low on his hip does not mean he is an old hand at gunfighting. Many reasons can explain this habit. During a workday, freedom of movement was essential. Though some men wore gun belts high on the hip, they were very good at handling their weapon at that height. Constant horseback riding often meant shifting a gun belt to a certain position in order to feel some comfort all day in a saddle. Belts were let out to the last notch for that reason, and the cowboy, during his hectic day of body movements, was free to manipulate in any position.

PLATE 31

95 Cowboy, 1880

96 Texan cowboy, 1888

97 Cowboy, 1890s

The chuck wagon was the social center for the cowboys and a meeting place for any riders encountered around on the trail drive. A huge coffee pot, dented and blackened by many fires, hung from a cooking tripod and offered a hot cup of 'Rio coffee' to anyone that dropped by. The cook, or 'cookie', reigned supreme, and getting on the good side of him meant bringing in quantities of wood or dried buffalo chips to help with the camp's fuel. Not until the late nineteenth century did chuck wagons go commercial and become a standard item with a few of the major wagon builders, including the Studebaker Company. Cattle outfits purchased these 1,600 pound 'open-air kitchens on wheels' for $75 to $100.

Cow ponies were small animals, but sturdy enough to carry a heavy saddle, often weighing from 35 to 50 pounds. The origin of the cow pony was the bronco, which was first used in Texas. A short pony of about 15 hands high worked better than a larger animal. The larger ponies were not always the best to work with. Each cowboy, when out punching cows, rode from five to eight ponies, using them in turns, riding one pony as many as 40–50 miles of which a good many of the miles might be fast riding. After the work day was over, the saddle and bridle were removed from the pony allowing him a little freedom on his own with the other horses grazing near by. He would not be used again for several days. The cow ponies got nothing to eat but the grass they foraged for themselves.

In those early days of cow punching, a cowboy's average pay was $25 a month, and he was obliged to furnish his entire outfit, except the horse, which belonged to the rancher. The cowboy's outfit was no trifling item. A genuine wide-brimmed fur Stetson would cost from $10 on up. His Mexican leggings, or chapperals, took another $12 from his pocket. The yellow slicker, one of the most important items on the list, cost around $3. A camp blanket brought $5; a lasso, of the best raw-hide, cost $12. His saddle drained his purse to the extent of $45, and the bridle sold for $10. A quirt . . . $3, spurs . . . $3, Colt revolver . . . $14, and looped belt and holster . . . $3. Ready made boots ran from $12 to $15 a pair. Summing up the cost of his entire equipment showed that it took $147 to outfit a cowboy before he could do a minute's work.

There was another way a cow puncher could be fitted out if he didn't have any money. The rancher that hired him would fit him up with the necessary gear and charge him $15 a month out of his meager wages to pay for the whole outfit. If the cowboy had good luck, he would have his outfit paid for by the end of the season, but he would soon discover that a large part of it would have to be renewed before he rode out on the range again the following year.

About the only entertainment a cowboy could look forward to was horse racing, card playing, dreaming up games of chance, and pulling 'Tomfoolery' on his bunkie. Cowboys sometimes got a reputation for recklessness. After being on a drive for six months and after having been paid off, they rode into town for some fun, and in their sport they rode yelling through the streets shooting a few lamps out, and getting into a saloon row. Immediately some imaginative newspaper correspondent would send an account of it to some Eastern paper, where the headlines read, 'Another Cowboy Outrage'. As one old-timer pointed out, 'I've cowboy'd all over the West and knew hundreds of these boys, many who never carried a revolver. They have strict ideas of honor, and they stand upon their honor. Sure, when they're off "Treeing a town", so to speak, they're a lot of big-hearted, rough boys, but not outlaws or outcasts with no regard for human feelings. They are not the class of men who rob trains or hold up people crossing the plains, and I believe that, taken all in all, the American cowboy will compare favorably in morals and manners with any similar number of citizens. I agree, that once in a while a bad apple will turn up – killing someone for no apparent reason, and souring the whole "apple barrel".'

An unknown writer wrote a brief sketch of a cattle stampede, and sent it back East to his newspaper publisher, explaining the event in detail.

One of the slickest things I ever saw in my travels, was a cowboy stopping a cattle stampede. A herd of six or eight hundred had got frightened at something and broke away pell-mell, with their tails in the air, and the bulls at the head of the procession. But Mr. Cowboy didn't get excited at all when he saw the herd was going straight for a high bluff, where they would certainly tumble down into the canyon below and be killed. You know that when a herd like that gets to going they can't stop, no matter whether they rush to death or not. Those in the rear crowd those ahead, and away they go. I wouldn't have given a dollar a head for that herd, but the cowboy spurred up his mustang, made a little detour, came in right in front of the herd, cut across their path at a right angle, and then galloped leisurely on to the edge of that bluff, halted, and looked around at that wild mass of beef coming right toward him. He was as cool as a cucumber, though I expected to see him killed, and was so excited I could not speak. Well, sir, when the leaders had got within about a quarter of a mile of him I saw them try to slack up, though they could not do it very quick. But the whole herd seemed to want to stop, and when the cows and steers in the rear got about where the cowboy had cut across their path, I was surprised to see them stop and commence to nibble at the grass. Then the whole herd stopped, wheeled, straggled back, and went to fighting for a chance to eat where the rear guard was.

You see that cowboy had opened a big bag of salt he had brought out from the ranch to give the cattle, galloped across the herd's course and emptied the bag. Every animal sniffed that line of salt, and, of course, that broke up the stampede. But, I tell you, it was a queer sight to see that fellow out there on the edge of that bluff quietly rolling a cigarette, when it seemed as if he'd be lying under two hundred tons of beef in about a minute and a half.

THE 'ROUND-UP'

We have said that, from November to May, cattle wandered where they pleased for food. Cowboys bestowed no special care upon them, except occasionally, after a severe storm, or during an unusually cold winter, they went out to find how it was with the herd. About the twentieth of May, however, the 'round-up' began. All the cattlemen in the district (the grazing country was divided into districts, under the control of necessary laws) met at a given place, each owner of a herd furnishing a given number of cowboys and horses, according to the size of his herd; an organization was formed by the choice of captain and other necessary officers; and the exciting and fascinating business began. The cowboys, upon their well-trained broncos, swept over the country, searching for and surrounding the scattered cattle, driving them towards an appointed locality, where, each day, each stockman 'cut out' his own cattle, branded the calves, guarded them at night, and drove them on the following day to another fixed locality, and so on, until the home ranch was reached, when they were again turned loose.

Many of the steers were wild as buffalos, and often started off into a dead run just where the cowboys objected to their going, and it was a neck and neck race often for miles, or until the wild creatures were exhausted. Here the excitement, as well as the dangers of the business, came in. Sometimes a wild bull turned upon his pursuer in a frenzy of madness, and the cowboy had but one thing to do – he had to turn from the enraged animal and run for dear life. Neither horse nor rider could wage successful warfare with a mad bull. Horses were trained so thoroughly to the business that they voluntarily chased a steer when it was necessary, but ran from him when that appeared advisable.

A writer in the *Boston Commercial Bulletin* describes his participation in a round-up in Colorado, from which we make a few extracts:

> All in a moment the earth seemed fairly sprouting with cattle, as they suddenly sprang into sight on all sides, the insatiate curiosity of the animals drawing them from miles across the country to take a good look at us. Breathing hard with excitement, they would stand viewing us with eyes large from fright and defiance, until as we started for them away they would go, bellowing wildly and with a noise as of hundreds of beaten drums from the falling hoofs.
>
> And wildly exciting was the chase, our aims quite marvellously aided by the excellence of our ponies, who it would seem might almost have accomplished the task themselves. The perceptions of a trained cow-horse become marvellously acute. Guided by the smallest twitch on the reins, he seems to divine by a subtle instinct the will of the rider. Out of a large herd the horse will seem to comprehend at once what cattle are to be cut out, sighting an animal apparently at the same instant with his rider, and seeming to take a diabolical sort of delight in running the creature down and frustrating all its clumsy, contrary efforts to run the wrong way.

When a cowboy left his outfit to join any other, or for an expedition of any kind, he always took his 'string' of horses, generally five or six, as well as all of his personal property, along with him. The tarpaulin – always pronounced as if spelled tarpaulion, and as we will therefore henceforth so call it – and the blankets, comprising his bed, were wrapped around the gentlest of his horses and made fast with a lariat in a good 'squaw hitch'; on top of this the precious war-sack was fastened with special care, and thus, driving his horses ahead of him, with all his earthly responsibilities directly before his eyes, the cowboy sallied forth. He got his 'grub' at any ranch he came to until he joined another grub wagon, and unrolled his tarpaulion on the ground wherever night overtook him, corralling his horses if he was so lucky as to find a corral, otherwise hobbling them, by tying the forelegs together with a bit of rope. One horse, however, ready for immediate use, he was always staked.

It so happens that the American cowboy is still around, branding cattle, rounding them up in the fall, and practising many old traditions used by old-timers. Over 120 years, he is more popular today, in real life, than he was at any time in history.

PLATE 32
98 Chuck wagon cook, 1880s
99 Cowboy, 1890–1900
100 Cowboy, 1900s

98. *He was called 'Cookie' by most of the hands, and you'd better treat him with some respect. He had to be good to qualify as a chuck wagon cook because he had to be both versatile and resourceful. He was depended upon to throw together three hot meals a day, come rain or shine, with enough grub to go around twice. Besides tending his outdoor kitchen, Cookie listened to complaints over a hot cup of 'Rio' coffee, acted as doctor for both man and beast, settled quarrels, held the stakes when heavy bets were made, and played a good hand in poker. Any assistant to Cookie was quickly labeled 'Little Mary', who usually was a young man in his teens and wanted desperately to be a cowboy . . . this was the closest he got to it. Here Cookie wears a warm Cardigan sweater with deep side pockets and a long four-by-six apron that looks like it has been soaked in a grease pit. He wears no weapon, but among his pots and pans there is an old .44/40 hog leg loaded and ready for action. The Dutch oven that he carries contains a full kettle of fresh baked sourdough bisquits. The chuck wagon was concocted by Charles Goodnight in 1866. It was an old army wagon with a mess box with many drawers and shelves added to the rear. The idea caught on years later and farm wagons were used, but were not durable enough. Not until the late nineteenth century did chuck wagons go commercial with a few major wagon builders. Studebaker built many, and sold them for $75 to $100 each.*

99. *The 'All Around Duster' can be traced back to the days of the Civil War, with a single row of six buttons running up and down the front and with one right-hand pocket. A small, split, flop-over collar topped it off. At the rear a split divides the bottom of the duster to enable a horseman to mount with ease and be seated comfortably, with the duster's sides lying over both sides of the horse's rib cage. In the small of the back an adjustable belt is attached, permitting either a tight or a loose fit. Field surgeons,* *Army scouts, contract haulers, and stagecoach riders were often seen wearing these dusters. After the Civil War when the cowboy became identified with the great cattle drives, the duster was once again popular – only with one difference. A few inches more were added to the bottom. The heavy trail dust had much to do with this decision. The material was either a heavy linen or a lightweight canvas, and was manufactured in colors of white or tan. In the late 1800s, a double-breasted duster with two rows of buttons (eight in all) was produced, along with one pocket on each side. The automobile made another drastic change in the duster. Instead of a split at the rear, there were splits on either side, enabling the driver of an automobile to climb in and out of his vehicle with free movement.*

100. *'Long Johns', or 'handlebars', took the place of shirts when sweat crystals caked on the cowboy's shoulders, normally ruining everyday cotton shirts. This one piece 'union suit' took a lot of rough wear. Sometimes the men would chuck off their boots and breeches and jump into a cool running creek still wearing their 'longies'. Submerging several times seemed to rid them of odor, sweat and dust. When first purchased, the underwear came in several colors: white, grey, and red. The white usually turned grey, the grey faded to a lighter color and the red turned pink. For the sake of illustration, this cowpuncher is wearing suspenders. Most of the men would shy away from this sort of apparatus, mainly because it could create a danger to man and animal. During the course of a hectic day the cowboy might hang himself up on the saddle horn or the steer's mighty crowned horns, rendering him useless while on a drive. Trousers were Levi's denim tan (in this case) or Army blues, as long as they didn't have a yellow stripe running down either of the outside seams. Any other pair made of heavy material was also worn. Leather cuffs, shown on the ground, were to protect the cowboy's wrist and forearms in brush country and from rope burns. Originating in Texas as early as the 1880s, the leather was either plain, handcarved, or Mexican nickeled studs.*

PLATE 32

98 Chuck wagon cook, 1880s

99 Cowboy, 1890–1900

100 Cowboy, 1900s

Bibliography

CHAPTER 1

Eastman, Chas. A., *Indian Heroes and Great Chieftains*; Little, Brown & Co., Boston, 1918.

Fighting Cheyennes, Geo. Bird Grinnell; University of Oklahoma Press; 1956.

Indian Tribes, Report on Conditions of the; Washington, 1867.

Manypenny, Geo. W., *Our Indian Wards*, Robt. Clarke & Co., Cincinnati, 1880.

McClemand, Edward J., *With the Indian and the Buffalo in Montana, 1870–1878*; Arthur H. Clark Co., Glendale, Calif., 1969.

Neihardt, John C., *Black Elk Speaks*; Wm. Morrow & Co., N.Y., 1932.

Paine, Boyard H., *Pioneers, Indians & Buffaloes*; Curtis Enterprise, Curtis, Neb., 1935.

Records of Engagements with Hostile Indians; Chicago, 1882.

Schmitt, Martin F., and Dee Brown, *Fighting Indians of the West*, Scribner's & Sons, N.Y., 1948.

Schields, G. O., *The Blanket Indian of the Northwest*, Vechten Waring Co., N.Y., 1921.

Standing Bear, Luther, *My People the Sioux*; Houghton Mifflin Co., Boston, 1928.

Stands in Timber, John and Margot Liberty, Cheyenne Memories, Yale University Press, New Haven, 1967.

Vestal, Stanley, *Sitting Bull, Champion of the Sioux*; Houghton Mifflin Co., Boston, 1934.

War Path & Council Fire; Random House, N.Y., 1948.

Westerners, Potomac Corral of the; Great Western Indian Fights; Doubleday & Co., Inc., N.Y., 1960.

CHAPTER 2

Firearms, Traps and Tools of the Mountain Man, Carl P. Russell, Publ. Alfred A. Knoph.

George Catlin and the Old Frontier, H. McCracken, Dial Press.

Letters & Notes on the Manners, Customs and Conditions of the North American Indians, Geo. Catlin, Vols. 1 & 2, Dover Publ.

The American Fur Trade of the Far West, H. M. Crittenden, 3 vols., Harper.

The Far Western Frontier, Ray Allen Billington, Harper and Row Publ.

CHAPTER 3

Billington, Ray A., *The Far Western Frontier, 1830–1860*; N.Y., 1956.

Botkin, B. A. (ed.), *A Treasury of Western Folklore*, N.Y., Crown Publ., 1951.

Custer, G. A., *My Life on the Plains*; N. Y., Sheldon & Co., 1874.

Devoto, Bernard, *Across the Wide Missouri*; Cambridge, Mass., Houghton Mifflin Co., 1947.

Eccleston, Robt., *Overland to California on the South-western Trail*; 1849, Berkley, U. of Calif. Press, 1950.

Ghent, W. J., *The Road to Oregon* (A Chronicle of The Great Emigrant Trail); N.Y., Tudor Publ. Co., 1934.

Hulbert, A. B., *Forty Niners: The Chronicle of The California Trail*; Little, Brown & Co., 1949.

Kincaid, Robert L., *The Wilderness Road*; Bobbs-Merrill, 1947.

McDermott, J. F., *Travelers on The Western Frontier*; Univ. of Illinois, 1970.

Rawling, Gerald, *The Pathfinders*; MacMillan, 1964.

Roenigh, Adolf, *Pioneer History of Kansas*; Publ. by Author, 1933.

Salisbury, Albert & Jane, *Here Rolled the Covered Wagons*; Superior, 1948.

Unruh, Jr., J. D., *The Plains Across; The Overland Emigrants & The Trans-Mississippi West, 1840–60*, Univ. of Illinois Press, 1979.

Winther, O. O., *The Old Oregon Country*; Stanford Univ. Press, 1950.

Winther, O. O., *Via Western Express & Stage Coach*; Stanford Univ. Press, 1950.

CHAPTER 4

Buck, Franklin A., *A Yankee Trader in The Gold Rush*, Boston, 1930.

Chidsey, Donald B., *The California Gold Rush*, Crown, 1968.

Coyle, C. W., *Gold! Adventure in the Nevada Desert*; Mass., 1931.

DeLorenzo, Lois M., *Gold Fever and The Art of Panning & Sluicing*; A.T.R. Enterprises, 1970.

Jackson, Sam B., *200 Trails to Gold*, Doubleday, 1976.

Jenkins, Olafp. (Ed.), *The Mother Lode Co.*; State of Calif., Div. of Mines, 1948.

Johnson, O. S., *Following the Trail to The Hidden Gold*; Tipton, Iowa, 1914.

Morgan, Murray, *One Man's Gold Rush*; Univ. of Washington Press, 1967.

Price, S. Goodale, *Ghosts of Golconda*, Western Publ., 1952.

Probert, Thom., *Lost Mines & Buried Treasures of The West*; Univ. of Calif., 1977.

Schoonover, T. J., *The Life & Times of Gen'l John A. Sutter*; Sacramento, 1895.

Spurr, J. E., *Through the Yukon Gold Diggings*; Boston, 1900.

Storm, Barry, *Thunder Gods Gold*; Southwest Publ. Co., 1945.

Walton, C. C., *An Illinois Gold Hunter in The Black Hills*; Ill. State Historical Society, 1960.

Watson, M. G., *Silver Theatre, Amusements of the Mining Frontier in Early Nevada, 1850 to 1864*, Glendale: Clark, 1964.

Wood, Daniel B., *Sixteen Months at The Gold Diggins*; N.Y., 1851.

CHAPTER 5

Brown, M. H. & Felton, W. R., *The Frontier Years*, Bramhall House, N.Y., 1955.

Gard, Wayne, *The Great Buffalo Hunt*, Knopf Publ., 1959.

Marcy, R. B., *The Prairie Traveler*, Harpers & Brothers, 1859.

Russell, Osborne, *Journal of a Trapper*, Univ. of Neb. Press, Lincoln, Neb. 1965.

Sellers, Frank, *Sharps Firearms*, Beinfeld Publ., 1978.

Smith, W. O., *The Sharp's Rifle*.

CHAPTER 6

Campbell, Walter Stanley (Stanley Vestal), *Warpath and Council Fire; the Plains Indians' Struggle for Survival in War and in Diplomacy*; Random House, Inc., New York, 1948.

Danker, D. F., editor, *The Journal of an Indian Fighter; the 1869 Diary of Major Frank J. North*; Nebraska History, June 1958.

Downey, Fairfax David, *Indian-Fighting Army*; Charles Scribner's Sons, New York, 1941.

Forsyth, George A., *The Story of the Soldier*; Appleton-Century-Crofts, Inc., New York, 1900.

Herr, John K., and Edward S. Wallace, *Story of the U.S. Cavalry*; Little, Brown and Co., Boston, 1953.

Hull, Myra, editor, *Soldiering on the High Plains: The Diary of Lewis Bryan Hall, 1864–1866*; Kansas Historical Quarterly, February 1938.

Mattison, Ray H., *The Army Post on the Northern Plains, 1865–1885*; Nebraska History, March 1954.

Ostrander, Alson Bowles, *Army Boy of the Sixties; A Story of the Plains*; World Book Co., Yonkers-on-the-Hudson, 1924.

Reedstrom, E. L., *Bugles, Banners and War Bonnets*; Bonanza Press, New York.

Rickey, Don, *War in the West – The Indian Campaigns*; Custer Battlefield Historical and Museum Association, Crown Agency, Montana, 1956.

Wellman, Paul Iselin, *Death on Horseback; Seventy Years of War for the American West*; Garden City Publishing Co., New York, 1950.

Welty, R. L., *The Army Post on the Frontier*, North Dakota Historical Quarterly, April 1928; *The Frontier Army on the Missouri River, 1860–1870*; North Dakota Historical Quarterly, January 1928.

CHAPTER 7

American Heritage, April 1963.

Carl Breihan, *Great Gunfighters of the West*, Naylor Publ.

Richard Erdoes, *Saloons of the Old West*, Knopf Publ. 1979.

George E. Virgines, *Fast Draw, Yesterday, Today*, private printing.

George E. Virgines, *Famous Guns and Gunners*, Leather Stocking Publ.

Special thanks to George E. Virgines, author of *Saga of the Colt Frontier Six Shooter*. Fred Fell; N. Y., where this artist has gained permission to reproduce the illustrations from that book. (Illustrations by E. L. Reedstrom.)

The Old West series, *The Women*, Time/Life.

CHAPTER 8

Aikman, Duncan, *Calamity Jane and The Lady Wildcats*, N.Y., 1927.

Adams, Ramon F., *A Fitting Death for Billy the Kid*, Norman, 1960.

Baker, Pearl, *The Wild Bunch at Robbers Roost*, N.Y., 1971.

Bartholomew, Ed., *The Biographical Album of Western Gunfighters*, Frontier Press of Texas, 1958.

Bartholomew, Ed., *Kill Or Be Killed, A record of violence in the early Southwest*, Houstin, 1953.

Breihan, Carl W., *Great Gunfighters of the West*, Naylor Co., 1962.

Connelley, Wm. E., *Wild Bill & His Era*, Press of the Pioneers, N.Y., 1933.

Chalfant, W. A., *Gold, Guns & Ghost Towns*, Staford, 1948.

Dacus, J. A., *Illustrated Lives & Adventures of the James & Younger Brothers*, St. Louis, 1882.

Fulton, Maurice, *The Authentic Life of Billy the Kid*, N.Y., 1927.

Grisholm, Noel, *Tame the Restless Wind, Legends of Sam Bass*, Austin, 1968.

Hall, Frank & Whitten, Lindsey, *Jesse James Rides Again*, Lawten, 1948.

Hardin, John W., *The Life of John Westley Hardin*; Sequin, Texas, 1896.

Hawkeye, Harry, *Rube Burrow, The Outlaw*, Baltimore, 1908.

Kelly, Charles, *The Outlaw Trail, story of Butch Cassidy & Wild Bunch*, N.Y.,1959.

Lloyd, Everett, *Law West of the Pecos – story of Judge Roy Bean*, San Antonio, 1960.

McConnell, W. J. & Driggs, H. R., *Frontier Law – Vigilante Days*, N.Y., 1924.

Odens, Peter, *Outlaws, Heroes, & Jokers of the Old Southwest*, Yuma, 1964.

O'Neal, Bill, *Encyclopedia of Western Gunfighters*, Norman, 1979.

Pinkerton, Wm. A., *Train Robberies & Train Robbers*, Jamestown, Va., 1907.

Raine, Wm. H., *Guns of the Frontier*, Cleveland, 1940.

Raine, Wm. H., *.45 Caliber Law.*, Evanston, Illinois, 1941.

Rasco, Burton, *Belle Starr, Bandit Queen*, N.Y., 1941.

Rasco, Burton, *The Dalton Bros., by an Eyewitness*, N.Y., 1954.

Sabin, Edwin L., *Wild Men of the West*, N.Y., 1929.

Waters, Wm., A. *Gallery of Western Badmen*, Kentucky, 1954.

Williams, Llew, *The Dalton Brothers in their Oklahoma Cave*, Chicago, 1883.

CHAPTER 9

Adams, Ramon F., *Six Guns & Saddle Leather*, Norman, 1954.

Aikman, Duncan, *The Taming of the Frontier*, N.Y., 1925.

Askins, Col. Charles, *Texans, Guns & History*, N.Y., 1970.

Atkin, Ronald, *Maintain the Right*, John Day, N.Y.

Breihan, Carl W., *Great Lawmen of the West*, N.Y., 1953.

Castleman, Harvey, *The Texas Rangers*, Girard, 1944.

Collier, Wm. Ross & Estrate, *Edwin Victor, The Reign of Soapy Smith*, N.Y., 1935.

Collins, Dabney, *Hanging of Black Jack Slade*, Denver, 1963.

Dillon, Richard, *Wells Fargo Detective*; N. Y., 1969.

Faulk, Odie B., *Dodge City*, N.Y., 1977.

Fetherstowhaugh, R. C., *The Royal Canadian Mounted Police*, N.Y., 1940.

Gish, Anthony, *American Bandits*, Girard, Ks., 1938.

Hayley, J. Evetts, *Jeff Milton; A Good Man With A Gun*, Norman, 1948.

Hanchett, Layfayette, *The Old Sheriff & Other True Tales*, N.Y., 1937.

Lake, Carolyn, *Under Cover for Wells Fargo*, Boston, 1969.

Lake, Stuart N., *Wyatt Earp – Frontier Marshall*, Boston & N.Y., 1931.

Lloyd, Everett, *Law West of the Pecas (on Judge Roy Bean)*, San Antonio, 1960.

Mason, H. M., *The Texas Rangers*, N.Y., 1967.

Metz, Leon C., *Dallas Stoudenmire; El Paso Marshall*, Norman, 1979.

Miller, Floyd, *Bill Tighman – Marshall of the Last Frontier*, N.Y., 1968.

O'Connor, Richard, *Bat Masterson*, N.Y., 1957.

Parkhill, Forbes, *The Law Goes West*, Denver, 1956.

Pike, James, *Scout & Ranger*, Princeton, 1932.

Pinkerton, Wm. A., *Train Robberies & Train Robbers*, Jamestown, Va., 1907.

Rockwell, Wilson, *Memoirs of a Lawman*, Denver, 1962.

Rose, Joseph, *The Gunfighter, Man or Myth*, Norman, 1969.

Schoenberger, Dale T., *The Gunfighter*, Caxton Printers, 1971.

Shirley, Glen; *Heck Thomas, Frontier Marshal*, Phil., 1962.

Turner, John Peter, *The North-West Mounted Police*, Vol. I–Vol. II, Edmond Cloutier (Ottawa), King's Printer (1950).

Virginis, Geo. E., *Arizona Rangers*, Arizona State Library and Archives, 1972.

Webb, Walter P., *The Texas Ranger*, Boston, 1935.

Wilstach, Frank J., *Wild Bill Hickok – Prince of Pistoleers*, N.Y., 1926.

CHAPTER 10

Adams, Andy, *The Log of a Cowboy*, Boston, 1903.

Adams, Ramon F., *Old-Time Cow Hand*, McMillan, 1961.

Brayer, Garnet M. & Herbert O., *American Cattle Trails – 1550–1900*, N.Y., 1952.

Clay, John, *My Life on The Range*, Chicago, 1924.

Cross, Joe, *Cattle Clatter*, Kansas City, 1938.

Dobie, J. Frank, *The Longhorns*, Boston, 1941.

Dobie, J. Frank, *On The Open Range*, Dallas, 1940.

Dobie, J. Frank, *Tales of The Mustangs*, Dallas, 1936.

Flanagan, Sue, *Trailing the Longhorns*, Sustin, 1974.

Fletcher, Sydney E., *The Cowboy & His Horse*, N.Y., 1951.

Fridge, Ike, *History of the Chisum War*, Electra, Texas, 1927.

Gard, Wayne, *Up the Chisholm Trail*, Houston, 1967.

Haley, J. Evetts, *Charles Goodnight*, Boston, 1936.

Haley, J. Evetts, *A Log of the Montana Trail*, Amarillo, 1932.

Johnson, M. L., *Trail Blazing*, Dallas, 1935.

Key, Della Tyler, *In the Cattle Country*, Quanah, 1972.

Krakel, Dean F., *Saga of Tom Horn*, Laramie, Wyoming; 1954.

Logan, Herschel C., *Buckskin & Satin*, Harrisburg, Penn., 1954.

McCracken, Harold, *The American Cowboy*, Garden City, N.Y., 1973.

Myres, Sandra, L., *S.D. Mures, Saddlemaker*, Kerrville, 1961.

O'Brian, Esse F., *The First Bulldogger*, San Antonio, Texas, 1961.

Ord, Paul, *They followed the Rails*, Childress, Texas, 1970.

Parker, Ben L., *The Origin of The Cowboy*, Jourdanton, Texas, 1970.

Pelzer, Louis, *The Cattlemen's Frontier, 1850–1890*, Glendale, 1936.

Rye, Edgar, *The Quirt & The Spur*, Chicago, 1909.

Siringo, Chas. A., *A Texas Cowboy*, N.Y., 1950.

Streeter, Floyd B., *Prairie Trails & Cow Towns*, Boston, 1936.

Treadwell, Edward F., *The Cattle King*, N. Y., 1931.

Walsh, C. C., *Early Days on the Western Range*, Boston, 1917.

Ward, Fay E., *The Cowboy at Work*, Hastings House, 1976.

Wright, Robt. M., *Dodge City, Cowboy Capital*, Wichita, Kansas, 1913.

Index

Figures in italics refer to page numbers of illustrations.